JUSTICE AND MERCY WILL KISS

JUSTICE AND MERCY WILL KISS
THE VOCATION OF PEACEMAKING
IN A WORLD OF MANY FAITHS

EDITED BY

MICHAEL K. DUFFEY

&

DEBORAH S. NASH

MARQUETTE
UNIVERSITY

PRESS

MARQUETTE STUDIES IN THEOLOGY
NO. 58
ANDREW TALLON, SERIES EDITOR

LIBRARY OF CONGRESS CATALOGING-IN-PUBLICATION DATA
Justice and mercy will kiss : the vocation of peacemaking in a world of many faiths /
edited by Michael K. Duffey & Deborah S. Nash.
    p. cm. — (Marquette studies in theology ; no. 58)
Includes bibliographical references and index.
ISBN-13: 978-0-87462-735-0 (pbk. : alk. paper)
ISBN-10: 0-87462-735-4 (pbk. : alk. paper)
1. Peace—Religious aspects. 2. Peace. I. Duffey, Michael K., 1948- II. Nash,
Deborah S., 1953-
BL65.P4J87 2008
201'.7273—dc22

                                                                                2008041608

© 2008 Marquette University Press
Milwaukee, Wisconsin 53201-3141
All rights reserved.
www.marquette.edu/mupress/

FOUNDED 1916

EDITORS' NOTE
Special thanks are due to Dr. Susan Mountin, Director of the Manresa Foundation,
who conceived of and carried out the "Justice and Mercy Conference" and directed the
production of this work. Without her vision, persistence and generosity it would most
likely never have come about. Thanks also to Dr. Patricia Marquardt and Dr. Stephen
Beall of the Classics Department of Marquette University for their excellent tutelage
in classical languages. It proved to be a valuable aid in preparing this volume.
                                                      Michael K. Duffey & Deborah S. Nash

∞ The paper used in this publication meets the minimum requirements of the
American National Standard for Information Sciences—
Permanence of Paper for Printed Library Materials, ANSI Z39.48-1992.

MARQUETTE UNIVERSITY PRESS
MILWAUKEE

The Association of Jesuit University Presses

TABLE OF CONTENTS

PREFACE

This text is the product of many hopes, dreams, stories, experiences and convictions. It is the result of joining the hearts and minds of people of diverse cultures and religions of the world who gathered at Marquette University in Milwaukee, Wisconsin in September 2005 for a conference entitled: *Justice and Mercy Will Kiss: The Vocation of Peacemaking in a World of Many Faiths*. When the conference planning committee began meeting, their expectation was to host a small conference of academicians and practitioners, of pastors and policy makers, who would bring their intellectual abilities, their lived experience as peacemakers and the cries of those around the world who suffer daily from the impact of violence into a creative and stimulating exchange.

Little did we know that this idea would capture the imagination of more than 500 participants from almost every continent and faith and nearly 100 presenters who shared experience, conversation, tears, smiles and promises to work for peace as a life commitment—a vocation sorely needed in a world fraught with violence.

The chapters that follow are based on the inspiring and informative presentations given at the conference. They may provide words for readers to ponder for a long, long time. The conference and this text share the following aims:

+ Promoting interfaith dialogue on peacemaking as a vocation
+ Encouraging multicultural and multidisciplinary dialogue
+ Disseminating research findings about contributions to the vocation of peacemaking
+ Building bridges between research, theory and praxis
+ Encouraging theological reflection on real life experience

We are grateful to the vision of the Society of Jesus (the Jesuits) for their mission especially as it was encouraged by their 1995 international meeting (General Congregation 34) calling for attention to justice, culture and interreligious dialogue in Jesuit work throughout the world.

We are especially grateful to the Lilly Endowment, Inc., and the Programs for the Theological Exploration of Vocation for providing financial resources to undertake this ambitious project as well, and to

countless individuals and departments at Marquette University and
the Wisconsin Province of the Society of Jesus for their support.
Special thanks to editors Michael Duffey, Ph.D. Department of
Theology at Marquette and doctoral candidate Deborah Peterson
(Nash), for doggedly moving this work from its initial stage as an as-
semblage of oral presentations and papers to a finished collection of
living chapters. Marquette Theology Professor Irfan Omar provided
significant guidance in planning the conference and contacted scores
of people across the ocean; he also contributed ideas for the title and
cover art. Thank you to Philip Rossi, S.J., for sharing his dream for the
conference and for the endless list of contacts in the world community
of passionate people seeking peace; to Ardene Brown, Ph.D. Manresa Faculty coordinator and Elizabeth Conradson Cleary, Manresa
graduate assistant and Mary Ferwerda, assistant director of the Manresa Project for the leadership and organizational skills they provided
to make the conference possible. Finally, thanks to super organizer,
Claire Anglim, Manresa student assistant for her skills in last minute
adjustments to the text.

The list of people to whom acknowledgment is owed for this text
is necessarily large, so undoubtedly, some deserving individuals will
inadvertently be overlooked. If that proves to be the case, realize that
your work has neither gone unnoticed, nor is it unappreciated. The
names are simply too numerous to mention them all.

We pray that the words that follow will touch our hearts and further
deepen our convictions about the need for us to be people of peace, to
work for a justice which reflects a God of love, mercy and forgiveness.

Susan M. Mountin, Ph.D.
Director, Manresa Project
Marquette University

INTRODUCTION

Exploring the resources of the world religions as guides to earthly peace is a vast undertaking, but also a promising one! The Lilly Endowment Inc. Programs for The Theological Exploration of Vocation (PTEV) through Marquette's Manresa Project provided the financial resources to Marquette University to sponsor a conference in September, 2005 entitled "Justice and Mercy Will Kiss: The Vocation of Peacemaking in a World of Many Faiths." It had several purposes: the promotion of interfaith dialogue, the encouragement of multicultural and multidisciplinary studies and the dissemination of new research in this area. It also aimed to help build bridges between theory and praxis and generally to encourage theological reflection.

Presenters spoke on behalf of five of the world's religions. Their essays, contained in this volume, appeal to adherents of these various traditions but also explore the problem of peacemaking in terms of both theory and praxis within and across those traditions. We believe that all of these papers will challenge readers on a number of levels. We are also of the conviction that the current global conditions require that we draw on the insights and claims of many, if not all, of the world's religions to foster peace among all who share life on earth. Doing so creates a basis for mutual understanding, one that can expand ever outward as dialogue continues. It can also render our labors for peace in the world's educational, social and economic institutions ever more efficacious.

The essays contained herein have been arranged in three groups. The first considers the formative texts of world religions; the second focuses on individuals from these traditions who have engaged in the work of peacemaking; the third considers models for promoting peace through education and economic development.

Some of the authors also provide an autobiographical reflection in which they comment on what has motivated them to commit to working for peace and justice.

In his work, *Revelation, the Religions, and Violence* (Orbis, 2000) Leo Lefebure cautions us against thinking about religious traditions as systems of doctrine that are reducible to a set of universal beliefs which are to be differentiated from each other only by their form of expression. Nevertheless, he writes that "although the major religious traditions often differ radically in their assumptions about ultimate reality, human existence, and the universe, they nonetheless agree to a significant, even surprising degree on many of the values that are most central for human existence." (170) He mentions agreement on such virtues as loving-kindness, compassion, and equanimity. In a final chapter, Lefebure examines the prospects of dialogue between Buddhism and Christianity, religious systems that he judges to be conceptually very different from one another. The Christian interlocutor in the chapter is theologian Karl Rahner. He stresses the limits of discursive reflection on the Transcendent Creator and invites us into the silence where the Buddhist is at home. It is fruitful to remind ourselves that our thoughts and actions in pursuit of peace require it as the starting (and returning) point. As Rahner states:

> Be still for once... Give these deeper realities of the spirit a chance now to rise to the surface: silence, fear, the ineffable longing for truth, for love, for fellowship, for God. Face loneliness, fear, imminent death. Allow such ultimate, basic human experiences to come first. (194; Rahner, *Practice of Faith*, 63)

PART I

RELIGIOUS TEXTS AS STARTING POINTS FOR DIALOGUE

Religious texts, whether read, recited or sung are a significant defining force in the development of religious communities. Each generation must enter into conversation with present and past co-religionists about how the texts are both to be *understood* and *lived*. Such texts are often closely connected with the founding figures of these religions: the Israelite Ancestors, Kings and Prophets, Jesus, Muhammad, the Buddha, Lord Krishna. Their lives illuminate the texts and make their teachings all the more compelling to ensuing generations.

(1) **Nancy M. Martin** begins by examining the notion of holiness in an interreligious context. She writes that "to become 'holy' is be transformed by the fire of love and realization to such a degree that one becomes transparent to the Transcendent and, in so doing, not only acts with love and compassion but manifests or embodies these in the world." Such transformative compassion, she argues, is recognized in saints, sages, and bodhisattvas across religions and cultures. It energizes struggles for justice, heals oppressed and the oppressor alike. Read-

ers will be indebted to Martin for her excellent study of transforming love across the traditions of Judaism, Christianity, Islam, Hinduism, Buddhism and Confucianism.

(2) **Patrick Hayes** explores the possibility of forgiveness rather than vengeance for harm suffered. "In the *Hebrew Scriptures*," he writes, "the sin against neighbor was nothing short of sin against God and so the need for reconciliation also involved a need to be reconciled with God by way of reconciliation with one's neighbor." Hayes finds in the Old Testament twin obligations: for the evildoer to repent and for the victim to accept repentance through forgiveness. Forgiveness re-establishes relationship with God and one's neighbor. The New Testament, Hayes claims, puts the forgiveness by victims ahead of repentance.

Hayes reflects on peacemaking in personal terms: *"Forgiveness has been a struggle for me. I am a stabbing victim and have gone through all the trials accompanying Post-Traumatic Stress Disorder. My assailant was never apprehended, so I haven't had much in the way of closure after being nearly murdered. And yet I am compelled by Jesus' admonition to forgive. I desire to follow this way of life. It is part of who I am. The world makes more sense to me if forgiveness is pursued as a viable form of living and it signals to me that living is indeed possible in the wake of horrendous evil."*

(3) **Jane Linahan** examines what is certainly the foundational text of Jesus' teaching, the *Sermon on the Mount*. She does so in dialogue with scripture scholar and theologian Jürgen Moltmann. Moltmann's conclusion is also Linahan's: Christians' encounters with so-called "enemies" offer them an opportunity "to respond in a new, unprecedented way…[to] form a relationship that no longer includes the idea of enemy." Taking responsibility for the very lives of "enemies" means renouncing retaliation and instead meeting their authentic needs, remedying injustices towards them, and refusing to demonize them. Love of enemies is the principle upon which true peace is founded.

(4) **Ed Grippe** compares the inspirational role of Jesus for his disciples and of Muhammad for his followers. He claims that Jesus rejected violence and the possibility that Caesar's wars could serve divine purposes; conversely, Muhammad taught that defensive wars could serve divine purposes. Grippe argues that the two positions are reconcilable. He sees convergence in the manner in which the disciples of both Jesus and Muhammad trust and submit to their masters. Rather than blind submission, both Christian and Muslim disciples must thought-

fully respond to their masters' examples and teaching. Jesus' response
was one of non-resistance. The scene in the Garden of Gethsemane
exemplifies this perhaps most clearly; also, he urged his disciples to do
the same. Muhammad led the *hajj* of 628 C.E. with a thousand unarmed disciples, hoping to avoid violence. The prophet quickly ended
the defensive violence that did break out at that point. "Magnanimity
and tolerance became the hallmarks of his leadership," writes Grippe.
By persuasion, the Prophet invited his followers to join the *ummah*
(reformed community). In both Jesus and Muhammad we see active
resistance to the evils of subjugation and oppression. Both beckoned
their disciples to submit ever more fully and humbly to the goodness
and truth revealed by God.

(5) **Ayse Oktay** examines the indebtedness of both Islam and Christianity to Aristotle's virtue ethics. Both teach that the practice of the
virtues is necessary to achieve rightly ordered human community and
to attain happiness in this life and the next. Oktay demonstrates that
in both traditions the virtue of justice is central, that Aristotle's virtue
of pride is replaced with humility in both Christianity and Islam. The
fact that Muslims and Christians share the same list of virtues and
vices is cause for optimism about any effort at peacemaking.

(6) **Brian Bloch** notes that fighting and war are central themes of
the *Mahābhārata*, so a superficial reading of the work does not lead to
discussion of non-violence. However, the *Mahābhārata* also distin-
guishes between action and contemplation and urges the reader to
unite these two modes of living.

(7) What exactly is the nature of the ongoing threats to American
cities subsequent to the 9/11 events? **Deborah S. (Nash) Peterson**
proposes that the enemy may, in fact, not be without but within—in
the psyche of the individual citizen, and so by implication also within
the collective consciousness. On this analysis, the work of peacemaking poses a somewhat different problem than is often thought to be
the case: We may need to first render ourselves peaceable before we
can become peacemakers. Doing this may require that we address
what in Buddhism are called the 'afflictive emotions' at work in each
of us, among them the *greed* that seems to drive the American mass
consumption of products related to the oil industry, and the *fear* that
seems to be provoked by the disinformation spread by the media.

When Buddhism's ethical principles, together with its meditative
practices, are brought to bear on these 'internal enemies' the indi-

vidual discovers the value of simplicity and restraint. This is hardly a revolutionary insight, but, when the practice of such 'mindfulness' is generalized, the result can be an expanded collective awareness of the conditions faced by others and so a sort of synergy of compassion. The events of 9/11 may have awakened in us the need for a different ethical paradigm and a more enlightened mode of living, one based in one-world thinking. If so, then the spiritual transformation which the individual can affect through study and work on him-or herself could be key to the development of such a global ethic of compassion.

PART II
TWENTIETH-CENTURY PEACEMAKERS

(8) **Vena Rani Howard** outlines Gandhi's interpretation of *ahimsā* (non-harm) as the greatest virtue expounded in the Hindu text, the *Mahābhārata*. For Gandhi *Ahimsā* as justice and mercy is in full agreement with praise of *ahimsā* in the *Mahābhārata* as the "highest justice" and the "greatest sacrifice." Self-sacrifice for the other is *ahimsā* and it is one's highest duty. Gandhi's justice is not blindfolded, but proceeds with the open eyes of wisdom overflowing with mercy.

(9) **Terrence Rynne & Michael Duffey** explore Gandhi's indebtedness to the Gospels and the profound impact that Gandhi's life and teaching have had on contemporary Christianity.

(10) **Irfan A. Omar** discusses the life and thought of a contemporary Gandhian Muslim theologian *Maulana Wahiduddin* Khan. He reflects on Gandhi's view of Islam in view of his [Gandhi's] theology of world religions and also on Khan's understanding of non-Muslims in light of his [Khan's] theology of Islamic nonviolence. He then goes on to examine what these two figures share in common, namely the ways in which they insist on seeing the "other" in respectful terms. One theme around which this comparison revolves is the much misunderstood notion of jihad.(11) The Jesuits, founded by Ignatius of Loyola in 1540, were among the first "internationalists" and often attempted to bring mutual understanding and peace to adversaries. **John Patrick Donnelly, S.J.** chronicles efforts of European Jesuits to mediate conflicts between Russia and Poland in the 16th century, between the Russian Czar and Chinese Emperor in the 17th century, and between the U.S. government and Native American leaders in the 19th century.

(12) **Hideyuki Koyama, S.J.** documents the contribution made by a community of Jesuit priests in a working class Catholic neighborhood of Belfast to bridging sectarian divisions.

(13) **Angela Hurley** profiles two Victorians, W.R. Inge and Jane Addams. Inge, an Anglican minister, lecturer and author decried the two world wars he witnessed as "the worst disease of civilization." He spent his life urging Christians to allow the New Testament's ethic of unselfish love to transform them—the only real alternative to the libelous labeling of others that fanned lethal nationalism and patriotism. Jane Addams is best known for her efforts to introduce "collective compassion" into the social systems of the U.S. She was also at the vanguard of movements for gender and race equality and international peace, and was convinced that the nurturing instinct in human beings was older and stronger than our inclination toward aggression.

(14) **Philip Naylor** offers a personal glimpse into the life of the Orthodox Patriarch of Istanbul, Athenagoras I, who ruled from 1948-72. Athenagoras was raised in a mixed Turkish-Greek and Orthodox Christian-Islamic village. From childhood, he was personally very familiar with Islam and respected its Abrahamic traditions, and, as patriarch, he would worked with Catholics, Protestants, Jews and Muslims. Naylor writes: "[Athenagoras] shocked the Orthodox and Christian world by praying in a mosque. Once when he was asked a confrontational question regarding Hagia Sophia's status as a museum rather than as one of Christendom's greatest churches, he responded: "In the time of Byzantium, Hagia Sophia was open to all. Today, as a museum, it is again open to all." The Patriarch was a symbol of rapprochement between the Greeks and the Turks throughout the crisis in Cyprus. He labored tirelessly on the question of the unity of Christianity, exchanging a fraternal "kiss of peace" with Pope John XXIII in 1964, the first meeting of a patriarch and pope since 1439.

(15 **Marc Ellis** asks what it means to be a faithful Jew today. The Holocaust and the state of Israel are primary symbols of contemporary Jewish identity. The Palestinians, however, he argues, are now also a permanent part of Jewish history. Their suffering is joined to that of the Jews, both of which constitute "an ever-broadening narrative that speaks truth to power." Ellis recalls the ancient Israelite prophets' critique of the wielding of military power and their stress on God's care for the victim. Rather than a "Constantinian Judaism" that places reli-

gion and power at the service of the state, he calls for Jews to use the memory of the Holocaust as a "bridge to all those suffering injustice."

(16) Michel Andraos explores the success of the Catholic Church of Chiapas Mexico, and its Bishop, Samuel Ruiz, in their roles as mediators and peacemakers in the struggle of the Mayas against the government of Mexico. Ruiz is a recent example of fostering "the creation of the conditions and space for civil, political and social forces to come together and become co-participants in building peace."

PART III

PEACEMAKING THROUGH EDUCATIONAL INSTITUTIONS
AND ECONOMIC DEVELOPMENT PROGRAMS

The final group of essays in this collection addresses peacemaking efforts from several perspectives: education, business entrepreneurship, and the consumer culture.

(17) Nathan Tierney examines the presuppositions and methodologies commonly drawn upon in peace programs, posing tough questions to the profession of peace education in order to more deeply engage students. He outlines "an expanded and more inclusive peace curriculum" that bridges cultures and ideologies in the same way that the most successful humanitarian and development non-governmental agencies (NGOs) have done. (e.g., Amnesty International, Doctors Without Borders, etc.)

(18) Lee Thomas and the late Paul Weber argue that given the increasing difficulties local suppliers are encountering in concealing unfair and unsafe labor practices from watchdog organizations such as the WTO, the IMF and other NGOs multinational businesses can act as instruments of justice and peace. The authors focus on the International Standards Organization founded in 1994, which monitors corporate performance with respect to environmental and worker rights. Social Accountability International includes in its worker standards (SA 8000) a living wage requirement. Although some U.S. corporations see this as a threat to short term profitability, others have signed on with SA 8000. Issues of accountability, compliance and transparency still remain to be resolved. The proliferation of codes of conduct has made it possible for some corporate players to plead innocence and confusion. Thomas and Weber point to a recent "successful effort to unite leading code of conduct organizations" that will allow

international businesses to bring ethical principles to bear in "order that people the world over can look forward to a better tomorrow."

Elsewhere, Thomas reflects on his life and the work of peacemaking by noting that, in August 1945, he was aboard a ship heading for Japan, to be part of the first invasion force. Over the ship's loudspeakers came news that an atom bomb had just destroyed the city of Hiroshima. Thomas was jubilant—until he arrived in Hiroshima as part of the U.S. occupation force: *"They were ordinary people, like we were. They carried pictures of loved ones, some of whom had been killed in the war. They were grieving, as we were."* He later joined the Quakers and has spent fifty years bringing their values (recognizing the inner light in all beings) to bear in the manufacturing business he led. He recently offered this prayer to pilgrims at Gethsemane Monastery as they passed through his hometown of Louisville, Kentucky:

> *Dear God, Father and Mother of us all, those of us that have fought in war have a special need for Thy mercy and forgiveness for we have killed Thy children.*
>
> *Bless and encourage those who would follow in the tradition of Mohandas Gandhi and Martin Luther King, Jr. Amen.*

(19) Luke Thompson addresses an enormous audience — and a politically complex one—namely, consumers and the sweatshop workers who labor to produce the goods which consumers purchase. Building on Marx's observation that workers suffer from alienation, Thompson describes how "the consumer is confronted with a vast economic system that depends on, and thus *demands*, the habitual purchase of goods." The sheer scale of modern multinational production, coupled with the powerful marketing techniques of the apparel industry, most often eclipse consumers' capacity for making ethical choices. "One must go the distance, become attached to the world community, and realize that both worker and consumer have a natural place in the market. The walls came down for me when a friend introduced me to his Cambodian fiancée whose family had worked in sweatshops across the ocean — a life changing moment indeed."

PART IV

CONCLUSION

(20) Daniel Maguire points out the powerful ironies embedded in the fact that we often tend to view war as a sort of spectator sport. A tacit endorsement of war and related undertakings seems to be suffused into the very sinews of our cultural imagination. War is effectively state-sponsored violence and, as such, requires an honest moral valuation of our involvement with it. It can perhaps never be referred to as "just." Maguire notes that the U.N. Charter was meant to put an end to the vigilante approach to war illustrated by Adolph Hitler as well as by the "preemptive war" policy of George W. Bush, and he claims that the primary challenge to contemporary ethics is to rethink the problem of the morality of war. Catholic moral theology has perhaps never really risen to the challenge put to it by some of its greatest historic figures (e.g., Pope John XXIII in *Pacem in Terris* [1963]: "it is irrational to believe that war is still an apt means of vindicating violated rights.") Still, stirrings of a "moral globalization" are perceptible today, as evidenced by such developments as the simultaneous anti-war demonstrations of February 15, 2003 in 80 nations around the planet. Maguire reminds us that citizenship in religious terms is not a privilege, but a *vocation*—one to which serious learning duties attach. Failure to respond to those duties is corrupt and evidence of the death of collective political consciousness. Tearless in the face of war is an indication that one is an enemy of peace; tears are, after all, Christic. (Jeremiah: "Unless your eyes run with tears you will come to a terrible ruin." 9:18-19). Finally, while we may be infected with a radical moral complacency (what Maguire terms the Imperial Comfort Syndrome), there is also reason to be hopeful about the future. It is evidenced in the various historic cases of successful nonviolent resistance to aggression and injustice.

Finally, the Manresa conference and the papers contained herein represent one effort at addressing the question of peacemaking. There are doubtless numerous other avenues which can be fruitfully explored to the same end. It is our hope that readers will find these essays informative and thought provoking, and that they will be able to draw on the insights they contain to enhance their own thinking and praxis. Given the complexities of the current world situation, no effort at peacemaking can be in vain. Any contribution toward the creation of more humane, conflict-free conditions of life for all human beings will prove valuable.

PART I
RELIGIOUS TEXTS AS
STARTING POINTS FOR DIALOGUE

I. TRANSFORMING LOVE:
HOLINESS AND THE VOCATION OF JUSTICE

NANCY M. MARTIN

The religions of the world suggest that in order for humans to live up to our full humanity and our full potential as spiritual beings, we are in need of transformation. Educating the mind is very necessary but insufficient. We must also educate the heart and transform our limited understanding of self. Religions put forward an ideal of holiness—or alternatively we might use the words "purity" or "sacredness"—toward which human beings might strive and with which we might align ourselves. In an inter-religious context, to become "holy" is to be transformed in the fire of love and realization to such a degree that one becomes transparent to the Transcendent and, in so doing, not only acts with love and compassion but manifests or embodies love and compassion in the world. Love then is not only something which one *does* but also something which one *is*. Few truly aspire to this state and few reach it fully, but those who do so inspire the rest of us, whether we are Hindus, Christians, Jews, Muslims, Buddhists, Confucians, followers of indigenous traditions or profess no religious affiliation.

We tend to call such people "saints," "sages" or "bodhisattvas," and they move among us transforming the lives of those they touch in great and small ways. And that transformative effect transcends the boundaries of religions and cultures as well as time, for it is recognizable to us, apprehended by the heart as well as the mind. This holiness, or love embodied, fuels the fight against injustice, as the saint acts in ways that radically deny hierarchies of difference in the universal power of love. That love, embodied by the saint or sage or bodhisattva, exposes and overwhelms injustice and reaches out to heal the suffering of both the oppressor and the oppressed. The holiness perfected in the saint guards against the subtle and not so subtle intrusion of self and self-righteousness into even our most charitable acts and sets the fight for justice and against injustice within the wider horizon of love. Understood in lesser terms, this fight can easily lead to forms of violence.

Though we may draw a distinction between the saint and the social or peace activist and though the activist may criticize the saint for being insufficiently socially engaged, I will argue that the pursuit of holiness is not an alternate path to the pursuit of justice. It is not to be practiced only by saints, bodhisattvas and monastics, but rather is an integral part of the religious vocation of justice. Indeed the cultivation of holiness is a key element of the vocation of pursuing peace and justice even as the pursuit of justice, arising within the wider horizon of love and compassion, is a key to the practice of the religious life, particularly in the twenty-first century. I will begin by examining the path to holiness and the nature of the holy person presented in the world religions—in the monotheisms of the West, and in Hinduism, Buddhism and Confucianism. I will then briefly explore the relationship between justice and the love and compassion embodied by such holy persons. This essay will conclude with a look at the lives of contemporary figures who bring together holiness and justice in their own vocations and therefore offer us models for living the religious life and working toward justice and peace in our time.

THE CULTIVATION OF HOLINESS
IN THE WORLD RELIGIONS[1]

To be holy, I have suggested, is to become transparent to the Transcendent. What I mean by this is that the individual comes to embody attributes of the Transcendent in the world. To reach this state of transparency or openness, a radical transformation of the individual is required, a move away from self-centeredness to other-centeredness and from false conceptions of the self to a true understanding of the nature of the human and the world. The cultivation of holiness, defined in this way, is a fundamental element of the religious path, though understandings of the Transcendent and the human vary across religious traditions. Further, a definitive mark of the Transcendent and of the fully realized holy person is love or compassion. This love has the power to transform the self and the world; and it is also a primary characteristic of the transformed individual.

LOVE AS AN ATTRIBUTE OF THE TRANSCENDENT

Whether we are talking about God in Judaism, Christianity and Islam or about Brahman in Hinduism, love is understood to be a principal attribute of the Transcendent. In the monotheisms of the West, the human-divine relation is characterized primarily by love, coupled with awe, and God's love is the wellspring of the human capacity to love. Jewish daily prayers speak of the deep and tender love God has for God's people, and according to Jewish mystical texts it is God's love which enlivens and governs the universe.[2] In Islam, Allah's compassion and mercy are continually invoked in the Qur'an, and in the Christian New Testament we find clearly articulated the understanding that God not only loves but *is* love: "God is love and the one who abides in love abides in God and God in that person."[3]

Alternately, in Hinduism, the Transcendent is understood to be Brahman, the One Reality behind all that is; and all existence (including human beings and the world) is a part of that divine reality. Brahman can be experienced by humans either as impersonal—a oneness into which the practitioner merges as in *advaita vedanta*—or as personal—a loving Lord who loves humans with a passionate and abiding love, as in *bhakti* or devotional forms of Hinduism. Brahman ultimately defies description, but in trying to move people toward a realization of the true nature of this transcendent reality, the Upanishads speak of Brahman as all encompassing, as no one thing and yet all things, as their source and end, as the Supreme Spirit and as *sat-chit-ananda* (being, consciousness and bliss). With respect to love, the Kena Upanishad says of this Supreme Being:

> His name is Tadvanam, which translated means "the End of love-longing." As Tadvanam he should have adoration. All beings will love such a lover of the Lord.[4]

Such a personalistic understanding of Brahman as Lord is more fully articulated in the *Bhagavad-gita* and comes into full bloom in the devotional forms of Hinduism. From a devotional or *bhakti* perspective, Brahman is the Divine Beloved, passionately loved and in love with the human devotee in a relationship that is both intimate and all encompassing.

Buddhism and Confucianism, in contrast, do not speak in such personal terms of the Transcendent, yet even in these non-theistic Asian traditions, compassion and human-heartedness are characteristics of the enlightened or fully-realized person, the person who has fully developed his or her own enlightened mind or whose life and character have been completely aligned with the Transcendent. Compassion in Buddhism is a fundamental characteristic of the *Dharmakaya* or uni-

versal Buddha Nature, while humanheartedness in Confucianism is
a principal aspect of a society and world which mirror the ordering
principle of all reality, *T'ien* or Heaven.

THE PURSUIT OF HOLINESS AND
THE TRANSFORMING POWER OF LOVE

In theistic traditions, the holy person is one who is steeped in love,
not only for God but also for fellow humans. Humans are created in
the image of God, according to Judaism, Christianity and Islam, and
our capacity to love arises out of this similitude. In Judaism, humans
are first and foremost called to love God "with all your heart, and with
all your soul, and with all your might."[5] This love is demonstrated
through action—through the study of the Torah, allowing humans
to know and love God more deeply and to become more and more
godly themselves, and through following the commandments, which
facilitate the cultivation of personal holiness and the instantiation of
justice in society.

These actions ultimately lead the human being into something
much more radical—a dynamic loving relationship with God that can
transform the self and dissolve the boundaries between self and God.
The language of romantic love found in the Hebrew scriptures in the
Song of Songs is used to describe the depth and passion of the love
between the soul and God. This text, referred to by Rabbi Akiba in
the Mishnah as the "Holy of Holies" among the writings of the Torah,
describes this human-divine love as "fierce as death, its jealousy bitter
as the grave. Even its sparks are a raging fire, a devouring flame. Great
seas cannot extinguish love, no river can sweep it away."[6] Like human
romantic love, this love takes delight in the presence of the Divine Beloved, but it is also marked by a deeper desire to "cleave to God" (*deve-
kut*).[7] This cleaving may begin with imitation of God, but it ends in an
experience of complete union in which the distinction between human
and Divine is dissolved.[8] According to followers of the Hassidic tradition, "God is love and the capacity to love is [the hu]man's innermost
participation in God. This capacity is never lost but needs only to be
purified to be raised to God himself. Thus love is not only a feeling;
it is the godly in existence."[9] The one who cleaves to God enters the
"Holy of Holies" of which Rabbi Akiba spoke, with the self now open
to and bound to God, but still retaining a distinct existence.

To love then is to be holy, to participate in God, and to be the presence of God in the world. The capacity to love *all* people as God does
is latent in every person but must be developed to the point that one's
empathy for another becomes identification, and their suffering becomes one's own. Thus the boundaries between self and other break
down in these human-human relations, and this outward flowing and
unbounded love is also a part of holiness and participation in God,
according to Jewish mystical traditions. Love of one's fellow humans
becomes inextricably bound up with love of God.

In Christianity, this realization of the dynamic nature of love is enshrined in the foundational love commandments:

> You must love the Lord your God with all your heart, with all your
> soul, and with all your mind. This is the greatest and the first com-
> mandment. The second resembles it: You must love your neighbor
> as yourself.[10]

Christian love for God, too, must be total, encompassing heart, soul
and mind, and it must be extended outward. Christians are called to
love not only those who love them (the realm of ordinary human love)
but to love even their enemies, and to manifest this love by acting not
for evil but for good and by helping those in need.[11]

The cultivation of love is the focus of the writing of Christian mystics across the centuries who describe their experiences of the love of
God in terms which fit what Joseph Runzo has called "seraphic love,"
an encompassing love incorporating the other-directedness and un-
conditionality of *agape* in dynamic tension with the passionate rela-
tionality and vulnerability of *eros*.[12] These Christian mystics also draw
on the Song of Songs, and indeed this text was the most often recited
and commented upon scripture in the monasteries of medieval Europe.[13] In one such commentary, the twelfth-century Cistercian Abbot
Bernard of Clairvaux claims that "Of all the motions, the senses, the
affections of the soul, it is love alone in which the creature is able, even,
if not on an equal basis, to repay the Creator for what it has received,
to weigh back something from the same measure."[14] To cultivate this
capacity to love is the highest pursuit. Human love offers a stepping
stone to deepen this capacity and Christ's humanity provides a bridge,
according to Bernard, "draw[ing] the soul into holiness."[15]

For the mystic, when the soul reaches the highest level of holiness, it
loves as it is loved, entering into a so-called "spiritual marriage" marked

by a loving union with God that "deifies" the soul. In so doing, the soul
not only loves but becomes love, its nature and its will conforming to
that of God. At times, this love bewilders and overwhelms the soul,
and St. Teresa of Avila speaks of it as a piercing pain that so overcomes
the lover of God, that "that the soul does not know either what is the
matter with it or what it desires."[16] To love God in this context includes
the willingness to let go of all else but God. The egoistic self is burned
away in the conflagration of love. French beguine Marguerite Porete
writes of this passing away of the self into the divine Beloved, declaring "I am so transformed that I have lost my name in order to love, I
who can love so little; it is into Love that I have been transformed;
for I love nothing but Love." [17] Such holy individuals stand outside of
the bounds of religious institutions, and the love they embody inherently challenges social hierarchies and religious authority. Marguerite
Porete was burned at the stake for her words, and many other mystics
were called before the Inquisition in an effort to silence them. Islamic
Sufi mystics sometimes suffered a similar fate.

In Orthodox Islam, the human-Divine relation is defined as one of
human submission to God, but that relation is understood to be submission motivated not by fear of punishment or desire for paradise,
but by pure love for God. God in turn is understood to be loving, compassionate and merciful, reaching out to those who seek a closer and
more intimate relationship. Indeed, in a well-loved *hadith*, Allah says

> My servant continues to come near to me by piety beyond what is
> required so that I love him…And if my servant approaches a hand's
> breadth, I go toward him and arm's length; and if he approaches
> an arm's length, I go forward the space of outstretched arms; and
> if he comes toward me walking, I go toward him running. And if
> my servant should bring to me sins the size of the earth itself, my
> forgiveness will be more than equal to them."[18]

The Sufi mystics of Islam, in particular, pursue this closeness to God,
and for them, divine love is so overpowering that all awareness of self
ceases and only God remains. [19] As with many Christian mystics, this
love is experienced by the Sufis as affliction, suffering and poverty, so
much so that they speak of the "martyrdom of love." The egoistic self
passes away in a love that knows no bounds. Such a state of awareness
led the tenth-century Sufi al-Hallaj to proclaim: "I am He whom I
love, and He whom I love is me," an utterance that led to his physical
martyrdom when others, misunderstanding his meaning, accused him

of claiming to be God's equal.[20] As in Christianity, the radical transformative power of this ecstatic love does not fit readily into the confines of religious authority and the divinely inspired law within Islam, but the mystic, like the moth drawn to the flame, cannot act otherwise.

The one who loves in this way becomes Divine Love and embodies that love in the world. Allah, it is said, has placed signs revealing God's nature in the world and in the human heart, so that human love reveals the nature of God's love and mirrors that love. Humans are called to love as God loves. Indeed a deep care for those in need and for the poor is enshrined in the required giving of alms, one of the five foundational pillars of Islam. In doing this, humans embody the generosity and compassion of Allah in the world. The saints of Islam, like the saintly figures of Judaism and Christianity, are those who have achieved a humility and selflessness that allows others to see and experience God's love and compassion through them.

In Hinduism, we find a different understanding of the Transcendent, not as creator God but as the One Reality underlying all that is, and the spiritual goal is to dissolve the veils of ignorance in order to be able to apprehend this truth. Yet the precise nature of this realization is variously conceived. For the follower of the way of knowledge, *jnana yoga*, described in the literature of the Upanishads, that realization leads to a merger into that One Reality, as all distinction passes away, like a drop of water merging into the sea. For those on the path of love, *bhakti yoga*, that One Reality is experienced not as an impersonal oneness but as loving Lord. The ideal human response to this loving Lord, and indeed the purpose of human life, is love. But it is hard for humans to love the Unmanifest One, and so this Lord lovingly appears to humans in multiple incarnational forms. Ultimately the devotee is not separate from the Divine Beloved, nor is the love which binds them. Rather together they are the manifestation, the play or *lila* of the Lord.

It is in the *Bhagavad-gita* (composed circa 200 BCE) that we first find the way of love portrayed as a path distinct from the way of knowledge found in the Upanishads. When Arjuna's charioteer Lord Krishna tells him that he must do what is right or *dharmic* only because it is right, letting go of any and all attachment to the fruits of his actions, he falters. He does want to fulfill his duties as a ruler and to act according to such universal dharmic virtues as "compassion for all creatures, patience, lack of envy...generosity and lack of greed" (also enumerated in Gautama's Dharma Sutra and elsewhere) and thus to align his life with the dharmic moral structure of the world. But to do so without attachment, without acting on behalf of self in any way, is no easy task. The self is capricious and tenacious and so must be disciplined and transformed. One way to achieve this goal is to follow the difficult meditational discipline taught by the Upanishads. Such a path necessitates no theistic or relational conception of the Transcendent but instead leads to the silencing of the mind—a silence out of which realization and self-transformation can emerge. But there is another path to selfless action advocated by Krishna—the path of devotion. Indeed Krishna tells Arjuna, "By devotion alone can I, as I really am, be known and seen and entered into,"[21] and he encourages Arjuna to offer up his actions as a sacrifice to him so that he may no longer act for self but for God.

The transformative power of this devotional relationship with the One is much more clearly articulated in the later *bhakti* literature which draws on all the dimensions of human love relationships to describe the breadth and depth of this intimate love. Devotees speak of their relation to the Divine as a romance marked by intense mutual longing, ecstatic union, and devastating separation. The union which the human devotee and Divine Beloved both long for is in dynamic tension with the separateness which makes love possible. The devotee is a part of the Divine Reality and thus not ultimately separate (as the creature is from the Creator in the monotheisms of the West), and yet it is the separateness of the manifestation and the One manifesting that allows love to arise. This separation is felt keenly by the devotee; the fifteenth-century North Indian saint Mirabai accuses her Lord Krishna of drawing her into love and then abandoning her. She begs him not to leave her but if he must go, then to build a funeral pyre of fragrant sandalwood and aloe, and light it with his own hand. "When I am burned away to cinders," she says, "rub this ash upon your limbs. Let flame be lost in flame."[22] Only God remains, and her words echo those of Christian and Muslim saints who speak of the conflagration of love and of annihilation.

If love can bring the human and the divine into a relationship of mutuality, then there are clearly no grounds in this *bhakti* religious worldview for human hierarchies of caste, gender or religious authority. Its saints include women and men and people of high and low caste, and their insistence on the equality of all before God has been a radical democratizing force within Hinduism. Yet attempts to fully establish this equality in the social realm have at times evoked extreme violence, as in the case of the twelfth-century community of Kalyana in the Kanada speaking region of South India where devotees succeeded for a time in creating a religious and social community some 150,000 strong in which only the depth of one's religious experience was grounds for authority and deferential treatment.[23] The songs of the bhakti saints, which are the principal religious texts in this strand of Hinduism, affirm the dignity and equality of all, unmask the prejudices embedded in social hierarchies, challenge intra- and interreligious squabbling, and offer an alternative value system based not on money, power or birth but on devotion to God and on love. These songs when sung by those who suffer oppression and deprivation have become a language of resistance, used to declare a "space to be human."[24]

In Buddhism, it is the deep experience of suffering and impermanence that leads to a radical transformation of conceptions of the self. This transformation lies at the heart of liberating realization, and a principal characteristic of the holy or realized person is his or her great compassion for others. As in Hinduism, the veils of ignorance must fall away from the mind as it comes to realize the true nature of reality. For the Buddhist this realization is that all things are made up of non-self elements and thus are radically interdependent—there is no hard and fast boundary between self and other—instead, things "inter-are," as Thich Nhat Hanh puts it. This is the realization of dependent co-arising and of anatman or no-self. Mistaken notions of the existence of independent and separate selves are shattered; and compassion, together with the other Buddhist virtues of loving kindness, magnanimous joy and equanimity, arise with this realization and flow out toward all sentient beings.[25] This compassion and love is embodied in the Mahayana Buddhist ideal of the *bodhisattva*, who vows to work for the liberation of all beings and who responds to the suffering of others not with objectifying pity but with a deep empathy which feels another's pain as one's own.

This compassion is both naturally arising and intentionally cultivated in Buddhist practice. Buddhists seek to develop *bodhicitta*, which can be translated both as "the mind of enlightenment" and "the mind of love," so that they might exercise a wise and universal compassion. Those who truly realize *anatman* and become fully transparent to reality as it is in itself manifest this wise compassion in the world. Indeed,

the ideal bodhisattva in early Mahayana literature is Vimalakirti, decidedly a man of the world and not a monastic living in isolation from
it.

Confucianism offers a different approach. From a Confucian point
of view, a person comes into the world not yet completely formed
and needs to become fully human, through cultivation of the self and
through aligning him or herself with the Transcendent. This Transcendent is T'ien or "Heaven," the ordering power shaping and enliv-
ening the world through the structuring principle of li and the dynamic matter-energy continuum of chi. The cultivation or development of
the self is the fundamental task of human beings and requires education in the "arts of peace:" literature and poetry, math and science, history and ritual, art and music. Further, to reach the culmination of this
humanizing process, they must learn to act in concert with "heaven,
earth and the myriad things," and in doing so to act according to li and
with ren or human heartedness, which are as inseparable as Buddhist
compassion and wisdom.[26]

Ren or human heartedness, like Buddhist compassion, requires being able to fully empathize with another, to put oneself in his or her
place to the extent that the fully realized person is, in the words of David Hall and Roger Ames, "an indivisible continuum between 'self' and
'other,' between 'I' and 'we,' between 'subject' and 'object,' between 'now'
and 'then.'"[27] Confucius himself refers to the ability to "love others" (ai
jen)—to take another "into one's sphere of concern, and in so doing
make [that person] an integral aspect of one's own person"—to be an
essential capacity of the fully developed person.[28] In Confucianism
this love is to be cultivated in specific and expanding relationships of
reciprocity, beginning with the family and moving outward to community, nation, humanity, and ultimately to "the myriad things."[29] These
structured, shared understandings of reciprocal social responsibilities
in specific types of love relationships were, in Confucius's mind, indispensable to the instantiation of love in a society, and thus he rejected
the general call for universal love put forward by his contemporary
Mo-Tzu as impractical and impracticable.

Confucius sought to sanctify the secular, to bring attitudes that one
might bring to a religious ritual to bear on the social interactions of everyday life. The ideal person in the Confucian tradition is the sage who
has completed a process of self-cultivation and self-transformation so
that he or she is neither mean-spirited nor small-minded, but rather

at home in the world and able to put others at ease, empathetic, loving and wise and able to inspire others to virtue and human-heartedness. The ideal society is one whose leaders most fully embody human-heartedness and lead by virtue and decidedly not by any form of force. If there are people in need in a society—the poor and destitute—then the society is failing its mandate of human-heartedness even as it is if it resorts to violent conflict.

Love, compassion and human-heartedness do have the power to transform the self and the world, dropping the boundaries of self to create a new shared identity and a new world. Such transformation of the self is a principal goal of the world's religions, though that self might be variously understood as soul, *atman*, or *anatman* and the underlying problem understood as willful disobedience, ignorance or the incompleteness of the process of becoming fully human. This transformation requires the complete dismantling of former limited and egoistic notions of the self so that a transformed self might arise. As the Sufi poet Rumi exclaims, "The way of love is not a subtle argument. The door there is devastation." [30] The pursuit of this transformation is the pursuit of holiness; love, compassion and/or human-heartedness grow in proportion to holiness as this change is effected.

Religions have developed disciplines for bringing about such transformation, but one need not be religious to undergo such an experience. Something of the same self transformation and holiness may also come unbidden to those whose "hearts are broken" and who have reached the point of devastation "somewhere between rage and despair," through their deep empathy for the suffering of fellow human beings. Such a transformation has been eloquently described by James Orbinski, Head of Mission for Doctors without Borders in Kigali during the Rwandan genocide. [31]

THE PURSUIT OF JUSTICE
WITHIN THE WIDER HORIZON OF LOVE

Where does the vocation of justice and peacemaking fit into this pursuit of self-transformation and holiness marked by love, compassion or human-heartedness? We have already seen that the actions of the holy have led to their persecution. The love and compassion which they embody affirms the equality of all before God and challenges those social and religious structures which instantiate inequality or are silent to suffering and injustice. To live the life of love necessarily exposes injustice and offers a concrete demonstration of an alternate way of being in the world, one which both embraces justice and actively seeks to relieve suffering.

Writing of morality generally, the philosopher William Frankena, argues that the "law of love" which he identifies with "the principle of benevolence, that is, of doing good," underlies the entire moral law. He insists that "it must be supplemented by the principle of distributive justice or equality," but that "the principle of benevolence is presupposed even by the principle of justice." This further leads Frankena to view the law of love as "underl[ying] the entire moral law even though this cannot all be derived from it. In this sense [he says], it is…true that on it hang all the law and the prophets," as the Christian scriptures suggest.[32] If Frankena is correct, and I believe that he is, then love or the principle of benevolence is the foundation for justice and morality, and distributive justice is an essential aspect of moral action and of love. The love or compassion embodied by the holy person does have this universal nature that moves him or her to feel and seek to alleviate the suffering of others and to act equally benevolently toward all. Thus it inherently carries within it a concern for justice.

Frankena goes on to argue that morality includes both character traits and principles, dimensions of both being and doing, a conception that is congruent with the cultivation of holiness of character which leads to actions guided by a love supplemented by justice.[33] Confucius would agree, arguing that a developed human character and structured relationships were necessary to instantiate the love and high moral behavior that mark human-heartedness in the world. Frankena, too, argues that "The life of pure love, unsupplemented by [a principle of justice], is not the moral life; it is not immoral, but it is beyond morality. And it is not possible on earth."[34] Yet were a person to exist who lived this life of pure love, that love would nevertheless also reveal injustice, through its attention to those who suffer, seeking to heal and also to put an end to preventable and dehumanizing suffering, as well as to the dehumanizing effect of imposing such suffering on others. Our world is one of divisions and of terrible injustice, violence and suffering. Our life of love within this world must also necessarily be a life which exposes injustice and actively works to promote justice out of the equality and universality of love. Pure justice unsupplemented by love is also not something we would want to advocate, for when it is untempered by mercy and compassion, justice carries an unrelenting and harsh retributive as well as distributive dimension. The pursuit of justice then rightly belongs within the wider horizon of love, which is its proper ground and foundation.

When we turn to those spiritual leaders we might call holy in our time, those who serve in some sense as our global saints, for example, Mother Teresa, Mahatma Gandhi, Reverend Martin Luther King Jr., Archbishop Desmond Tutu, the fourteenth Dalai Lama, and Thich Nhat Hanh (and many others), the love which they embody clearly includes this concern for justice and for peace. These people have acted counter to injustice and in ways that expose suffering and injustice, particularly inequalities in the ways in which people are treated. As holy persons, they have affirmed the dignity and value of all, with regard to social hierarchies and divisions by focusing on a common humanity, and in the case of the Buddhists among them, of our inextricable inter-being. Notably, they have also often affirmed the value of multiple religious traditions, and quote sacred scriptures from many of them. As the embodiment of love and compassion, they feel the suffering of other beings and respond to that suffering with loving action.

In some cases, as with Mother Teresa of Calcutta, their vocation may not be to directly confront structures of oppression; nevertheless, their very lives challenge those structures and the power which keeps them in place. She saw herself as following in the footsteps of Jesus, who, at times, disregarded rules of holiness in favor of healing the sick and feeding the hungry, and moved among the socially outcaste— prostitutes, tax collectors, lepers, the impure and the poor. She felt him calling her

> to serve the most miserable, the poorest of the poor in Calcutta: those who have nothing and nobody; those whom others refuse to approach because they are filthy and teeming with germs and parasites; those who can't go out and beg because they are naked, don't even have a piece of rag to put over them, and can't bear going naked in public; those who collapse in the street, exhausted and emaciated, conscious of the fact that they are dying; those who no longer cry because they don't have any more tears. These are the people [she says] that Jesus told [her] to love. [35]

A well-loved teacher in a sheltered Catholic girl's school, she heard this calling as she watched the suffering of the most marginalized people during a wave of communal violence that racked Calcutta be-

fore the partition of India, and she took up the work of offering these
people love and dignity. Descriptions of Mother Teresa's life speak of
the depth of her prayerfulness—her pursuit of holiness. She herself
speaks of seeing Jesus in each person to whom she extended this love,
and at the heart of her ministry and her teachings was love.

"Each individual," she says," has been created to love...and to be
loved." And her words continue to encourage others to "Do small
things with great love. It is not how much we do, but how much love
we put into giving." That love knows no boundaries of caste, gender,
nationality or religion. For she says, "It is your love of God that is the
main thing. Religion is meant to help us to come together. It is not
meant to separate us...that is, true religion. You can't call it religion
if it destroys us. We have all been created for the same purpose... To
love and be loved." And, according to Mother Teresa, "all works of love
are works of peace."

Her favorite prayer was that of St. Francis which begins,

> Lord, make me an instrument of your peace,
>
> Where there is hatred, let me show love.
>
> Where there is injury, pardon...
>
> Where there is doubt, faith.
>
> Where there is despair, hope.
>
> Where there is darkness, light.
>
> Where there is sadness, joy...
>
> Grant that I may not so much seek to be consoled as to console, to
> be understood as to understand; to be loved as to love...[36]

St. Francis's words are as relevant today as they were in the twelfth
century. Still, they take on new layers of meaning as we become increasingly aware of the roots of injustice and as we work toward interreligious and inter-cultural understanding.

The other figures I have mentioned—Gandhi, Tutu, King, Hanh,
and the Dalai Lama—have engaged more overtly in the work of peacemaking and the pursuit of justice. Gandhi and the Dalai Lama challenged colonial domination, Tutu and King confronted institutionalized racism, and Hanh pursued an end to the brutality of war. And
they have done so from a distinctly religious perspective. We are familiar with their work. In each case, they have embraced a path of
nonviolent activism, a path of empathy and reconciliation which al-

lows no room for the demonizing of opponents, a path of speaking the Truth to power and of working actively to address the needs of the poor and marginalized and championing their rights. And each of these figures has also pursued holiness with discipline and cultivated love and compassion to such a degree that they have come to embody it for us and for our time.

This is all wonderful, we may say, but I am not Gandhi or Tutu or King or Hanh or Mother Teresa. They are, after-all, saints. They are holy, but we more ordinary people cannot hope to aspire to their transparency to divine love. Yet the twin pursuits of justice and holiness are not merely the vocation of saints. Christian engagement in the battle against slavery and racism, Hindu engagement in the struggle against colonial domination, caste oppression and communalism, as well as the rise of Liberation Theology within Christianity and of Engaged Buddhism in the 1960s, all reflect a widening sense of the importance of love and compassion as forces for healing in the world. Individuals who wed holiness to justice have emerged as those who can lead our global community toward lasting peace and the honoring of human rights and human dignity.

Our saints encourage us to act even as others have in these struggles. His Holiness the Dalai Lama writes,

> If we are unable to use our human intelligence in a positive way, there is no purpose to human life. We will simply be machines to produce manure. Human beings should be able to use their intelligence, their discriminating awareness, to contribute to the welfare of all sentient beings. That is how to make life meaningful. That is the way to bring about peace, both temporarily and in the long run.[37]

Engaged Buddhist Thich Nhat Hanh, speaking out of his experience of the horrors of war in Vietnam, asks us to look deeply into the suffering of others:

> The essence of love and compassion is understanding, the ability to recognize the physical, material, and psychological suffering of others, to put ourselves "inside the skin" of the other. We "go inside" their body, feelings, and mental formations, and witness for ourselves their suffering.[38]

He challenges us further, saying:

Do not avoid contact with suffering or close your eyes before suffering. Do not lose awareness of the existence of suffering in the life
of the world. Find ways to be with those who are suffering, by all
means, including personal contact and visits, images, and sound. By
such means, awaken yourself and others to the reality of suffering
in the world.[39]

In the face of such suffering, Archbishop Desmond Tutu rallies us to
hope and action, saying

There may indeed have been moments when God regretted creating
us. But I am certain there have been many more times when God
has looked and seen all these wonderful people who have shone in
the dark night of evil and torture and abuses and suffering; shone as
they have demonstrated their nobility of spirit, their magnanimity
as they have been ready to forgive, and so they have dispelled the
murkiness, and fresh air has blown into that situation to transfigure
it. It has filled people with new hope that despair, darkness, anger
and resentment and hatred would not have the last word. There is
hope that a new situation could come about when enemies might
become friends again, when the dehumanized perpetrator might be
helped to recover his lost humanity. This is not a wild irresponsible
dream. It has happened and it is happening and there is hope that
nightmares will end, hope that seemingly intractable problems will
find solutions and that God has some tremendous fellow-workers,
some outstanding partners out there.

He marvels that humans might indeed be called to be the presence of
God in the world in the pursuit of justice and compassion and in an
effort to sanctify creation:

Each of us has a capacity for great good and that is what makes God
say it was well worth the risk to bring us into existence. Extraordi-
narily, God the omnipotent One depends on us, puny, fragile, vulnerable as we may be, to accomplish God's purposes for good, for
justice, for forgiveness and healing and wholeness. God has no one
but us. St. Augustine of Hippo has said, "God without us will not,
as we without God cannot.[40]

Yet if the pursuit of peace and justice is integral to the religious vocation and to the life of love, compassion and human-heartedness as advocated by religion, how are we to know how to act and how are we to
keep from falling into rage and despair when we look into the depths
of suffering? In order to act wisely, we do need to learn the history of
particular situations, train ourselves and others in nonviolent action,

listen to needs of those who suffer, and work to empower others to act, to find their own solutions to the problems they face. All of this is very important, but our saints would also suggest that we need to pursue holiness as a part of this vocation.

Thich Nhat Hanh writes of the bodhisattva of compassion Avelokiteshvara who is portrayed as having a thousand arms and a thousand hands with an eye in the palm of each hand, representing understanding, and whose name in Chinese means "listening to the cries of the world." Our hands must have eyes, our actions filled with a deep understanding of both the situation and the suffering that arises. Yet beneath both understanding and training must be love, as Thich Nhat Hanh affirms:

> The essence of nonviolence is love. Out of love and the willingness to act selflessly, strategies, tactics, and techniques for a nonviolent struggle arise naturally. Nonviolence is not a dogma; it is a process. Other struggles may be fueled by greed, hatred, fear, or ignorance, but a nonviolent one cannot use such blind sources of energy, for they will destroy those involved and also the struggle itself. [41]

It is the pursuit of holiness that will allow us to act without hatred toward those who perpetrate atrocities, without ignorance and with true compassion and love. For the Buddhist, the path to holiness is the path of the cultivation of mindfulness and meditation, a path open to all, for each of us is a bodhisattva in training.

For the Christian as for the engaged Buddhist, the vocation of justice entails the pursuit of holiness, even as the pursuit of holiness entails the pursuit of justice. Christian liberation theologian Gustavo Guttierez sees this call to holiness—"to abandon [ourselves] to God's embrace, and, in the words of Deuteronomy [to] 'cleav[e] to' God, thereby choosing life (30:19-20)"—as an essential message of the book of Job. [42] Job is in a terrible situation of suffering, a point of utter devastation not unlike that spoken of by the mystics, and his supposed friends argue the retributive idea that those who suffer are justly being punished by God for some sin, and so Job must repent. Job resists this understanding of God and of justice. Part of his defense is that he realizes that he himself has come to the aid of the poorest of the poor, something which he comes to see as a core element of living an upright life according to God's will. He does not claim to be sinless, but nevertheless asserts his innocence based, in part, on these actions undertaken to address the suffering of others. He asks God to do the same with respect to his own suffering.

God responds to Job, first by recounting the wonders of creation and reminding Job that God is not handcuffed to some idea of retributive justice. Rather, God's love is free and gratuitous, cause and not effect, limited only by God's self-limitation in choosing to allow and to respect human freedom.[43] Job is called into the experience of God. To enter into this experience, he must choose to leave behind his friends' vision of a controllable and predictable retributive God and his own limited understanding and "cleave to God," a God who is love and who is free. God's concern for justice and for the poor, variously defined, is not thereby negated but rather placed within this wider horizon of love. To fully understand this God and this love, Job must leave behind his former more limited conception of the righteous life and of the nature of God's love to embrace holiness. Only then is he truly able to understand suffering and justice and the freedom which God gives to humans to choose our vocation. In respecting human freedom, and, to use James Orbinski's phrase again, in allowing people the "space to be human," God "stops at the threshold of their freedom and asks for their collaborative help in the building of the world and in its just governance." [44] Job's encounter with God and his journey into holiness through the experience of both suffering and love transform him and lead him into a profound humility and a deeper empathy for those who suffer and into the practice of justice within love. Archbishop Tutu, in his work against apartheid and as a member of the Truth and Reconciliation Commission (TRC), offers but one example of what such a transformed life might look like in our time.

Even as he challenges us to take up that vocation of love and peacemaking which is deepened and fulfilled through the pursuit of holiness, Archbishop Tutu also speaks of the transformative holiness of peacework done in this way, offering encouragement to those in Belfast "working away in strife-torn communities to build bridges between alienated and traumatized people," whom he lauds as "extraordinary agents of peace and reconciliation." He compares the effect of their work to the holiness one feels in a church where people have prayed. Their actions for reconciliation and peace sanctify the world in a similar way, imbuing it with a palpable hope and love, and though we may not be able to see the change right now, in the fullness of time, the effects of this work will become apparent. Thich Nhat Hanh speaks in similar terms of the struggle of Buddhists in Vietnam:

> Despite the result—many years of war followed by years of oppression and human rights abuse—I cannot say that our struggle was a failure. The conditions for success in terms of political victory were not present. But the success of a nonviolent struggle can be measured only in terms of love and nonviolence attained, not whether a political victory was achieved. In our struggle in Vietnam, we did our best to stay true to our principles. We never lost sight that the essence of our struggle was love itself, and that was a real contribution to humanity.[45]

To live our religious lives authentically in our time, I believe, we must take the call to work for justice and peace seriously as an integral expression of the love, compassion and human-heartedness that our religious traditions teach us lie at the heart of what it means to be truly and fully human and to live a truly meaningful life. To be able to do this with wisdom and in a way that brings healing into the world, we ourselves also need to pursue the holiness that makes possible the most complete love and the wisest compassion. Such holiness is not confined to those who are religious. It can also be pursued by those who stand outside the institutional structures of religion who are willing to look deeply into suffering and into the self and to walk into the fires of love and its realization. The love that flows from holiness and impels us to work for justice and peace is a manifestation of the Transcendent in this world which sometimes seems so intractably violent and unjust. We become that manifestation as we embody this love.

I will close with a quotation from an author who is not overtly religious in his writing at all. War correspondent, Chris Hedges, in his book *War is a Force that Gives Us Meaning*, concludes his analysis of the seductive but ultimately false sense of connectedness and meaning that war gives with the following words:

> Love alone fuses happiness and meaning. Love alone can fight the impulse that lures us toward self-destruction...Love may not always triumph, but it keeps us human. It offers the only chance to escape from the contagion of war. Perhaps it is the only antidote. And there are times when remaining human is the only victory possible."[46]

It is love, then, which must be our vocation, our calling, a love that is perfected in holiness and made manifest in our work to alleviate suffering and to establish justice and peace in our world.

ABOUT THE AUTHOR

Nancy M. Martin is Associate Professor of Religious Studies at Chapman University; Life Member of Clare Hall, Cambridge University; and co-Founder and Associate Director of the Global Ethics and Religion Forum (www.GERForum.org). Dr. Martin's research interests include comparative religious ethics, gender and religion, and the religions of India. She has done extensive field research in India, focusing particularly on the religious traditions of low-caste Hindus and Muslims and on women's religious lives, and has lectured internationally on devotional Hinduism, comparative religion, human rights, and environmental issues.

NOTES

1 I have written more extensively on the emotion of love in religion in my essay "Love," coauthored with Joseph Runzo and published in *The Oxford Handbook of Religion and Emotion* (New York: Oxford University Press, 2007). The following discussion of love in the world religions is a condensed version of this material.

2 Ben Zion Bokser, 1981. *The Jewish Mystical Tradition*. New York: The Pilgrim Press, p. 117. The hidden Godhead, the En-Sof or the Infinite, manifests in ten aspects, the Sefirot, and among them are love (Hesed) and compassion (Rahamim, sometimes also called beauty or Tifereth) which mediates between God's love and God's power.

3 I John 4:16b (RSV).

4 *Kena Upanishad*, in *The Upanishads*, trans. Juan Mascaro. Harmondsworth, England: Penguin Books, 1965. pp. 53-4.

5 Deuteronomy 6:4-5 (RSV).

6 *Song of Songs* 8:6-7.

7 Shneur Zalman of Lyady (1745-1813), in *Iggeret haKodesh* 18, in *The Jewish Mystical Tradition*, trans. Bokser, p. 218.

8 Moshe Idel, 1996. "Universalization and Integration: Two Concepts of Mystical Union in Jewish Mysticism," in *Mystical Union in Judaism, Christianity and Islam: An Ecumenical Dialogue*, ed. Moshe Idel and Bernard McGinn. New York: The Continuum Publishing Company, p. 28. See also Moshe Idel, 1988. *Kabbalah: New Perspectives*. New Haven: Yale University Press.

9 Maurice Friedman, 1955. *Martin Buber: the Life of Dialogue*, third edition, revised. Chicago: The University of Chicago Press, p. 22.

10 Matthew 22:34-40 (RSV).

11   Matthew 5:43-38; Luke 6:27; Eg. I John 3:17-18.

12   Ibid., p. 195.

13   Jean Leclercq, O.S.B., 1982. *The Love of Learning and the Desire for God: A Study of Monastic Culture*. New York: Fordham University Press, p. 84.

14   Sermon on the Song of Songs 83.2, quoted by Bernard McGinn, "The Human Person as Image of God: Western Christianity," in *Christian Spirituality: Origins to the Twelfth Century*, eds. Bernard McGinn, John Meyendorff, and Jean Leclercq . New York: Crossroad, 1988, p. 325.

15   M. Corneille Halflants, 1977. "Introduction," in Bernard of Clairvaux, *On the Song of Songs I*, trans. Kilian Walsh, Cistercian Fathers Series: No. 4, Bernard of Clairvaux, volume 2. Kalamazoo: Cistercian Publications, xx.

16   St.Teresa of Avila, 1960. *The Autobiography of St. Teresa of Avila: The Life of Teresa of Jesus*, ed. and trans. E. Allison. Peers Garden City, NY: Image Books, p. 273.

17   Marguerite Porete, 1989. Quoted in Emilie Zum Brunn and Georgette Epiney-Burgard, *Woman Mystics in Medieval Europe*. New York: Paragon, p. 154.

18   John Renard, 1996. *Seven Doors to Islam: Spirituality and the Religious Life of Muslims*. Berkeley: University of California Press, p. 16-17.

19   Qur'an 50:16.

20   Annemarie Schimmel, 1982. *As Through a Veil: Mystical Poetry in Islam*. New York: Columbia University Press p. 32.

21   *Bhagavad-gita* 11:54, in *The Bhagavad Gita: Krishna's Counsel in Time of War*, trans. Barbara Stoller Miller (New York: Bantam, 1986), p. 108.

22   Translated by Nancy M. Martin.

23   A.K. Ramanujan, *Speaking of Siva*, pp. 61-4.

24   "The space to be human" is James Orbinski's phrase. Marquette University, September 2005.

25   His Holiness the Dalai Lama, 1998. *The Joy of Living and Dying in Peace*. Hammersmith: Thorsons, p. 14.

26   For a detailed discussion of *chi* and *li*, see Mary Evelyn Tucker, 2001. "Confucian Cosmology and Ecological Ethics," in *Ethics in the World Religions*, eds. Joseph Runzo and Nancy M. Martin. Oxford: Oneworld Publications.

27   David L. Hall and Roger T. Ames, 1987. *Thinking Through Confucius*. Albany: State University of New York Press, p. 119.

28   Hall and Ames, *Thinking Through Confucius*, p. 121.

29   Tucker, "Confucian Cosmology and Ecological Ethics," p. 334.

30   Rumi, 1995. *The Essential Rumi*, trans. Coleman Barks. San Francisco: Harper Collins, p. 243.

31   James Orbinski, Marquette University, September, 2005.

32   William Frankena, 1963. *Ethics*. Englewood Cliffs: Prentice-Hall, p. 44.

33   Ibid., p. 53.

34   Ibid., p. 45.

35   Renzo Allegri, 1996. *Teresa of the Poor: The Life of Mother Teresa of Calcutta*. Ann Arbor: Charis Books, p. 53.

36   Mother Teresa, *Everything Starts with Prayer: Mother Teresa's Meditations of Spiritual Life for People of All Faiths*, edited by Anthony Stern (Ashland, OR: White Cloud Press, 1998), p. 46.

37   H.H. The Dalai Lama, 1998. *The Joy of Living and Dying in Peace*. London: Thorsons, p. 85-6.

38   Thich Nhat Hanh, 1991. *Peace is Every Step: The Path of Mindfulness in Everyday Life*. New York: Bantam Book, p. 81.

39   Ibid., p. 127-8.

40   Desmond Mpilo Tutu, 1999. *No Future Without Forgiveness*. New York: Doubleday, p. 157-8.

41   Thich Nhat Hanh, 1993. *Love in Action*. Berkeley: Parallax Press, p. 39.

42   Ibid., p. 75

43   Gustavo Guittierez, 1987. *On Job: God Talk and the Suffering of the Innocent*. Maryknoll: Orbis Press, p. 75.

44   Ibid., p. 79.

45   Thich Nhat Hanh, 1993. *Love in Action*. Berkeley: Parallax Press, p. 47.

46   Hedges, Chris, 2002. *War is a Force that Gives Us Meaning*. New York: Anchor Books, pp. 160, 168.

2. DISARMING RETRIBUTIVISM: TOWARD AN AUTHENTIC FORGIVENESS AS A BASIS FOR PEACEMAKING

PATRICK J. HAYES

Recent philosophical thought on retributivism, which I take to mean the set of values that creates a space for vindictive or retaliatory forms of punishment for crimes demanding redress, has sought to offer critique of its weaknesses. Little has, however, been put forth by way of a practical alternative that restores balance to disordered relationships and honors victims' rights without allowing them to cave into the baser emotions that are the hallmark of revenge.[1] Retributivists have marshaled impressive arguments for their position. However, forgiveness may be a powerful antidote to retributivism, an edifying and concrete means of re-establishing justice between oppressors and their victims. The kind of forgiveness I am talking about does not just say, "Oh, well, forgive and forget." Those nations that have sought to establish truth and reconciliation commissions will attest to the fact that it is never easy to ensure that forgiveness takes root; they would also acknowledge that it is sometimes entirely unrealistic to forget.[2] This may be due, in part, to some rather abstract notions

---

1 Cf. Jeffrie Murphy and Jean Hampton, *Forgiveness and Mercy* (New York: Cambridge University Press, 1988); Susan Jacoby, *Wild Justice: The Evolution of Revenge* (New York: Harper and Row, 1983); J. L. Mackie, "Morality and Retributive Emotions," *Criminal Justice Ethics* (1982): 3-9.

2 Cf. e.g., Russell Daye, *Political Forgiveness: Lessons from South Africa* (Maryknoll: Orbis Books, 2004); Tomas Forsberg, "The Philosophy and Practice of Dealing with the Past: Some Conceptual and Normative Issues," in ed. Nigel Biggar, *Burying the Past: Making Peace and Doing Justice after Civil Conflict* (Washington, DC: Georgetown University Press, 2001); Brandon Hamber, "Remembering to Forget: Issues to Consider when Establishing Structures for Dealing with the Past," in ed. B. Hamber, *Past Imperfect: Dealing with the Past in Northern Ireland and Societies in Transition* (Derry/Londonderry: INCORE/University of Ulster, 1998); Martha Minow, *Between Vengeance and Forgiveness: Facing History After Genocide and Mass Violence* (Boston: Beacon Press, 1998); Alletta Norva,

of forgiveness, particularly when they are applied to specific, political circumstances. There remains therefore the need to give forgiveness "teeth." I argue below that this can be done through a probing examination of this Biblical concept. Far from being antiquated, the notion is still useful and flexible enough to apply to a broad range of situations that call for forgiveness over vengeance.[3]

An immediate goal of theology, as a discipline contributing to the dialogue on peace, is to try to render a Biblical concept of forgiveness intelligible, practicable, and desirable to aggrieved parties. The canonical Hebrew and Christian scriptures point to ways in which current philosophical critiques of retributivism could be strengthened by recourse to an authentic hermeneutic of forgiveness. The interpretive key lies less in instances where forgiveness is demonstrated within a given narrative and more in cases where rules for forgiveness are laid down, for example, those concerning the importance of integrating memory into the process, or considerations of the degree to which one ought to forgive. In the Biblical context, forgiveness is hardly considered to be "cheap" precisely because it attends to these rules. This is the product of a thoughtful and sometimes arduous struggle, one whose goal is genuine and lasting peace and not a mere palliative doubling as a therapeutic.

The Biblical aim is not merely to satisfy some spiritual need for healing. Christianity has sought ways to show how, especially in the last ten years, forgiveness is seen as a crucial social goal, too. Pope John Paul II placed this conviction at the forefront of the celebration of the millennial year, but he also underscored the connection between

---

"Memory, Identity, and the (Im)possibility of Reconciliation: The Work of the Truth and Reconciliation Commission in South Africa," *Constellations* 5:2 (1996): 250-265; Sarah Nuttall and Carli Coetzee, eds., *Negotiating the Past: The Making of Memory in South Africa* (New York: Oxford University Press, 1998); Robert I. Rotberg and Dennis Thompson, eds., *Truth vs. Justice: The Morality of Truth Commissions* (Princeton: Princeton University Press, 2000).

3 Here I disagree with some, for example, Donald Shriver, that the religious patrimony on forgiveness must of necessity "escape its religious captivity and enter the ranks of ordinary political virtues." Cf. Shriver, *An Ethic for Enemies: Forgiveness in Politics* (New York: Oxford University Press, 1995), 7. I would argue that the contribution of a religious perspective—as long as it is useful—is also political and so there is no need to liberate forgiveness from any one domain.

forgiveness and civil justice at several other points.[4] His personal experience of systematic violence perpetrated against whole peoples led him to wonder: *"How do we restore the moral and social order subjected to such horrific violence?"* My reasoned conviction, confirmed in turn by Biblical revelation, is that the shattered order cannot be fully restored except by a response that combines justice with forgiveness. *"The pillars of true peace are justice and that form of love which is forgiveness."* [5]

Moreover, Catholic theologians such as Georges Cottier have sought to explain the Church's internal need to bring itself into right relation and to offer itself as a model by which aggressors might be reconciled with their victims. In his view, the sin of one impacts all, one wrongdoer acts necessarily within the social realm, infects it, and contributes to the breakdown of justice, holiness, and peace.[6] More politically nuanced studies of forgiveness have been advanced through the series of discussions and white papers on conflict resolution issued by the Woodstock Theological Center, which has tried to bring Catholic ethicists into conversation with those working in government and non-governmental agencies (Catholic or otherwise) who have the power to affect the direction of policy.[7] It is in the hope of adding something to the discussion on forgiveness that the remainder of this essay will attempt to articulate a foundational perspective by surveying those Biblical texts that supply an alternative to a vacuous and dehumanizing retributivism. The second part of the paper offers a theoretical model by which forgiveness can be embraced in various situations of conflict—from human rights abuses to the aftermath of

---

4 Cf. Pope John Paul II, 2002 World Day of Peace Message, "No Peace Without Justice, No Justice Without Forgiveness" (January 1, 2002); Message for the Celebration of the XXX World Day of Peace, "Offer Forgiveness and Receive Peace" (January 1, 1997); Encyclical Letter *Dives et misericordia* (1984), 14; and Apostolic Exhortation *Reconciliatio et paenitentia* (2 December 1984). All are available on the Vatican website, www.vatican. va (accessed August 2005).

5 Cf. Pope John Paul II, 2002 World Day of Peace Message, "No Peace Without Justice, No Justice Without Forgiveness" (January 1, 2002), #1 (author's italics).

6 Cf. George Cottier, *Mémoire et repentance: Pourquoi l'Eglise demande pardon* (Paris: Parole et Silence, 1998), 11-13.

7 Cf. William Bole, Drew Christiansen, and Robert T. Hennemeyer, eds., *Forgiveness in International Politics: An Alternative Road to Peace* (Washington, DC: USCCB, 2004).

war. I contend that an authentic Biblical concept of forgiveness can provide consolation and that such a concept suggests that the restoration of justice is hardly dependent upon aggressors' recanting of their ways. Instead, justice lies with the victim.

A BIBLICAL HERMENEUTIC OF FORGIVENESS

The theology of forgiveness is linked to atonement.[8] It is a consequence or effect of atonement, occurring subsequent to the atoning act and removing enmity between parties. Atonement, however, has its own largely subjective litmus tests. We do better to ask what forgiveness requires in the moral life of Christians. What does it mean for us to say, "I forgive you..."? Similarly, what does it mean to display or enact "just vengeance?" In the Old Testament especially, the language of forgiveness is closely integrated with that of vengeance. "I wipe away

8 For the OT, see Raymond Abba, "The Origin and Significance of the Hebrew Sacrifice," *Biblical Theology Bulletin* 7 (1977): 123-138; Klaus Koch,
"Is there a Doctrine of Retribution in the Old Testament?" in James Cren-
shaw (ed.), *Theodicy in the Old Testament* (Philadelphia: Fortress Press,
1983), 57-87; Rolf Rendtorff, *Studien zur Geschichte des Opfers im alten
Israel* (Neukirchen: Neukirchener Verlag, 1967); and Angel M. Rodri-
guez, *Substitution in the Hebrew Cultus* (Berrien Springs, MI: Andrews
University Press, 1979). For the NT, see Robert Daly, *Christian Sacrifice:
The Judeo-Christian Background Before Origen* (Washington, DC: Catholic
University of America Press, 1978); Paul Garnet, *Salvation and Atonement
in the Qumran Scrolls* (Tübingen: JCB Mohr (Paul Siebeck), 1977); Fran-
çois Marty, "Le péché sans rémission dans l'Epître aux Hébreux," in Michel
Perrin (ed.), *Le Pardon: Actes du Colloque Organisé par le Centre Histoire des
Idées de l' Université de Picardie* (Paris: Beauchesne, 1987), 29-47; and An-
thony Tambasco, *A Theology of Atonement and Paul's Vision of Christianity*
(Collegeville, MN: Liturgical Press, 1991). See also the bibliography of
H. Vorländer and C. Brown in s.v., "Reconciliation," in Colin Brown (ed.),
New International Dictionary of New Testament Theology, v. III (Exeter, UK:
Paternoster Press, 1978): 174-176. For the theological development, see
J. Patout Burns, "The Concept of Satisfaction in Medieval Redemption
Theory," *Theological Studies* 36 (1975): 285-304; John Goldingay (ed.),
Atonement Today: A Symposium at St. John's College, Nottingham (London:
SPCK, 1995); Paul Jensen, "Forgiveness and the Atonement," *Scottish Jour-
nal of Theology* 46 (1991): 141-159; Stanislas Lyonnet and Leopold Sab-
ourin, *Sin, Redemption, and Sacrifice: A Biblical and Patristic Study* (Rome:
Pontifical Biblical Institute, 1970); and David Wheeler, *A Relational View
of the Atonement: Prolegomenon to a Reconstruction of the Doctrine* (New
York: Peter Lang, 1989).

your sins like a cloud, your transgression like a mist" (Is. 44:22); or again, "I will forgive their iniquity, and I will remember their sin no more" (Jer. 31:34); but, "Vengeance is mine, and recompense. ... I will take vengeance on my adversaries and will requite those who hate me" (Deut. 32:35, 41).[9]

Over the last several decades, the matter of forgiveness and retributive justice has been treated more within the preserve of philosophy of law.[10] Some Biblical ethicists also take a legalistic approach. Seen this way, forgiveness is not undertaken for its own sake, but is rather part of a social ethic of order for the early Christian community.[11] Such an idea of forgiveness *per se* must be developed within the context of a model of community building, and not be seen merely as a vehicle of restoration of relations between the penitent and her victim and, more importantly, the living God. If anything, *that* is the thrust of the Hebrew legacy—and it is given still greater emphasis in the New Testament corpus. The sin against neighbor was nothing short of sin against God and so the need for reconciliation also involved a need to be reconciled with God by way of reconciliation with one's neighbor.

---

9 From the start, Christian disciples read the Old Testament as reserving retribution to God alone: "Bless those who persecute you; bless and do not curse them. ... Repay no one evil for evil, but take thought for what is noble in the sight of all. ... Beloved, never avenge yourselves, but leave it to the wrath of God; for it is written, 'Vengeance is mine, I will repay, says the Lord.'" (Rom. 12:14, 17, 19). See further, Klaus Koch, "Is there a Doctrine of Retribution in the Old Testament?" in James Crenshaw (ed.), *Theodicy in the Old Testament* (Philadelphia: Fortress Press, 1983), 57-87, and Brian E. Kelly, *Retribution and Eschatology in Chronicles* (Sheffield, UK: JSOT, 1996).

10 For philosophy of law, Herbert Fingarette, "Punishment and Suffering," *Proceedings and Addresses of the American Philosophical Association*, 50:6 (1977): 499-525; H. L. A. Hart, *Punishment and Responsibility: Essays in the Philosophy of Law* (New York: Oxford University Press, 1968), esp. 230ff; Marvin Henberg, *Retribution: Evil for Evil in Ethics, Law, and Literature* (Philadelphia: Temple University Press, 1990); and C. L. Ten, *Crime, Guilt and Punishment: A Philosophical Introduction* (New York: Oxford University Press, 1987), esp. 38-65.

11 Thomas Ogletree, *The Use of the Bible in Christian Ethics* (Philadelphia: Fortress Press, 1983), 119- 121. Similarly, Richard Hays views the Biblical material as espousing a kind of social control. See his *The Moral Vision of the New Testament: A Contemporary Introduction to New Testament Ethics* (San Francisco: Harper Collins, 1996), 101-104.

Understanding the way these matters are conceived of in the Old Testament will assist in subsequent reflection on how they are taken up in various New Testament contexts.

The basic term for forgiveness in the Old Testament is *slh*. It occurs about fifty times.[12] There, forgiveness is typically used either in the form of supplication, that is, either asking God's forgiveness (e.g., Ex. 34:9) or, in the context of confession, proclaiming God's forgiveness (e.g., Ex. 34:6-7; Is. 55:7). Later rabbinic writings on God's ability to purge sin from the people concentrate on the Day of Atonement. Thus Rabbi Yehudah b. R. Simeon commented around 300 CE: "For all the sins with which the Israelites soil themselves in the course of the year, the Day of Atonement atones (Lev. 16:30)." Eventually, the atonement was extended to New Year's Day, as reflected in the anonymous statement of a fourth-century writer: "On this day all men are standing in judgment before God and the world is found to deserve annihilation, because the creatures are soiled with sins, but God declares His world not guilty."[13]

In each of these instances, there are no criteria for God's appeasement other than purgative suffering of some sort. In the case of sins against God, genuine repentance must accompany the atoning agony. Divine judgment is presumably more merciful to the contrite because they attain company with the Almighty (cf., Is. 57:15).[14] Sometimes, though, the line between atonement and forgiveness is blurred. Some texts indicate that a wholesale cleansing of the impurities coursing through the land may warrant God's forgiveness and that an offender's repentance isn't worth one farthing to God. This is especially true of capital crimes whose blood-guilt (*damim*) does not simply accrue to the perpetrator but to the whole people. As a consequence of the abomination of shedding blood, the community becomes polluted and so cries out for expiation of the capital offense, "for blood pollutes the land, for the blood that is shed in it, except by the blood of

---

12   Cf. John S. Kselman, s.v., "Forgiveness," in ed. David Noel Freedman, *Anchor Bible Dictionary* (New York: Doubleday, 1992), II:831.

13   Cf. A. Büchler, *Studies in Sin and Atonement in the Rabbinic Literature of the First Century* (London: Oxford University Press, 1928), 302-303.

14   Cf. Patrick D. Miller, *Sin and Judgment in the Prophets* (Chico, CA: Scholars Press, 1982).

him who shed it" (Num. 35:33). That the whole community incurs blood-guilt when one man murders another was a generally accepted principle. That the perpetrator himself was liable and had to suffer was assumed.[15]

Consider Deut. 21:7-8: "Our hands did not shed this blood, neither did our eyes see it shed. Forgive, O Lord, your people Israel, whom you have redeemed, and set not the guilt of innocent blood in the midst of your people Israel; but let the guilt of blood be forgiven them." The point here is not to display the narcissism of an objectively innocent group of people seeking forgiveness for a sin they did not commit. Rather, the reader's attention should be directed to the fact that a conscious separation occurs between the community and the guilty, even though the stain of blood blemishes the entire society.[16] No thought is given to the repentant heart, nor can a murderer hope to bribe his way out of punishment. This is stressed elsewhere in the Old Testament: "You shall not take forgiveness monies for the soul of a murderer who deserves to die" (Num. 35:31). Without some reparation, there is a continued and manifest need for expiation: "the redeemer of blood shall slay the murderer" (Num. 35:19). That there was an appointed redeemer of blood (*go'el haddam*) is a curious matter. We know nothing about such people. As referenced in both Num. 35:16-21 and Deut. 19:11-13, their sole function is to purge the community of the guilt of intentional homicide. We can also gather that their activities were condoned by the people, just as killing in battle was accepted. But for these exceptions, human blood, as a seat of life (cf., Lev. 17:11), could be expected to "cry out" for vindication if it was deliberately shed (Gen. 9:6; cf. Gen. 4:10-11).[17] 'Satisfaction' could only be achieved by terminating the offending party.

---

15   Cf., Gen. 9:5-6: "I will surely requite your own blood. I will exact it from every beast, and from every human being I will exact the life of a person. Whoever sheds human blood, by a human shall that person's blood be shed. " This was not a principle peculiar to the Israelites. See further D. M. MacDowell, *Athenian Homicide Law* (Manchester, UK: Manchester University Press, 1963), passim.

16   Cf., Aaron Schreiber, *Jewish Law and Decision-Making: A Study Through Time* (Philadelphia: Temple University Press, 1979), 51.

17   Shed blood was interpreted as an assault on 'the image of God' (cf., Gen. 9:6), especially the 'blood of the innocent' (Deut. 27:25; 1 Sam. 19:5; Jer. 7:6; Pss. 94:21; 106:38; Prov. 6:17) spilled through violence.

Retribution permits of negative social rage under the Old Testament's understanding of blood-guilt, but we must ask why and search out the context. The *lex talionis*, the law of retaliation, prescribed death for anyone guilty of taking another's life, but unlike other statements of the law, only Gen. 9:5-6 referred to blood in expressing this life-for-life punishment.[18] In ancient Israel, *lex talionis* has an "if" - "then" character: "if" party *x* offends party *y*, "then" party *y* has an obligation to match the offence, but with an additional compensatory sanction. While not strictly retaliatory, an example of this may be seen in Ex. 22:1-2, where the 'if' is the theft of an ox and the 'then' is the fact that the thief must pay back five times over. The crucial difference between Hammurabi's code and Israel's law lies in a refined sense of the meaning behind punishment. For the Babylonians, injury to another is a liability to oneself in a one-to-one correspondence, but an offence against Yahweh is an individual *and* collective liability and so carries with it the additional burden of squaring both.

It is difficult to tell where genuine remorse fits into this picture. Clearly, the shame of a person's sin (= pollution) is in the foreground. I believe the Old Testament regards repentance—especially public repentance—as an important component in the process of forgiveness. In several places the transgressions of Israel, once acknowledged, are met with God's gratuitous forgiveness. It is precisely at this point where the language of obligation is inserted. One is obliged to forgive when the penitent seeks it in earnest. But this is not an absolute. It is probably a mark of the deep distrust of those involved in capital crimes that no manner of sorrow is to be taken into account. Execution is imminent and no obligation to forgive exists in such instances. That is left for Yahweh.

THE NEW TESTAMENT

As the foregoing suggests, forgiveness in the Old Testament seems overshadowed by God's initiative and good pleasure. Seen through the lens of the covenant, Israel was under obligation to forgive for matters other than capital crimes. For such infractions no possibility of creaturely forgiveness was to be obliged or countenanced. This changed

---

18   In fact, the *lex talionis* appears in only three passages of the Torah: Exod. 21:22-25, Deut. 19:19-21, and Lev. 24:17-21. Cf. Marvin Henberg, *Retribution: Evil for Evil in Ethics, Law, and Literature* (Philadelphia: Temple University Press, 1990), 69ff for discussion of these passages.

when the developing Christian community began to see an alternative in the actions and words of Jesus, a new state of affairs made all the more stark by his crucifixion. How was forgiveness then understood? We can begin with the Greek verb *diallasomai* which, as I. Howard Marshall points out, is found only once in the New Testament: "*be reconciled* to your brother" (Matt. 5:24).[19] It is closely related to the more passive Pauline usages (as in Rom. 5:10; 1 Cor. 7:11; 2 Cor. 15:18, 19, 20), where the sense is to act to remove enmity from antagonistic parties or, more positively, to reconstruct a good relationship between enemies. Some dictionaries include *aphiēmi*, let go, cancel, remit, leave, forgive; or *aphesis*, release, pardon, cancellation, forgiveness. The LXX uses *aphiēmi* in many places in the sense of letting go (e.g., Jud. 3:1; 9:9, 11, 13), leaving behind (2 Sam. 15:16; 20:3), or release (Deut. 15:2). It is used relatively seldom as meaning 'to forgive.' Where it is, it usually captures the Hebrew *nāśā*, to release from guilt or punishment (Gen. 18:26; Ps. 25:18; 32:1, 5; Isa. 33:24) or *sālah*, to forgive or pardon (Lev. 4:20ff; 5:6ff; Num. 14:19, 15:25ff; Is. 55:7). Sometimes it stands for *kippēr*, to cover or make atonement (Is. 22:14). Paul uses the term *katallassō*, to reconcile (e.g., 1 Cor. 7:11, a reconciliation between individuals, and Rom. 5:10-11 and 2 Cor. 5:18-19, a reconciliation between individuals and God). Clearly, it involves putting two parties into positive relation again. Where the disease of ill-will or maliciousness had existed, the balm of reconciliation restores (*apokathistēmi*) the health of relationship, sealing the very fact of relationship (cf., Mk. 3:5; Lk. 6:10).

This is done through atonement. It is important to distinguish between disputants because the requirements of atonement will be different between God and creatures, on the one hand, and in human affairs on the other. The idea of the *apokatastasis* works to bring about an eschatological restoration, a cosmic healing (cf., Acts 3:19ff). Nearly always in the New Testament creaturely forgiveness is held against the backdrop of God's forgiveness, usually with special reference to individuals (cf., 2 Cor. 2:7, 10; Eph. 4:32; Col. 2:13; 3:13). However, the New Testament rarely takes up social forgiveness as a central theme apart from the covenant. In Mk. 11:25 the precondition for under-

---

19   Cf. I. Howard Marshall, "The Meaning of Reconciliation," in Robert A. Guelich (ed.), *Unity and Diversity in New Testament Theology: Essays in Honor of George E. Ladd* (Grand Rapids, MI: Wm. Eerdmans Publ., 1978), 118.

taking prayer is a forgiving heart, "in order that your Father who is in heaven may forgive your transgressions."[20]

The call to forgive as we are forgiven by others is not peculiar to the synoptics. The Pauline literature also contains this same formula: "Put on then, as God's chosen ones, holy and beloved, compassion, kindness, lowliness, meekness and patience, forbearing one another and, if one has a complaint against another, forgiving each other; as the Lord has forgiven you, so you also must forgive" (Col. 3:12-13, cf., Lk. 6:37; Eph. 4:32). Again, it is not correct to read into these lines an end of social cohesion any more than if we took this to mean that redemption is guaranteed through forgiving others.

It is striking that there is no mention in the New Testament of the avenger of blood or someone who is under orders to make the guilty pay for their crimes. Where the avenger of blood is particularly absent is in the passion narratives, but it is the reader who is the true go'el haddam, who is required to proclaim the saving deed. Not only does Jesus mediate forgiveness from the cross, "Father, forgive them, . . ." (Luke 23:34), his very act is seen in Pauline doxology as an expiation (hilastērion = "mercy seat") in Rom. 3:24-25 (cf., Rom. 5:6-11).

Still, this kind of language is difficult to square with what God wants, viz., "I desire mercy, not sacrifice" (Hos. 6:6; Matt 9:13; 12:7). The call to mercy is also of a particular form. It plants the seed for reconciliation by speaking to the heart. It grounds right relation to God, as well as the enacting of forgiveness. Consider the need for reconciliation over the demands of sacrificial worship (Matt. 5:24), where Jesus wants his disciples to forgive their transgressors even before they formally come and seek forgiveness (cf., Mk. 11:25). Mercy is active— deliberately omitting the retributive reprisal of vengeance and making way for love — "Repay no one evil for evil, but take thought for what is noble in the sight of all" (Rom. 12:17; cf., Prov. 20:22; II Cor. 8:21; 1 Thess. 5:15); "Beloved, never avenge yourselves, but leave it to the wrath of God; for it is written, 'Vengeance is mine, I will repay, says the Lord'" (Rom. 12:19; cf., Lev. 19:18; Deut. 32:35). This is precisely the

---

20 However, "forgive us as we forgive others" is not an absolute remark. Unforgivable sins (such as blasphemy against the Holy Spirit) are in evidence in, for instance, Heb. 6:4-6; and 1 Jn. 5:16. Cf., M. E. Boring, "The Unforgiveable Sin Logion: Mk. 3:28-29; Matt. 12:31-32; Lk. 12:10: Formal Analysis and History of the Tradition," Novum Testamentum 18 (1976): 277.

2 ❧ *Disarming Retributivism: Authentic Forgiveness & Peacemaking*   51

same attitude demonstrated in certain African cultures. They would use the phrase *m'bara hake to an ye*—an expression that conveys the idea of being powerless to retaliate against an offense but at the same time activating a choice to move on with life knowing God will right the wrong.[21]

We see example after example in which mercy feeds forgiveness in Jesus' own ministry. In Mk. 2:1-12, Jesus offers forgiveness to distressed persons (the paralytic and the impudent scribes). The parable of the prodigal son shows us a forgiving father (Lk. 15:11-32). In the encounter with the woman taken in adultery, sin is acknowledged but overcome by pardon's grace (Jn. 8:1-11). A repeated retributivist claim based largely on these texts is that to forgive without punishing is to condone evil, "to reduce grace to sentimentality" or to hold the idea that to forgive is to "let someone off."

This does not, however, resemble my concept of forgiveness. Instead I side with Timothy Gorringe who notes, "When Jesus forgives the woman taken in adultery, he neither insists on her punishment nor condones her sin. Forgiveness is a creative act, *sui generis*, which heals by restoring people to community."[22]

A THEORETICAL MODEL OF FORGIVENESS
EMERGING FROM INTERNATIONAL CONFLICT

How would the Biblical material come into play in a way that is both coherent and effective in shaping attitudes of victims toward aggressors? How, for instance, can the United States learn to appropriate the language and intent of a Biblical perspective on forgiveness toward groups like Al-Qaeda? How can countries like the United States begin

---

21   Cf. Michael Jackson, "The Prose of Suffering, The Practice of Silence," *Spiritus* 4:1 (2004): 44-59, here at 51. The author notes that the expression "i hake a to nye" means "I am freeing myself of the effects of your hatred. I am refusing to hate back. But this doesn't mean that justice will not be done." See also Thomas Talbott, "Punishment, Forgiveness, and Divine Justice," *Religious Studies* 29 (1993): 166: "Divine forgiveness is one of the essential means by which God protects the innocent from irreparable harm and will eventually vindicate his righteousness in the face of unjust suffering." For challenges to this view, see further Anne Minas, "God and Forgiveness," *Philosophical Quarterly* 25 (1975): 138-150 and Meirlys Lewis, "On Forgiveness," *Philosophical Quarterly* 30 (1980): 236-245.

22   Timothy Gorringe, *God's Just Vengeance: Crime, Violence and the Rhetoric of Salvation* (New York: Cambridge University Press, 1996), 265.

to acknowledge some of its own transgressions toward, for example, Central and South America, and to bring itself to the point of asking these regions for forgiveness? [23] We must admit that these kinds of questions seem to run counter to a *realpolitik* and in fact can be considered to emerge from a deep, deep well of *chutzpah*.[24] In the case of Al-Qaeda, our nation's policies reflect a disposition of revenge as the only legitimate option, one that is often found in the tone of the President's own rhetoric.[25] In contradistinction, it is useful to recall the words of Pope John Paul II's 2002 World Day of Peace message. It offered all humanity, "and particularly the leaders of nations, the opportunity to reflect upon the demands of justice and the call to forgiveness in the face of the grave problems which continue to afflict the world, not the least of which is *the new level of violence introduced by organized terrorism.*"[26]

Let me suggest that the daunting task of trying to convince Americans of the errors of their ways is nothing compared to convincing

---

23   One thinks of the efforts at regime change in Guatemala (Jacobo Arbenz), the support of juntas in Chile and Panama, the undermining of the Sandinistas in Nicaragua, training those who eventually murdered several Jesuits and members of their staff in El Salvador, and so forth. And as he signed the CAFTA provisions in August 2005, President Bush spoke no words of remorse for all the genuine harm the United States has brought to the regions south of our border, as if this trade agreement will nullify all past sins.

24   Realism is necessary, but it ought not be determinative. In this regard, Pope John Paul's message for the 1997 XXX Day of World Peace, "Offer Forgiveness and Receive Peace" mirrors my sentiment: "With deep conviction therefore I wish to appeal to everyone to *seek peace along the paths of forgiveness.* I am fully aware that forgiveness can seem contrary to human logic, which often yields to the dynamics of conflict and revenge. But forgiveness is inspired by the logic of love, that love which God has for every man and woman, for every people and nation, and for the whole human family. If the Church dares to proclaim what, from a human standpoint, might appear to be sheer folly, it is precisely because of her unshakable confidence in the infinite love of God."

25   Cf. Tammy Greer, et al., "We Are a Religious People; We Are a Vengeful People," *Journal for the Scientific Study of Religion* 44:1 (2005): 45-57.

26   Cf. Pope John Paul II, 2002 World Day of Peace Message, "No Peace Without Justice, No Justice Without Forgiveness" (January 1, 2002), #3.

them that a retributivist attitude is ultimately unjust and unhealthy.[27] For "political forgiveness" to work, several elements must be in place. I would argue that these square admirably with a Biblical ethic of forgiveness as sketched in the previous section.

First, forgiveness is not necessarily dependent upon two parties, but one: the victim. This is so for at least three reasons. To begin with, only the victim has the authority to forgive. Second, immediately upon becoming a victim, he or she has a right and often a duty to forgive. Where no victim exists, no forgiveness can be granted. Third, the act of forgiving should not be triggered by anything that the offender hopes to receive, rather forgiveness can be made available depending upon what the offender does by way of atonement. On an Old Testament reading, a perpetrator is owed nothing based upon that person's remorsefulness or some other intervening compensatory act. If part of a definition of justice is to set relationships back into balance by granting each their rightful due, then to victimize with the expectation of future forgiveness tends to make a mockery of the process.[28] Not incidentally, the victim would be wronged twice. But forgiving helps to establish reciprocity in relationships, where there is give and take. This is Pope John Paul II's point when he notes that "in reciprocal relationships between persons merciful love is never a unilateral act or process."[29] The granting of forgiveness always has benefit for the forgiver as well as for the offender.

---

27   However, these errors are not miniscule. Recall the sinking thud heard by many when, on December 1, 1991, then President George H. W. Bush declined to issue an apology for the dropping of atomic bombs on Hiroshima and Nagasaki. The point is explored in Jerald Richards, "Keys to Political Forgiveness in International Relations," in ed. Nancy Nyquist Potter, *Putting Peace into Practice: Evaluating Policy on Local and Global Levels* (New York: Rodopi, 2004), 165-176.

28   Cf. P. E. Digeser, *Political Forgiveness* (Ithaca: Cornell University Press, 2001), 78-81.

29   Cf. Pope John Paul II, Encyclical letter *Dives in Misericordia* (30 November 1980), #14 accessed August 2005 via the internet at www.vatican. va. Drucilla Cornell and others have developed this notion of relation as "dialogic reciprocity." Cf. Cornell, "In Defense of Dialogic Reciprocity," *Tennessee Law Review* 54 (1987): 335-342 and Beth J. Singer, "Nationalism and Dehostilization," in ed. Nancy Nyquist Potter, *Putting Peace into Practice* op. cit., 157-163.

Second, forgiveness does not necessarily require atonement, though it helps. Redress is also sometimes not possible. At times, the need for atonement is manifest, but there is no identifiable agent who must come forward to atone. Justice requires atonement; forgiveness does not.[30]

Third, where restorative measures are exacted, they must be reasonably proportionate to the crime.

Fourth, invoking what some have called "global realism," it is important to understand that forgiveness of the personal sort cannot be translated easily to the social realm and that it takes time and consistent effort of large segments of a population.[31] The corollary is that it is not impossible to do this.

Fifth, the symbolism behind forgiveness cannot be underestimated with respect to its psychological power to heal the victim of his or her resentment and anger and "rob an atrocity of its perpetual power to ... corrode the bonds of humanity."[32] Symbols are found in stories. Expression of these stories is not a necessary condition of forgiveness, since one can forgive from the heart without verbalization, but, as the experience of truth and reconciliation commissions indicates, articulation of pain and the words of sorrow go a long way toward effecting better relations.

Sixth, forgiveness is not necessarily opposed to forgetfulness, but it creates space for the dissolution of enmity; this, in turn, gives way to the freshness of a newfound relation. Bitterness is cast off over time; memories fade depending upon the magnitude of the transgression.

---

30   Note the remarks of Pope John Paul II in his message for the 1997 XXX Day of World Peace, "Offer Forgiveness and Receive Peace," #5: "Another essential requisite for forgiveness and reconciliation is *justice*, which finds its ultimate foundation in the law of God and in his plan of love and mercy for humanity. Understood in this way, justice is not limited to establishing what is right between the parties in conflict but looks above all to re-establishing authentic relationships with God, with oneself and with others. Thus there is no contradiction between forgiveness and justice. *Forgiveness neither eliminates nor lessens the need for the reparation* which justice requires, but seeks to reintegrate individuals and groups into society, and States into the community of Nations."

31   Cf. Bole, Christiansen, and Hennemeyer, *Forgiveness in International Politics*, op. cit., 31.

32   Cf. ibid., 37.

Dealing with the past in these terms opens new vistas for the future.[33]

Seventh, offering forgiveness demonstrates that the victim has not been extinguished; that is, he or she can muster the resolution to assert personal power as a living being who controls his or her destiny. When opting for forgiveness, victims are witnessing to positive, life-affirming goals for themselves and others. Shriver notes that this is nothing short of "moral courage"[34] and the previous pontiff has called it "heroic."[35]

CONCLUDING REFLECTIONS

The material discussed in the preceding sections will not satisfy all of the subtly nuanced objections to the role played by forgiveness. The Biblical witness does, however, provide some ground for discerning the application of principles that should regulate our behaviors and attitudes toward the wronged and wrongdoers. For instance, real harm must be done if one is to forgive and real forgiveness—unfettered by considerations of revenge—must then be granted. As the Biblical reading indicates, there are specific ways to arrive at this point. In the Old Testament, capital crimes require recompense for blood guilt incurred in and by the community, a requirement that cannot be scotched by the payment of fees. Forgiveness does not depend upon the amount

---

33   Here again the words of Pope John Paul II are appropriate: "The difficulty of forgiving does not only arise from the circumstances of the present. History carries with it a heavy burden of violence and conflict which cannot easily be shed. Abuses of power, oppression and wars have brought suffering to countless human beings and, even if the causes of these sad events are lost in the distant past, their destructive effects live on, fuelling fear, suspicion, hatred and division among families, ethnic groups and whole peoples. These are facts which sorely try the good will of those who are seeking to overcome their past conditioning. The truth is that *one cannot remain a prisoner of the past*, for individuals and peoples need a sort of 'healing of memories,' so that past evils will not come back again. This does not mean forgetting past events; it means re-examining them with a new attitude and learning precisely from the experience of suffering that only love can build up." Cf. Pope John Paul's message for the 1997 XXX Day of World Peace, "Offer Forgiveness and Receive Peace," #3.

34   Cf. Donald Shriver, *An Ethic for Enemies*, op. cit., 67.

35   Cf. Pope John Paul II, message for the 1997 XXX Day of World Peace, "Offer Forgiveness and Receive Peace," #4.

of retributive suffering one has gone through, nor does withholding forgiveness always rest on the amount of harm inflicted on a victim, at either the personal or the community level. The conditions under which forgiveness is granted and demanded are hardly capricious, and the stakes are high in realizing the new disposition between enemies. Questions still need to be raised about this though. For example, one might want to ask what role, if any, resentment plays in forgiving someone if the victim is to preserve some shred of dignity.[36] There is also the question of the role played by repentance in making a determination to forgive.[37] Is forgiveness a requirement between individuals or merely a supererogatory act? I.e. Is it an act that is praiseworthy but not required? And, how might we determine what is required or what is supererogated? In the end, can we, with Saint Augustine, "hate the sin, love the sinner"?[38]

In both the Old and New Testaments, to forgive is to obey the call to love in such a way that love becomes the binding force in all moral decision-making.[39] I depart from Lauritzen and others who hold that in the absence of repentance, there can be no forgiveness.[40] Often crime victims do not know their assailant(s) because they have not been ap-

36   Cf. Margaret Holmgren, "Forgiveness and the Intrinsic Value of Persons," *American Philosophical Quarterly* 30:4 (1993): 341-353. Holmgren writes: "The victim of wrongdoing is morally required to respect himself and must therefore resent a responsible agent who wrongfully harms him. Not to do so is a sign of servility" (345-346). For me it is too great a leap to *require* resentment toward wrongdoers who harm us. After all, we harm ourselves in varying degrees, sometimes willfully, too. On Holmgren's logic, we would be the object of perpetual self-loathing.

37   Thus, Vincent Brümmer, "Atonement and Reconciliation," *Religious Studies* 28 (1992): 441: "Although my penitence is a *necessary* condition for your forgiveness, it is not a *sufficient* condition. My penitence can neither cause nor earn your forgiveness. … It takes two to repair a personal relationship just as it takes two to establish it in the first place." (author's italics)

38   St. Augustine, *Ep.* 211.

39   This is the basic assumption of Victor Furnish who has pointed out with respect to the love command in the New Testament that love does not wait for a repentant soul to make overtures for our forgiveness. See Furnish, *The Love Command in the New Testament* (Nashville, TN: Abingdon, 1972), 67.

40   Cf. Paul Lauritzen, "Forgiveness: Moral Prerogative or Religious Duty," *The Journal of Religious Ethics* 15:2 (1987): 141-154. See also, e.g., Joanna North, "Wrongdoing and Forgiveness," *Philosophy* 62 (1987): 499-508

prehended. The process of victimization would continue if those who have been harmed could not offer forgiveness, if they so chose, as a way of overcoming the violence done to them. Carrying the tremendous burden of resentment and bitterness toward an unknown assailant can be tiresome. That does not mean the innocent have somehow acquiesced to the harm perpetrated against them. Certainly none of this should imply that victims condone what happened to them. To what profit could something like this lead, either for them or for the victimizer? [41]

In sacred scripture, all forgiveness needs to ground itself in a willing heart aimed at healing a breach between parties. [42] It is not a mere pleonasm to say that the love that arises from this is stronger than the grief initially caused. It enables victims to integrate an injurious calamity into the fabric of their lives and promotes good mental health. It may appear that the forgiveness of the cipher is really coming in the form of transferring animus toward some higher end, a channeling of resentment into some good. But the objection that this is not real forgiveness, only repression (or forgetfulness), is cynical in my view. Again, an awareness of wrongdoing and its concomitant forgiveness on the part of the victim is not tantamount to condoning the act. To the contrary, it is a deliberate choice to assail evil with love by recognizing the wrong for what it is and dealing with it appropriately. This is why an elderly rabbi once told me that he had to forgive the Nazis for what they inflicted on his family and friends: "Not to forgive would be to play into the hands of evil." Still, forgiveness does not preclude remembering.

and John Wilson, "Why Forgiveness Requires Repentance," *Philosophy* 63 (1988): 534-535.

41   Where Lauritzen and I concur is in his reading of Bishop Butler, "Forgiveness is the remission of resentment, but—and this qualification is crucial—not the remission of our legitimate indignation at an injury, rather only the excess and abuse of this feeling.'" Lauritzen, op. cit., 146. Cf. Joseph Butler, *Fifteen Sermons Preached at Rolls Chapel* (London: Bell and Sons, 1964), 136.

42   Cf. Robert C. Roberts, "Forgivingness," *American Philosophical Quarterly* 32:4 (1995): 289-306. "Forgiveness has the advantage over mere control of anger that it involves a genuinely benevolent view of the other person and thus fosters attitudes, and not just behavior, characteristic of the various kinds of happy relationships. Unlike moral offenses, forgiving them does not compromise the moral integrity of the offended one" (p. 289).

Finally, it should be said that our *intention* to forgive is also part of the Biblical picture. It serves to undergird more developed notions of right living in extra-biblical contexts. We can gather from sacred scripture that this intention feeds or precedes the obligation to forgive and it is based on a principle of mercy. The act of forgiving demonstrates Christian love, an empowering love that is freely given. This liberating freedom from hostility toward the wrongdoer is modeled after Jesus' message of reconciliation. It is a belief that punitive attitudes in fact interfere with our collective striving toward the redemption of the world. [43]

PERSONAL REFLECTION BY PATRICK J. HAYES:

Forgiveness has been a struggle for me. I am a stabbing victim and have gone through all the trials accompanying Post-Traumatic Stress Disorder. My assailant was never apprehended, so I haven't had much in the way of closure after nearly being murdered. And yet I am compelled by Jesus' admonition to forgive. I desire to follow this way of life. It is part of who I am. The world makes more sense to me if forgiveness is pursued as a viable form of living; this also signals to me that living is indeed possible in the wake of horrendous evil.

---

43   Cf. Lyonnet and Sabourin, op. cit., p. 56: "How is man liberated from the slavery of sin? Since sin dwells in man's inmost being, in the very heart of his free will, it follows that God cannot grant a genuine pardon without producing in man himself a radical change: *aphesis,* 'pardon,' will necessarily be *apolutrōsis,* 'redemption' (Col. 1:14; Eph. 1:7)."

3. THE SERMON ON THE MOUNT AND THE CREATION OF PEACE

JANE E. LINAHAN

Does the Sermon on the Mount count as valid? And is it something that has to be practised?
... [A]nyone who considers the Sermon on the Mount to be in principle impossible of fulfillment, mocks God; for God is the creator and lover of life, and ... gives no commandments that cannot be fulfilled. Anyone who considers that the Sermon on the Mount is fulfillable only in the sentiments of the heart, but not in public action, says that Jesus is wrong; for he preached the sermon precisely in order that it might be put into practice. Anyone who considers that it is fulfillable only for himself personally, but not in the context of his *responsibility for other people*, does not know God the Creator.[1]

INTRODUCTION

These words of the German theologian, Jürgen Moltmann, make the powerful claim that the Sermon on the Mount constitutes a serious mandate for those who believe in the God of Jesus Christ: faith in this God must be lived out in a very concrete way—particularly, in "responsibility for other people." But what does such responsibility entail? What specifically, in light of the Sermon's fundamental orientation to the making of peace? And what might the Sermon itself mean for today's world, a world desperately in need of finding the ways that lead to peace?

Moltmann himself offers some thought-provoking suggestions for responding to these questions. He argues that the true import of the Sermon's command to love of enemies is not to encourage the "negative" stance of passive non-resistance to evil, but to call forth the positive act of *creating peace*, particularly by taking *responsibility for the enemy*. My reflections, which focus especially on the love-of-enemies command, will attempt to draw out the implications of Moltmann's

---

1 Jürgen Moltmann, *The Way of Jesus Christ: Christology in Messianic Dimensions* (San Francisco: HarperCollins, 1990), 132, 127 (author's italics).

ideas and thereby, it is hoped, make the case for the supreme relevance and urgency and the compelling validity of the Sermon's call to the creation of peace. The challenge of this call, however, can be considerable. Surely, the Sermon is not a guide for real life in the real world! Is it not asking the impossible to expect fallible, weak and threatened human beings to love their enemies? Is it not foolish, unrealistic, or even irresponsible to put oneself in a position of such vulnerability? Some misconceptions indirectly lend fuel to these objections by taking the edge off the Sermon's mandate or allowing us to evade its challenge. They must first be addressed here. Subsequent to doing this I will consider some implications of its call to the creation of peace: What does it mean to be responsible for the enemy? What does the Sermon say about how one is to relate to the Other? And how can this lead to the creation of peace?

EVADING THE SERMON'S CHALLENGE

The Sermon on the Mount (Matthew 5-7) or, as it is depicted in the Gospel of Luke, the Sermon on the Plain (Luke 6:20-49)[2] is a key collection of Jesus' teachings on the meaning of the Kingdom of God and what is required of those who would share in it. Although the Sermon as a whole is a call to radical commitment and integrity, perhaps the teaching on love of enemies is most challenging. Luke's Jesus urges, "Do *good* to those who *hate* you" (6:27, emphasis added). Such idealism is attractive but it nevertheless runs counter to deeply-held sensibilities. The love-of-enemies command has provoked scorn and been dismissed outright as unrealistic and irrelevant.[3] This writer has

---

2   The present discussion is based on both texts. Unless otherwise noted, biblical quotations are from the New Revised Standard Version.

3   E.g., Pinchas Lapide, *The Sermon on the Mount: Utopia or Program for Action?*, trans. Arlene Swidler (Maryknoll: Orbis, 1986), 96, quotes a statement made by Herbert Marcuse at a 1968 Berlin student gathering: "Nothing is more abominable than the preaching of love: 'Do not hate your opponent'—this in a world in which hate is everywhere institutionalized." Lapide also cites statements by both Bismarck and the West German chancellor in 1981 to the effect that the Sermon on the Mount cannot be used in governing a political state. It seems that these are not the only "Christian" government officials to have held such sentiments. Might the real issue here be not so much the supposed *impracticality* of the Sermon as its *inconvenience*?

herself heard the remark that it is just not possible to love someone who has hurt us or with whom we do not have an intimate relationship. Such resistance to the counter-cultural message of the Sermon is encouraged by particular tendencies in interpreting the ministry of Jesus, especially by what I refer to in what follows as a *spiritualizing* approach.

The Sermon is strategically placed in both Matthew and Luke as the first of Jesus' teaching discourses. This important inaugural teaching provides a fundamental orientation to the meaning and ethos of the Kingdom of God, the primary focus of his ministry. In each Gospel, the distinctive placement of the love-of-enemies command within the structure of the Sermon gives it a particular emphasis.[4] In its own way, each focuses on the signal importance of this teaching for understanding both what the Kingdom *means* and how one is to *live* if one is to be part of it.

These two issues, the meaning of the Kingdom and its ethical imperative, illustrate how spiritualizing tendencies can deflect the Sermon's critical, prophetic edge. The meaning of the Kingdom itself may be distorted if it is interpreted as a strictly other-worldly reality ("heaven") or an "internal," personal state of union with God (e.g., "the Kingdom of God is *within* you" [Lk. 17:21]).[5] Even though they acknowledged that the Kingdom of God was the primary concern of Jesus' ministry, some scholars believed that he thought of its coming

---

4 In *Matthew*, the teaching on love of enemies is the culmination of the series of "antitheses" (Jesus' commands in contrast to and surpassing the old understanding of the Law) which begin eight verses after the opening Beatitudes; the sayings about "non-retaliation" lead up to the love-of-enemies section in Matthew, whereas they are incorporated into it in Luke. In Luke, this teaching immediately follows the opening series of Beatitudes and Woes.

5 Rheims translation, emphasis added. See Joseph A. Fitzmyer, *The Gospel According to Luke*, The Anchor Bible (Garden City, N.Y.: Doubleday & Co., 1985), 2:1161, for discussion of various possible meanings of ἐντός in this verse, and his argument that "within you" is not consonant with Luke's outlook: "elsewhere in Lucan writing the kingdom is never presented as an inward reality or an inner condition of human existence." (Note the NRSV translation: "the kingdom of God is among you.")

as an eschatological act of God which would take place *beyond* history, rather than an event with significance *for* history.[6]

It is likely that Jesus, however, did not regard the Kingdom as a purely spiritual reality. Biblical thought does not separate the "spiritual" from the bodily, material, social and historical. In his view, the Kingdom would have been understood as a reality impinging on *this* world, as God's acting *within* human history to bring justice and righteousness to those suffering from oppression.[7] The Gospels portray Jesus as convinced that his ministry constituted the arrival of God's reign, bringing with it healing and wholeness to people in every area of their lives (what we would call the spiritual, emotional, physical, and social dimensions). The coming of God's Kingdom is God's act of bringing the world into correspondence with God's goodness: *this* is what the world can be when God reigns, when the devastation of injustice, violence, and wretchedness is wiped away and God's intentions for creation, its wholeness and fullness of life are realized.[8]

Understanding the Kingdom as encompassing the whole of life rather than just the other-worldly phase of it, seeing it as inclusive of all creation rather than of just the heavenly sphere and recognizing God's lordship over all existence rather than only over the spiritual life, lead to the realization that the divine justice, care, and concern encompass *everything*. Nothing stands outside of God's domain. This has implications for all areas of life, including the ethical: the Kingdom calls human beings not only to accept God's reign, but to live in a way that *corresponds* to it. Thus, the tendency toward spiritualizing the Kingdom and its claims can, once again, dull the Sermon's prophetic edge.

Particularly problematic in this regard is the injunction against resisting an evildoer (Mt. 5:39). Does it command us to comply passively with evil? It has sometimes been so interpreted, especially in the context of a spiritualized understanding of the Kingdom: Christians should submit to abuse as a mortification of self for the sake of their spiritual welfare. The unfortunate implication of this is that one should not challenge the existence of evil, be concerned with condi-

---

6   See Richard A. Horsley, *Jesus and the Spiral of Violence: Popular Jewish Resistance in Roman Palestine* (Minneapolis: Fortress, 1993), 168-69, for a critique of the "eschatological" interpretation of the Kingdom.

7   Ibid., 167-77.

8   See Moltmann, 94-109, passim, esp. 97-99, 103, 104-109.

tions on earth, or take responsibility for confronting injustice.[9] But compliance with evil can amount to complicity in it, and urging compliance on others can amount to implicit violence against them. As Walter Wink puts it, "[T]o ask the poor and powerless to acquiesce in injustice when that is all they have ever known is itself an act of complicity in injustice. For those who are struggling for a more human world, these readings of the text are themselves laden with political repression and demagoguery."[10]

It could be argued that the Jesus of the Gospels is not himself a model of non-resistance to evil, but is, rather, like the prophets before him, outspoken and defiant of convention for the sake of those burdened by suffering and injustice. These texts depict him as strong, assertive, and self-assured ("he taught them as one having authority" [Mt. 7:29]), not shrinking from criticism and conflict, and not averse, even, to initiating confrontation. They portray him engaging evil rather aggressively. And, given that the texts are a call to "follow him," it seems unlikely that they are championing a passive acquiescence in evil. Non-resistance allows harm not only to oneself, but to potential victims as well. Living in correspondence with God's reign cannot mean being a passive accomplice in injustice. Injustice has no place in the Kingdom. And it makes the creation of true peace impossible.

While it is beyond the purpose of this discussion to examine every interpretation of the Sermon on the Mount, I have highlighted a few issues in regard to which problematic approaches, such as a tendency to spiritualize its meaning, can and have obscured its relevance for life in this world. Such approaches can fail to encourage responsibility for justice on this earth here and now, and can dissipate the critical, prophetic call of the Sermon to the making of peace as well as the wisdom it contains. It is to that wisdom that we now turn.

---

9 "Neither Passivity nor Violence: Jesus' Third Way (Matt. 5:38-42 par.)," in *The Love of Enemy and Non-retaliation in the New Testament*, ed. Willard M. Swartley, Studies in Peace and Scripture (Louisville: Westminster/John Knox, 1992), 102. Walter Wink briefly summarizes various such views, including some which imply that justice is the responsibility of others (e.g., God or civil authorities), but not of the Christian.

10 Ibid., 103.

TAKING THE SERMON SERIOUSLY: THE CREATION OF
PEACE

Jürgen Moltmann has noted how Matthew, in particular, portrays Jesus as the Wisdom of God, the Wisdom that was present with God at the creation of the world and that is the foundation of its existence. The Wisdom of God "from the beginning gives life to all created beings, and does not desire their death." On the Mount, Jesus teaches wisdom for life, that which is necessary for sustaining and fostering the life of all creatures, all of whom are loved by their Creator.[11] Matthew's beatitudes at the beginning of the Sermon include a blessing on peacemakers, who are called "children of God" (5:9). Being a child of this God calls one to be a *maker of peace*: peace is this Father's will for his beloved children, because peace is what makes life in its fullness possible for all. Although Luke does not include a similar blessing on peacemakers, his "love of enemies" text contains a greater number of commands to positive action and thus speaks in an even more positive tone. It urges us to counter evil directly with good (6:27-28, 31), rather than to merely "go along with," *not* resist, or *not* refuse it. (cf. Mt. 5:39-42). That is, Luke's text, implies a call to take *initiative* and *responsibility* in bringing about a different relationship with the "enemy." The making of peace consists in just this: creating a new, life-giving relationship with the Other. In Luke, it is as if Jesus is urging us to be *proactive* in creating peace, instead of merely *reacting* to the "enemy": the "enemy's" act is to be taken as an opportunity to respond in a new, unprecedented way, to begin something brand new, to go in a totally new direction. And this "pro-action" is to take the specific form of *love*.

"LOVE YOUR ENEMIES"

The command to "love your enemies" is sometimes dismissed as impossible of fulfillment because of the way love itself is often understood: we simply cannot conjure up warm feelings for those who have hurt us or those whom we do not even know. The gospel, however, views love as more than warm feelings. Love of enemies is not so much an emotion as a thoroughgoing putting-into-practice of radical and selfless care for the Other's well-being: "*Do good* to those who *hate you*." Of all the love commands in the New Testament, this one—requiring

---

11   Moltmann, 123-27.

love for the one by whom one is hated—is the most extreme. Love is to be inclusive of the entire range of persons encountered in life, to the entire range of humanity, even to those at the furthest extreme from oneself. It is love such as *this* that is like God's, who is "kind to the ungrateful and the wicked" (Lk. 6:35). (Cf. Rom. 5:6-10, where Paul states that the proof of God's love is that Christ died for us "while we were *enemies*" [author's italics].) A love that includes even one's enemy is a love that excludes no one.[12] This is how to understand Matthew's τέλειος in 5:48, "Be *perfect* … as your heavenly Father is *perfect*": the Father's love is whole, complete, non-exclusive, all-encompassing.[13] It is radical, absolute, unconditional, and thoroughgoing. This is what our love, too, is to be like—as wide and comprehensive, as *complete*, as God's.

The love of enemies command is not merely a warm, generalizing sentiment about love and good will. There is nothing sentimental about putting love of enemies—or any authentic love—into practice; sentimentality may even muffle and distract from the critical, concrete challenge of doing good to those who hate. What, then, does this concrete challenge to love of enemies entail? How is love of enemies consonant with resisting injustice? What does this mean for the creation of true peace? And who *is* the enemy? (Cf. Lk. 10:29, in keeping with the statement of the love of neighbor command: "And who is my neighbor?") Our discussion now turns to these questions, with the last being addressed first.

---

12   An important principle in Catholic social teaching is the *preferential option for the poor*, which requires that our primary concern is to be for the most vulnerable and marginalized in society: if their well-being is made a priority, then the well-being of *all* is assured. Might a parallel principle be suggested by the love-of-enemies command? If love is structured according to a *preferential option for the enemy*, then the well-being (*shalom*) of *all* is assured.

13   I. Howard Marshall, *The Gospel of Luke: A Commentary on the Greek Text*, The New International Greek Testament Commentary (Grand Rapids: Eerdmans, 1978), 265; G. Delling, *Theological Dictionary of the New Testament*, ed. Gerhard Kittel and Gerhard Friedrich, trans. Geoffrey W. Bromiley (Grand Rapids: Eerdmans, 1964-76), 8:67-78.

AND WHO IS MY ENEMY?

For our purposes, debating the identity of the "enemies" envisioned in these texts—e.g., whether they are "national," "local," or "personal"[14]— distracts from the concern at the heart of this teaching. Luke elaborates the meaning of "enemies" as "those who hate you ... those who curse you ... those who abuse you" (6:27-28). This could include a wide range of people, all those by whom one feels wronged. If Jesus' words were originally addressed to the poor of Galilee, victims of both Roman oppression and Jewish collaboration with that oppression, his hearers may have thought that they had many enemies, of various stripes. The situation is different but no less complex today, especially for people in the first world who may not think of themselves as victims of oppression, and who may be unwitting accomplices in the oppression of others, but who feel threatened, nevertheless, by many "enemies." Usually, however, they have no direct, personal knowledge of their "enemies." Today's social complexity and privatizing individualism can insulate them from meaningful contact, even with those in their own communities ("neighbors"). The control of information can keep them in ignorance of their complicity in injustice and can shape their opinions of other peoples of the world. Those hearing Jesus' words today may not *know* that they are implicated in exploiting others and that *they* are justifiably considered the enemy by many; they may have no understanding of the web of enmity that is woven through the manipulation of global economics and politics. Most importantly, they often do not *know* the people their news media teach them to call the "enemy"—people who are, in many cases, innocent targets of blame. Today's global realities, coupled with the realities of human shortcom-

---

14   For example, Richard A. Horsley, "Ethics and Exegesis: 'Love Your Enemies' and the Doctrine of Nonviolence," in Swartley, 85-86 argues that "the content of nearly all the sayings indicates a context of local interaction with personal enemies, not one of relations with foreign or political foes." This could be used to argue, in turn, that the Sermon on the Mount applies only to "personal" ethics, to relations with immediate acquaintances, but not to "social" ethics or to global contexts—to relations with those who are necessarily unknown to us, yet seriously affected by our actions. Such an argument deflects the relevance of the Sermon for what is precisely *the* fundamental ethical reality for human beings: our essential relatedness with all those with whom we share this planet.

ings and sinfulness, make it almost inevitable that *all* are implicated, justly or unjustly, in a deadly vortex of enmity.

Jesus, however, completely subverts all assumptions about who the "enemy" is. Those who would enter the Kingdom of God are to transcend the tendency to categorize other persons as "neighbor" or "enemy," "friend" or "the Other." The enemy is rather someone to be *loved*, just as one's neighbors/friends are. The parable of the Good Samaritan (Lk. 10:29-37), a multi-layered story about the meaning of love and the true identity of "neighbor," has as its fundamental point the total subversion of assumptions about who deserves to be considered "neighbor": the one who was regarded as the despised "*Other*," the Samaritan, turns out to be the true *neighbor* to the one in need.[15] The Sermon on the Mount calls for transcending the neighbor-enemy dichotomy altogether, particularly when Jesus invokes the action of God as the model for human behavior: "Your Father ... makes his sun rise on the evil and on the good, and sends rain on the righteous and on the unrighteous" (Mt. 5:45); "the Most High ... is kind to the ungrateful and the wicked" (Lk. 6:35). God does not discriminate between "good" and "bad," "friend" and "enemy," but provides for the needs of *both* with care and kindness.

TAKING RESPONSIBILITY FOR THE ENEMY

Love of enemies must take concrete form if it is to be made real: "Do good ... ." Luke's text implies that a certain "pro-action" should characterize dealings with the "enemy." Moltmann argues that love of enemy in concrete form means *taking responsibility for the enemy*.[16] This goes far beyond a "negative" not resisting of evil. As argued above, non-resistance can be problematic if it is understood as acquiescence in injustice, because injustice ultimately leads, not to peace, but to the erosion of persons and of their relations with each other. *Taking responsibility for the enemy* is a positive, pro-active imperative, which is intrinsically linked with *resisting injustice*. Both are necessary for *creating the peace, shalom*, that God's rule entails. *Shalom* is more than the absence of conflict: it is the realization of the comprehensive wholeness and well-

15　It is interesting that the Good Samaritan story is placed in Luke's narrative (10:29-37) not long after the incident in which the disciples want to call down fire on the Samaritan village (9:51-56)—as if it is an indirect critique of their attitude on that occasion.

16　Moltmann, 130-32.

being that can be manifested when human beings conform to God's righteousness.[17] Peace means that life in its fullness is possible for all.

Taking responsibility for the enemy is a thought-provoking idea that has at least two connotations. First, it can mean holding oneself accountable for the "enemy's" person, life, and well-being; second, it can mean accepting responsibility for having created an "enemy" through unjust action or by demonizing the "Other." The Sermon on the Mount is directed toward aspects of both meanings: toward accountability for the "enemy's" life insofar as it requires us to refuse violence and attend to human needs; toward the search for justice (a concern which bridges both meanings); and toward surmounting enmity itself by discovering commonality and moving toward solidarity with the other.

REFUSING VIOLENCE AND ADDRESSING NEEDS

Holding oneself accountable for the "enemy's" life and well-being has at least two dimensions. One is necessarily refusing to use violence against them. Non-retaliation has been one of the lenses used for interpreting the Sermon on the Mount, but by itself it provides too narrow a focus. The renunciation of violence, the refusal to respond to violence with violence and thereby escalate the spiral is, however, necessary to the creation of peace. But such a refusal is more than a passive avoidance of conflict at any cost. It is a conscious choice, a deliberate act of resistance. Specifically, it is a choice to resist the violation of any person, even the one who happens to be an "enemy," and to safeguard that individual's well-being. Refusing violence breaks the cycle associated with it. It activates in us a "sovereign power over violence":

> The wickedness is not merely the first act of violence but the vicious circle of violence and counter-violence. ... Non-resistance to evil shows up the absurdity of evil. Evil's strength is violence. Evil's weakness is its wrongness. Counter-violence supplies evil with its supposed justification, and often enough stabilizes it. It is only the nonviolent reaction which robs evil of every legitimation and puts the perpetrator of violence in the wrong ... .[18]

Forgoing violence, breaking the cycle of violence, resisting the violation of persons are the very least that is required if we are to be accountable for the "enemy."

17   Lapide, 33-35.
18   Moltmann, 129.

The Sermon implies a second dimension of this accountability: acknowledgment of and concern for the basic human rights and needs of the "enemy." Peace entails not merely the absence of conflict, but also wholeness and well-being, and generally the fulfillment of the conditions that make for the fullness of life. According to the Sermon, no matter how wicked, dishonest, or ungrateful human beings are, God is kind to them, providing for their needs by sending the sun and rain without fail. Persons and their needs are of far greater concern to God than are their moral deserts. Even the "enemy" is our fellow creature, loved and cared for along with ourselves by the Father. The Sermon urges us to see the "Other" with new eyes, to see that we are all very much alike and have a great deal in common, in particular basic human needs. And it is these needs that the Father is concerned about: sustenance, shelter, health, security, dignity, love—for the sake of peace.

SURMOUNTING THE CREATION OF ENMITY

Responsibility for the enemy can also mean holding oneself accountable for what one has done to create an "enemy," either through injustice or by demonizing the "Other." The call to concern for the needs and rights of the "enemy" has as its corollary the necessity of addressing the values, interests, attitudes, actions, policies, and structures which violate the enemy's needs, rights, dignity, and autonomy. Being complicit in, or benefiting from, injustice implicates one in that injustice and in the creation of the enmity of its victims. It thus entails responsibility for alleviating that injustice, by engaging those "enemies" in a positive way—"loving" them.

> What is in question is ... the intelligent conquest of the hostility. In loving one's enemies one no longer asks: how can I protect myself and deter my enemies from attacking me? The question is then: how can I deprive my enemy of his hostility? Through love, we draw our enemies into our own sphere of responsibility, and extend our responsibility to them. [19]

The reason the Other has become an "enemy" must be addressed if a just peace is to be created—and if one is truly to love them, for love cannot be authentic if the Other is not respected enough to be accorded justice.

A particular challenge to love of the enemy in the search for justice arises when one is oneself a victim. Perhaps this was the situation of

19 Ibid., 131.

many in the Sermon's original audience. What response is called for by those who are *not* responsible for injustice, but who are its victims? By those who are at the mercy of "enemies," individuals who have anything but their well-being at heart? Simplistic answers may not do justice to the experience of those who know such danger firsthand. Is the Jesus of the Sermon counseling the powerless to be compliant and good-natured in order to preserve their lives at any cost? To show a friendly face to their abusers, while fearing and hating them in their hearts? Such strategies may be necessary, short-term survival tactics but they lead neither to justice nor to true peace. What Jesus does call for, at the very least, is not to return evil for evil,[20] not to respond to it with violence. Non-retaliation at least breaks the cycle of overt violence. Still, it does little to resist the perpetuation of injustice, little to change the relationship with the enemy, little by way of engaging the enemy as a fellow human being. Or does it?

Walter Wink argues that the responses recommended in Matthew—offering the *left* cheek (after a backhand on the right, a humiliating blow to a social "inferior"), the second garment or the second mile (when only one is allowed by law)—are acts of resistance that enable the victim to maintain personal dignity and initiative, put the abuser in an embarrassing or awkward position, and thereby expose the absurdity and tenuousness of an unjust system.[21] But embarrassment and ridicule alone do not create peace; they may even exacerbate violence. Insofar as they assault the humanity and dignity of their target, they are themselves forms of violence. Luke's Jesus says to treat enemies, not the way they treat us, but in exactly the opposite way ("bless those who curse you"), and further, to treat *them* the way we would like them to treat *us*, and, most extreme of all, to treat them the way God treats them (6:27-28, 31-35). This is true resistance: it resists the temptation to violence; it resists the proliferation of violence; and, at the same time, it resists the proliferation of injustice because it acknowledges, and reminds the perpetrators of their own humanity and dignity and calls them to conversion. Love of enemies means caring enough about their humanity to hope and work for its healing and wholeness. An example is Dr. Martin Luther King, Jr. who used nonviolent resistance to work for justice and who counseled his followers to accept violence without retaliating in kind. This form of resistance

20   See Wink, 116-17.
21   Ibid., 104-12.

had a powerful impact on the consciences of those who witnessed it. His movement profoundly challenged the structures of racism and helped bring about sweeping changes in American society. It is worth noting that in the course of his campaign for justice, he came to realize that the pursuit of justice and the search for peace are inextricably linked.[22]

But "enemies" are also created through demonizing the Other. Fears and insecurities are projected onto those who are different, who do not share one's values, attitudes, race, religion, or history. "Outsiders" are blamed for social problems: it is often easier for a group to marshal its energies against an "external" target, a scapegoat, than to deal with its own internal tensions.[23] We in the first world can be arrogant and yet feel powerfully threatened at the same time, despising and yet distrusting those who are not like us: surely, we are the most advanced of all peoples; surely, our worldview is the right one. Yet any alternative must be combated vigorously, for it calls us and "all we hold dear" into question. The creation of peace, on the other hand, requires that we see things quite differently, that we see the Other not as a threat but a gift. The Sermon on the Mount speaks of the sun rising and the rain falling on the "bad" as well as the "good." Are "bad" and "good" not labels we all use to judge and categorize others according to our *own* particularities and prejudices? Might the point of the Sermon be the call to transcend labels and self-serving presumptions about who is "good" and who is "bad"?

We demonize Others insofar as we deny their common humanity, the rights and needs that all human beings yearn to have fulfilled. This entails a refusal to see that Others are very much like us and yet have their own distinctive truth, a refusal to see them for who they really *are*. Instead, they are the "enemy" which has been manufactured by our distorting biases. The Sermon on the Mount proposes a way of seeing others that transcends all such rationalizations. It calls us

---

22   Among the many writings on these themes are Martin Luther King, Jr., "A Time to Break Silence," 231-44, and "A Christmas Sermon on Peace," 253-58, in *A Testament of Hope: The Essential Writings and Speeches of Martin Luther King, Jr.*, ed. James Melvin Washington (Harper SanFrancisco, 1986; New York: HarperCollins Paperback, 1991).

23   See the analysis of the scapegoat mechanism by René Girard, *The Scapegoat*, trans. Yvonne Freccero (Baltimore: Johns Hopkins University Press, 1986).

to recognize basic human needs and so to realize a *common humanity*
with the "enemy." "Treat others as you would like them to treat you"
(Lk. 6:31, REB). In other words, "Realize that the Other is someone
very much like you, who would like to be treated the way you want
to be treated—and , furthermore, that he or she is actually capable of
treating *you* that way." Such re-visioning opens possibilities not only
for transcending demonizing stereotypes but also for building positive
relationships for transforming "enemies" into friends.

COMPASSION: TOWARD SOLIDARITY WITH THE OTHER

Luke's Jesus urges something still more radical: "Be compassionate, as
your Father is compassionate" (6:36, REB).[24] It is demanding enough
that one's treatment of others, particularly enemies, must be like God's:
loving those by whom one is hated is easy for God, the all-good, all-
loving, and all-*powerful*, but extremely difficult for vulnerable human
beings! It is daunting enough that one's love must be all-encompassing
("perfect"). What is natural to God, loving everyone, being "perfect," is
surely beyond our limited capacities! But here the command to love
one's enemies culminates in a call for a most radical love, a love that
suffers with the Other. The Greek οἰκτίμων can mean both *compassionate* and *merciful*; it has the particular sense of having the *sympathy*
(feeling with) that moves one to help someone who is suffering and in
need (including need caused by unworthiness). Mercy in this sense of
being moved to help is a "basic characteristic" of the Biblical God, for
whom it "is not simply an emotion; it is always manifested historically
in personal actions."[25] Being compassionate or merciful, therefore,
means being *moved* to *do* something to help those in need, no matter
who they are, particularly those who do not or cannot deserve it: "the
ungrateful and the wicked" (Lk. 6:35).

Being so deeply moved by the suffering of another that one *must* help
them happens only when we can allow ourselves to be open and vulnerable, to enter into what the other is going through, to be wounded
by it, to *feel* it *(com-passio)*, almost physically, in one's very core. Compassion invokes the humanity that all people share: bodies that can be

---

24   The NRSV and NAB have "merciful"; the REB and NJB, "compassionate."

25   D. E. Garland, *The International Standard Bible Encyclopedia*, ed. Geoffrey W. Bromiley (Grand Rapids: Eerdmans, 1986), 3:322-23; Marshall,
265; R. Bultmann, *Theological Dictionary of the New Testament* 5:159-61.

twisted in pain, lives that can be devastated by tragedy, hearts that can be broken with grief—everything that every human being has in common with every other. It makes us deeply, and sometimes uncomfortably, aware of how much we are like the Other. To enter into another's suffering marks a significant movement toward *identifying* with them, and identifying with the Other means no longer seeing them as "over against" oneself, someone to be kept at arm's length, demonized and denied: the "enemy." The true companion in suffering is then no longer an "enemy" when we share deeply in an elemental human experience, when we "enter into" one another and one another's feelings, relate to one another in a profoundly intimate way. Identifying with the Other thus brings one into solidarity with them and subverts the very possibility of enmity. It is difficult to think of someone as an enemy when one feels what they are feeling on the deepest of human levels, namely that of suffering. Compassion transforms enmity into solidarity.

Although Jesus of the Sermon resorts to "enemy" language to describe the thinking and behavior to be transcended by love and compassion, when he invokes the Father's treatment of the unworthy as a model for human conduct, the word "enemy" is conspicuously absent. The divine compassion—*suffering with*—precedes and supersedes the division of the world into friend and foe. It encompasses both the good and the wicked and cannot even recognize such distinctions for it goes deeper than either of these.

CONCLUSION: THE VALIDITY OF CREATING PEACE

Does the Sermon on the Mount count as valid? And is it something that has to be practised? It makes compelling sense to work for peace in a world so direly threatened with violence and devastation. But the imperative for peace is much more than a common-sense response to the practical exigencies of a particular moment in history. It could be argued that it is deeply-rooted in the very structure of creation itself and in the nature of its Creator. The "creator and lover of life," in whose Wisdom the world was created, "from the beginning gives life to all created beings, and does not desire their death." Faith in this Creator God presents a non-negotiable mandate to take this God's concerns seriously—the God that the Sermon depicts as caring compassionately for each beloved creature. It challenges us to realize our intrinsic relatedness with one another, to take seriously our "responsibility for other people," so that life in its fullness may be possible for all.[26] The challenge of the Sermon is directed to something fundamental to the creation of peace, and, even more so to that which is fundamental to creaturely existence: it is, in the end, a call to relate to our fellow human beings in the way God intended from the beginning, in the way God relates to them.

To create means to bring something completely new into being. To create peace means to bring about a new reality, to introduce new possibilities for new life out of what seemed to be possibilities for only violence and death. It requires that we see with new eyes, especially, that we see the Other with new eyes. It means finding new ways of being with one another, new forms of relating which no longer involve the idea of "enemy." Moltmann says, "Love of our enemies is not recompensing love that returns what it has received. It is creative love. Anyone who repays evil with good has stopped just reacting. He is creating something new."[27] He or she is participating with God in the re-creation of the world!

---

26   Moltmann, 132, 127, 124.
27   Ibid., 131.

4. THE COMPLEMENTARY PERSPECTIVES OF MUHAMMAD AND JESUS: AN ANALYSIS OF MORAL LEADERSHIP AND DISCIPLESHIP WITH SECULAR APPLICATION

EDWARD J. GRIPPE

This essay will be an inquiry into the interrelationship between leadership and discipleship necessary for human moral development. To make a very complex subject more manageable, I will focus on but two aspects: submission to responsibility and the responsibility of submission. I will draw on one example from each of the religions of Christianity and Islam (the Passion of Jesus in the Garden of Gethsemane and Muhammad as a great *sayyid* of the Muslim's bloodless *jihad* over Mecca in 630) in order to explore to what extent it is the duty of a leader to serve and the obligation of one who submits to lead.

How to lead people to a more moral, just, and fair world? By the spirit and pacifism, or the spirit and the sword? Christianity was founded on the first style of leadership, Islam on the second.[1] But are these two forms of moral leadership or two aspects of the same mode? Both the Qur'an and the New Testament remind their readers that wealth and power will not aid them when they stand at the Last Judgment and are asked why hadn't they helped the poor and the sick, or why did they not give comfort to those in need with the blessings they had received from Allah/God? Since they disdain political power for its own sake,[2] Jesus and Muhammad could be spoken of as prophets or *nadhir* (warner) who alerted people (*ummah*) to their need to live a moral, humane life.

---

1 I use this phrase here mindful of the fact that the Qur'an explicitly states "there shall be no coercion in matters of faith" (2:256). My aim is only to distinguish Mohammad's inclusion of the *Lesser Jihad* (the effort of self-defense) as part of the effort to live in the way Allah intended people to live (the *Greater Jihad*) from Jesus' unequivocal rejection of violent self-defense as a means to the realization of the Kingdom of God (Matt. 26:47-55).

2 Qur'an 74:1-5, 8-10; 88:21-22; Matt. 4:8-11; Lk. 4:5-8.

Nevertheless, while he was cognizant of the role politics plays in all human undertakings, Jesus separated the political duty one owes to a "Caesar" from moral responsibility one has to God [3] even in the face of his inquisition by Pilate and his death.[4] On the other hand, Muhammad's appreciation of the Oneness of Allah [5] caused him to see everything in terms of the will of God. Politics, economics, the military, etc. were more than human constructs when placed in service to God.[6] Even the violence of war could be perceived as an instrument of Allah's will—as it was, for example, at the Battle of the Trench—if it is done in self-defense *and* if Muslims used every means possible to seek a peaceful settlement to the hostilities in the shortest possible time (as was attempted by the first Muslim *hajj* in 628).[7] Thus, a significant difference is evident between Muhammad and Jesus. Whereas the latter stresses to his disciples that the moral way into God's Kingdom is through loving one's enemies and doing "good by those who hate you," [8] the former, while not forcing anyone to become Muslim, employed both the olive branch of peace and the marching armies of war to establish the *ummah* dedicated to social justice and practical compassion.

Given this significant difference in methods of moral guidance, do we also find incommensurate types of leadership? Can there be reconciliation between a holy man who proclaims that those who live by the sword will die by it and a prophet whose sword helped found the religion of Islam?

3 Lk. 16:9-15; 20: 20-26. Jesus' rejection of political power as a way to salvation is not apolitical, but constitutes a political position, namely radical moral democracy achieved through self-awareness and nonviolent action.

4 Jn. 18:33-38; 19:9-11

5 Qur'an 6:159, 161-162.

6 This presents a problem when considering the killing of seven hundred men of the Qurayzah (a Jewish tribe particularly hostile to the Muslims) and selling their women and children into slavery. If a slaughter of this magnitude is thought to be part of the will of God to bring the hostilities to an end after the Battle of the Trench, then how can one distinguish between this sort of act and Papal crusades against Arabs of the Middle East in the name of Jesus Christ, the aim of the latter having been to bring Christianity to the "heathen infidels" and thereby move mankind as a whole one step closer to salvation?

7 Qur'an 8:16-17.

8 Lk. 6: 27-38.

Reconciliatory dialogue was the hope of John Paul II, [9] and it is also the current wish of Pope Benedict XVI. In this context, Benedict gave an address to an academic audience at the University of Regensburg, Germany on September 12, 2006, on the main theme of the intrinsic need for a rapprochement between faith and reason. One of his concerns was with the Muslim teaching, alluded to above, that God as an absolutely transcendent Being "is not bound up with any of our categories, even that of rationality. … Ibn Hazn went so far as to state that God is not bound even by his own word, and that nothing would oblige him to reveal the truth to us. Were it God's will, we would even have to practice idolatry."[10] Benedict also cites Duns Scotus's *voluntarism*. As humans we are aware only of God's *voluntas ordinata*. "Beyond this is the realm of God's freedom, in virtue of which he could have done the opposite of everything he has actually done. This gives rise to positions which clearly approach those of Ibn Hazn and might even lead to the image of a capricious God, who is not even bound to truth and goodness."[11] This is unacceptable for the Christian faith as one of its central beliefs is that God's will is bound up with *logos*" (i.e., reason). Benedict concluded his remarks with an invitation to other faiths to engage with him in a dialogue of cultures in the spirit of "this great logos."

I therefore suggest an affirmative answer to the question posed here initially: "Can there be reconciliation between the principles exemplified by Jesus and those proclaimed by Muhammad?" Both spiritual figures were men of vision as well as faith; they were also facilitating leaders and responsive disciples. This is clear if one appreciates the *logos* of leadership and discipleship which each of them exemplified and is not distracted into thinking that differences in style amount to differences in substance.

It has been said that a leader is defined as such by having followers. Those who follow the lead of another usually do so to get what they want or need. What they think they want or need might be benefi-

---

9 John Paul II said "And given that Islam and Christianity worship the one God, Creator of heaven and earth, there is ample room for agreement and cooperation between them. . . ." Newsweek. "The Pope's Holy War." September 25, 2006, p. 37.

10 "Pope's speech at University of Regensburg" in http://www.cwnews.com/news/viewstory.cfm?recnum=46474.

11 Ibid.

cial to them, or it could prove destructive to their real interests. Also, followers might place an emphasis on external benefits over intrinsic ones,[12] preferring signs to that which is being signified. In short, those who follow in this way do so because they think they know what is in their best interest. Associating themselves with some leader seems like it will get them what they want or need in immediate or concrete terms. *In contrast to a mere follower*, a disciple is a person who is someone who recognizes that he or she is ignorant of what constitutes her best interest and is therefore in need of the direction of another, someone who can fill the void in his or her self-understanding. Thus the disciple is open to moral influence, potentially vulnerable to the counsel and commands of a leader. This openness can be absolute or tentative. If the disciple submits unquestioningly, then, his or her action is done out of unconditional trust. Trust is necessary for authentic human interaction. However, one can place one's trust in another prematurely, thereby relinquishing one's ability to distinguish between authentic and misguiding leadership, and short-circuiting one's sense of responsibility to oneself. History is replete with the tragedy of the blind dedication of disciples to erroneous definitions of success (material or spiritual) set by others.[13] Thus there seems to be a need for wise judgment on the part of would-be disciples as well as on the part of leaders. It is critical that disciples actively assess the beliefs and goals set forth by their leader. Here we get to the core of the problem: How can a seeker (disciple) exercise wise choice when they seek wisdom from a seer (leader) who may or may not be wise?

Blind submission to Yahweh, Allah, or God the Father can always lead to a situation in which an abusive leader imposes demagogic interpretations of the Divine will onto unsuspecting and trusting

---

12 Plato's *Apology* touches on this distinction at 36c when he has Socrates say: " ... I went to each of you privately and conferring upon him what is the greatest benefit, by trying to persuade him not to care for any of his belongings before caring that he himself should be good and as wise as possible, not to care for the city's possessions more than the city itself, and to care for other things in the same way" (Grube, G. M. A. [1981]. *Plato: Five Dialogues*. Indianapolis, Indiana: Hackett Publishing Company, p. 40).

13 The suicide and murder of 900 of Jim Jones' disciples in the late 1970s is one such example.

disciples,[14] hence passive belief cannot bring us closer to the answer to the above problem. Responsible discipleship must be a vital element in making a wise decision as to which prophet or messiah one chooses to esteem. Responsibility in this context includes being "clever like a snake."[15] Awareness of the possibility that injustice may be done to naive disciples by overzealous leaders awakens the disciple to deeper aspects of the moral life: autonomy and integrity.

Unjust acts are great teachers of justice. Paradoxically, the ways in which the unjust can rob an individual of personhood highlight the elements necessary for a human life. We can see this at work in the Passion and Death of Jesus. In the Garden of Gethsemane, Jesus calls to his disciples three times to stay awake with him as *he* surrenders to the will of the Father (and the reality of his situation). Jesus is modeling the path of submission to the pains of death. It requires that he simultaneously be a follower *and* a leader. Through events that could be called anything but successful from an ordinary perspective, Jesus demonstrates the nature of integrity and autonomy to those who would remain awake precisely through the humiliation of arrest and questioning, the embarrassment of being put on display, the agony of being scourged, and the horror of death on the cross. By enduring the ordeal of his Passion without striking back, he remained steadfast in his principles of nonviolence and compassion, and by remaining self-possessed throughout, he did not acquiesce to those who would redefine him as a "failure" or a "victim" even as they scorned him. In this intentional example of nonviolent resistance to the violent oppression and coercive exploitation that pressed in on him, Jesus revealed to mankind the essence of justice and the virtue of the moral life. Furthermore, by being existentially one with his narrative to his last moments, he changed the meaning of suffering and loss of life from an inevitable affliction visited upon a person by either God, nature, or human action into an opportunity for personal and communal transformation. And, as a model for such transformation, he forces his

14   The Sufis understand the danger of even the best-intentioned leader bending text and experience to fit his expectations of the way the world ought to be. This is why they challenge all constructs in favor of the mystical unity in God (*baqa*) by direct awareness through *fana* (the passing away of the self).

15   Matt. 10:16. This passage continues, stating that the disciples must be as "innocent as doves" in addition to being quick-witted and resourceful.

disciple to confront unquestioned assumptions about the nature of creaturehood, community, and mortality. As an exemplar of non-coercive engagement, he opens the way for the disciple to evaluate freely the merits of Christ's way of life. Thus, even as he dutifully acquiesced to life's exigencies, Jesus both provided a model of wise judgment and allowed his disciples the freedom to evaluate critically that example. In other words, in the very act of submission to the will of the Father, he simultaneously offers the disciple a model for leadership *and* demonstrates that leadership itself; the disciple can therefore avoid the trap of blind submission.

Muhammad's situation at the time of his success in Mecca, is somewhat different from Jesus' predicament. In 628 C.E. with the recent military victories over Mecca and the opposition in Medina still fresh in people's memory, he dared to make the *hajj* with approximately one thousand unarmed Muslim pilgrims. Avoiding those who would harm him and reaching Hudaybiyyah on the outskirts of Mecca only with great difficulty, he took advantage of the Sanctuary of Mecca during the *hajj* to press the Quraysh [16] for peace. However, this treaty lasted for less than two years. It took the threat of an army of ten thousand men to seal the peace and set the stage for the spread of the *ummah* throughout the Arabian Peninsula.

Muhammad's aim had been to avoid force, and when that failed to bring hostilities to a quick conclusion in accordance with the teachings of the Qur'an.[17] Thus his goal was not that of a ruler, but a servant of Allah.[18] This is evident when it is noted that none of the Quraysh were forced to become Muslim,[19] something which would have been easy to demand once resistance to the Prophet had come to an end. But

16   The Quraysh was Muhammad's original tribe and one that was most hostile to Islam prior to 630.

17   *Qur'an* 8:16-17

18   "I never said that God's treasures are in my hands, that I knew the hidden things, or that I was an angel. I am only a preacher of God's word, the bringer of God's message to mankind." (From Ameer Ali's *The Spirit of Islam*, as cited in Huston Smith (1991). *The World's Religions*. New York: Harper Collins, p. 227.)

19   *Qur'an* 2:257; Karen Armstrong. (2000). *Islam: A Short History*. New York: A Modern Library Chronicles Book, p. 23. In fact, the Medina charter incorporated the principle of religious tolerance in accordance with *Qur'an* 5:28.

the circumstances did not warrant this response and God hates an aggressor.[20] Muhammad, obedient to Allah, refused to pay back persecution with persecution.[21] The return of good for evil motivated the victorious Muhammad to open the *ummah* to those who recognized their part in the old corrupt system which Islam was aiming to reform. Once the attacks against Muslims had ceased and the terrible social ills had begun to be redressed, persuasion and example came to the fore, even for those who still remained non-Muslim.

Magnanimity and tolerance were hallmarks of Mohammad's leadership. The *hadith* has him saying to a Meccan, "We have returned from the lesser *jihad* (war) to face the greater *jihad* (the battle of the enemy within ourselves)."[22] Muhammad's assessment of this situation is critical, for it mirrors Jesus'. In his submission to pain and loss, Jesus teaches how disciples can be leaders; in his triumph, Mohammad teaches how leaders can be disciples. The latter understood that the use of power is corruptive when it is idolized through *ghaflah* (i.e., forgetfulness, as in the case of the paternalist or pseudo-facilitator who loses sight of the divine due to philotyranny) or *kufu* (i.e., thanklessness, as in the case of an egoistic ruler's abusive embrace of the trappings of power and rejection of their Source and purpose). Thus a leader who models his behavior on Muhammad's must use power only when necessary *and* in submissive service to the good.

It appears that Muhammad's and Jesus' styles of leadership differed. In truth, however, that difference was one of perspective only, not substance.[23] Whether by the parry of a sword in self-defense or the turn of a cheek in a dynamic act of nonviolence, what both prophets had in common was the active resistance against the evils of subjugation and exploitation. They also both rejected the notion that one can return

---

20 Ibid., 2:190.

21 Ibid., 42:37.

22 Op. Cit., Smith, p. 257 (parenthetical statement added).

23 It is obvious that much more work needs to be done relative to Jesus and Muhammad's divergent attitudes toward the use of force for purposes of self-defense. Unfortunately, the space limitations of this short essay do not allow for this. Still, it is noteworthy that both men resisted tyranny in its obvious form as well as in the deceptive guise of philotyranny. And, if they both recognized each kind of tyranny for what it is, then it can perhaps be tentatively stated that neither of them succumbed to the allure of either form of the abuse of power.

evil for evil, however, each emphasized a different aspect of leadership: Muhammad modeled the leader-as-disciple by using his leadership role *not* for ego appeasement or to advance a sort of messianic paternalism, but rather in service to Allah. He sought to create the conditions under which an opponent might more readily choose to become like Muhammad: a disciple of God. Jesus, on the other hand, exemplified the disciple-as-leader, the individual who, though he is afflicted by adverse conditions and suffers under corrupt leadership, is not swayed from a life devoted to God's goodness and truth.

Both of these men exemplify a human life well-lived, even if they do so from opposite perspectives; and, their actions point to the answer to the perplexing issue of how a disciple can exercise wise choice when seeking wisdom from a leader who may or may not be wise. Muhammad sets the example of a just life, one that creates the conditions which are conducive to a disciple's making the free choice to allow a good leader to guide them to the acceptance of such a life; Jesus shows the seeker that a good disciple must cultivate self-knowledge so as to be able to discern critically the traits of good leadership (as defined here) and, through humble submission to all that is good, become a moral leader him or herself.

In terms that may be applicable to the question of human moral development in general, a good leader is one who facilitates his or her followers' becoming moral leaders themselves; a good follower allows, with open eyes, the leader to guide them toward moral leadership. And the good judgment that is necessary to be a facilitating leader and a discerning disciple is born from the humble wisdom that in life (secular and religious) we are, in fact, and ought always consciously to be, both facilitators of and disciples to truth—both seekers and leaders in the quest for an honest and just life. [24]

My interest in peace and justice issues was awakened when I began to take philosophy courses at Fordham University as a graduate student. Up to that point, I had been interested in such questions but had lacked a process by which to make the content of the debates coherent. Several teachers, beginning with Fr. Gerald McCool and culminating in Professor Kenneth Gallagher, provided a solid basis for exploring these issues with both reason and a sense of humanity.

---

24 My gratitude is extended to the Pawling Discussion Group for inspiring this essay with their thoughtful insights and constructive skepticism. They are indeed disciples and also facilitators of truth.

The character of Socrates has exerted a deep influence on me. He demonstrated the virtues into which he inquired and did it with both courage of his convictions and humility in regard to his beliefs. As Plato's *Crito* makes clear, Socrates is a person of peace, someone who is willing to sacrifice his life in a nonviolent manner for the good of the youth of Athens [It can, of course, be argued that we are the youth of Athens since we are the inheritors of the Greek cultural tradition].

My views have been challenged by what I take to be a Machiavellian worldview tacitly held by those in power who profess to be interested in peace and human freedom. What I am therefore called to do is, as Gandhi exhorts, to find some sort of common ground with those who would exploit situations and hence also people, in order to ensure victory in *their* own battles, allegedly against "evil" and for "good".

5. ISLAM AND CHRISTIANITY
AGREE ON CORE VALUES: JUSTICE AS A BASIS
FOR UNIVERSAL MORALITY AND PEACE

AYSE SIDIKA OKTAY

The many violent acts that occur in today's world are often thought to be the result of a conflict between two different religious civilizations, Islam and Christianity. But, are the moral values of these religions really so different? Is it not possible for the members of these civilizations to meet on common principles such as equality, justice, and respect for human life? Both religions aim to make people happy in this life as well as in the next. Globalization is, however, a force which has intervened in the lives of many and caused great problems both material and spiritual.

When acts of violence increase in a region, they effect a sort of chain reaction. In other words, one of the consequences of globalization is the spread of violence. It causes societies to suffer from security problems, both internal and external. The need for security, peace and a means of ensuring the common welfare on a global scale is perhaps greater now than it has ever been. The current global order has created large-scale problems of this sort. Deepening conditions of poverty lead to increased drug traffic and terrorism by both individuals and nation-states. Natural disasters seem to be on the rise as well, often resulting from environmental degradation. These problems can only be corrected through collaborative work. Furthermore, the forces of globalization tend to corrode traditional religious values and encourage societies to center on alternate (and by religious standards, false) values such as money, power and fame. Much current investment in third world economies aims to ensure the material welfare of the human person (e.g. physical health, beauty etc.), but it neglects the spiritual aspect of people's lives. We are trying to conquer nature through continually improving science and technology at the same time as we are consuming both it and ourselves. Our moral and ethical values have not improved as fast as science and technology have, yet human moral development may be far more important than any other aspect of human life.

Human moral development is central to peacemaking because, in the end, it is the human person, as defined by the moral values of his or her religion and society, who makes choices regarding the use (or abuse) of science and technology. Regional or national values and the moral rules which accompany these are not sufficient to solve the current global problems. Instead, we need to agree on a system of global ethics, one based in universal values. A wide-ranging consensus among world societies is necessary in order to realize such a system of ethics. It will not otherwise receive global approval and nor will it have continuity with the respective traditions. The world's religions are perhaps the most viable tools for establishing a global consensus of this sort, because, at their very core, virtually all of them contain universal ethical principles and values. The work of developing a global ethic therefore hinges on agreement on these core values, i.e., on uncovering them and identifying what is shared across cultures.

Islam and Christianity have both drawn on Aristotle's theory of virtue to develop their respective ethical traditions. Since both originate from the same Abrahamic source and have the largest global membership, it is relatively easy to identify the core principles which they hold in common. Collaborative work can therefore proceed along these lines. Both religions respect living creatures, aim to be tolerant and practice forgiveness. Given that all of us are children of Adam and Eve, we are, in some respect, brothers and sisters. We all respect the human being as a creation of God, honor individual rights, seek to ensure social and economic equality, and generally advocate justice.

The goal of Islamic ethics, like Christian ethics, is to guide the believer to eternal happiness. According to Islam, material life is finite. It is a period of time allocated to us to prepare for the next life. Therefore we must work out the conditions of our material life in a manner that enables us to proceed on this spiritual journey. As the Qur'an explains, a just social order facilitates our living properly in this world and focuses the individual on attaining happiness in the next.

Happiness can be attained only by the practice of virtue. And to form the soul virtuously, knowledge and action must coincide. Such inner harmony is possible only when it is undergirded by justice. Many philosophers, e.g. Plato, Aristotle and al-Farabi have discovered this subtle balance between knowledge and action, between theory

and praxis. It is a sort of golden mean which makes it possible to realize justice on a larger scale and, ultimately to attain wisdom.

It is noteworthy that justice is emphasized in the Qur'an, and this
because, as mentioned, it creates the conditions under which human
beings can live happily. Justice is, however, a composite of other concepts and values: Equality, fairness, or their opposites, tyranny, injustice are some of them. In Islam it is studied from various perspectives
such as morality, politics, law, philosophy, etc.

Justice is regarded as one of the basic virtues, indeed the very first
and foremost, and it is taken to be indispensable to proper human
moral development. Where it does not exist, tyranny rules, peace and
tolerance cannot flourish. Allah describes himself in Qur'an as the one
who judges his creatures with complete justice and without the slightest unfairness. He refers to himself as the one who is equitable and
fair. Justice is there described as manifesting itself in spiritual equilibrium, moral maturity (the perfect man) and autonomy. The "Perfect
man" is the one whose behaviors are fair and who has himself become
emblematic of justice.

Equality is the primary concept from which justice derives. In the
words of Allah,

> O mankind! We created you from a single (pair) of a male and a fe-
> male, and made you into nations and tribes, that ye may know each
> other (not that ye may despise each other). Verily the most honored
> of you in the sight of Allah is (he who is) the most righteous of
> you. And Allah has full knowledge and is well acquainted (with all
> things). (Qur'an, Al-Hujraat [The Private Apartments], 49/13)

All human beings are equal in the eyes of Allah. Differences of gender,
nationality, wealth, race or post are of no importance. Everyone is created from man and woman and the reason for different genders, races
and nationalities is not to bring about superiority and inferiority, but
mutual understanding. According to Allah, everyone is equal; superiority among human beings is only determined by their level of piety,
something which can only be discerned by Him. Muslims believe that
the message of the Qur'an is universal and available to all, and that
it encompasses past, present and future. Equality is therefore taken
to be a universal principle, one that has religious roots and extensive
implications for moral living.

Prophet Muhammad also draws attention to the relation between
equality and justice. He is taken to be a role model because he was so

thoroughly able to apply these principles in his life. Usama, a friend of
the Prophet, asked him to forgive a woman who had committed theft.
She was rich, respected and important in society, but the Prophet
said,

> The people before you were destroyed because they used to inflict
> the legal punishments on the poor and forgive the rich. By Him in
> Whose Hand my soul is! If Fatima (the daughter of the Prophet)
> did that (i.e. stole), I would punish her too. [1]

Many Bible verses also require that human beings treat each other
fairly and justly, for example:

> Masters, give unto your servants that which is just and equal; know-
> ing that ye also have a Master in heaven. (Col. 4:1)

Many verses from both the Qur'an and the Bible also dwell on justice
and related concepts. Human beings are ordered to act fairly, for example:

> O ye who believe! Stand out firmly for justice, as witnesses to Allah,
> even as against yourselves, or your parents, or your kin, and whether
> it be (against) rich or poor: for Allah can best protect both. Follow
> not the lusts (of your hearts), lest ye swerve, and if ye distort (jus-
> tice) or decline to do justice, verily Allah is well-acquainted with all
> that ye do. (Qur'an, An-Nisa (Women), 4/135)

In the Bible,

> Thus speaketh the Lord of hosts, saying, Execute true judgment,
> and shew mercy and compassion every man to his brother. (Zach.
> 7:9)

And, the Qur'an states,

> Say: "My Lord hath commanded justice; and that ye set your
> whole selves (to Him) at every time and place of prayer, and call
> upon Him, making your devotion sincere as in His sight: such as
> He created you in the beginning, so shall ye return" (Al-Araf (The
> Heights), 7/29)

The Bible states,

> Who through faith subdued kingdoms, wrought righteousness, ob-
> tained promises, stopped the mouths of lions. (Heb. 11:33)

In Islamic thought, the word "injustice" is not used as the antonym of
the word "justice"; "tyranny" is used instead, because where there is no

---

1 Bukhari, Sahih, Volume 8, Book 81, Number 779:

justice, tyranny prevails. In such circumstances, there is nothing but wickedness, bitterness, torment and fighting. Still, Allah is just and orders human beings to be fair to each other. He also cherishes those who are: "Whoever works righteousness benefits his own soul; whoever works evil, it is against his own soul: nor is thy Lord ever unjust (in the least) to His Servants." (Qur'an, Fussilat (Explained in Detail), 41/46). Human beings will be held responsible for their good and bad deeds because of Allah's fundamental fairness.

> (It will be said): "This is because of the deeds which thy hands sent forth, for verily Allah is not unjust to His servants." (Qur'an, Al-Hajj (The Pilgrimage), 22/10)

And,

> We shall set up scales of justice for the Day of Judgment, so that not a soul will be dealt with unjustly in the least, and if there be (no more than) the weight of a mustard seed, We will bring it (to account): and enough are We to take account. (Qur'an, Al-Anbiya (The Prophets), 21/47)

These passages indicate that the slightest vices and virtues will be punished or rewarded accordingly; they also point out how carefully Allah treats His creatures in order to sustain justice. Biblical verses also refer to divine justice:

> For God is not unrighteous to forget your work and labour of love, which ye have shewed toward his name, in that ye have ministered to the saints, and do minister. (Heb. 6:10)

Allah is not a tyrant, and does not torture His creatures. So he also does not approve of human beings treating each other unjustly:

> The recompense for an injury is an injury equal thereto (in degree): but if a person forgives and makes reconciliation, his reward is due from Allah: for (Allah) loveth not those who do wrong. (Counsel, 42/40)

This verse prescribes punishment of criminals in keeping with the magnitude and nature of the crimes they have committed, but, excessive punishment is a crime in itself. It amounts to a sort of tyranny of one human being over another. Conversely, forgiving a criminal and encouraging peace receive the blessing of Allah and are divinely rewarded.

One of the main reasons that Allah sends his messengers along with His messages, his holy books, is to ensure social justice. As the Qur'an says, "We sent aforetime our messengers with Clear Signs and sent down with them the Book and the Balance (of Right and Wrong), that men may stand forth in justice..." (Al-Hadid (The Iron), 57/25) The Bible also states

> Behold my servant, whom I have chosen; my beloved, in whom my soul is well pleased: I will put my spirit upon him, and he shall shew judgment to the Gentiles. (Matt. 12:18)

Muslim thinkers have tried to examine the Qur'anic notion of justice with the help of reason. Generally, they have held that revelation and reason were not in conflict, but harmonious: What comes to us via revelation and what is known via reason are merely expressions of the same truth. Their thoughts about justice are, for the most part, extensions of the opinions of Plato and Aristotle, since these thinkers' views were in general agreement with Islamic moral theory.

In the Qur'an, justice is an instrument by which we can attain peace and individual happiness. The Islamic philosophers also took it to be a virtue which conduced to happiness, not only one of the cardinal virtues like wisdom, temperance and courage - virtues that make human beings happy - but also one that grounds moral standards altogether. "Justice is a virtue that coordinates and balances other virtues."[2] It is therefore also related to moderation.

As the foundational principle of ethical and political philosophy, justice has been the focus of the work of many Muslim philosophers. Ibn Miskawayh, for example, studied ethical philosophy exclusively and reinterpreted the concept of justice that originated from Ancient Greek sources, looking at it from a unique Islamic perspective. He developed his thinking about it in terms of individual and political ethics[3] and also concurred with the Aristotelian claim that justice was one of the cardinal virtues:

> When the activity of rational soul is moderate and not extraneous to itself, and when this soul seeks true knowledge, not what is presumed to be knowledge but is in reality ignorance, it achieves the virtue of knowledge followed by that of wisdom. Similarly, when the activity of the beastly soul is moderate, when it yields to the rational soul and does not reject what the latter allots to it, and when it does not indulge in pursuit of its own desires, it achieves the virtue of temperance followed by that of liberality. When the activity

2 Macid Hadduri, *The Islamic Conception of Justice*, p. 116.
3 Mustafa Çağrıcı, *İslam Felsefesinde Ahlâk*, p. 167.

of the irascible soul is moderate, when it obeys the rational soul in what it allots to it and is not aroused at the wrong time nor becomes unduly excited, it achieves the virtue of magnanimity followed by that of courage. Then, when all these three virtues are moderate and have the proper relation one to another, a virtue is produced, which represents their perfection and completeness, namely, the virtue of justice. Thus, the philosophers are agreed that the virtues are four genera: wisdom, temperance, courage and justice.[4]

He goes on to explain why justice is the most important virtue:

> As for justice, it is a virtue of the soul which it gets from the union of the three above-named virtues when the three faculties act in harmony one with another and submit to discerning faculty so that they do not combat among themselves or follow their desires according to the dictates of their natures. The fruit of this virtue is the acquisition of an attitude which induces a person to choose always to be fair to himself in the first place, and, then, to be fair to others and to demand fairness from them.[5]

Ibn Miskawayh added the virtue of liberality (generosity) to temperance and that of magnanimity (forbearance) to courage, since these are central to Qur'anic ethics. He enumerated and subsumed a number of Islamic virtues under the traditional cardinal virtues. One of his most important insights, one that has exerted considerable influence over other Muslim philosophers, concerns the relations that obtain among justice, love and friendship. In his view, love is a force that can prevent or annul other harmful forces. He associates it with human fellowship (gregariousness). One of the main reasons for Islam's requirement of prayer five times a day, particularly on Fridays, for gathering together twice a year on feast days, and for meeting once in a lifetime at Mecca is to encourage and deepen our natural sense of fellowship, love, goodness and happiness, and thereby create social solidarity. Love, however, is virtue that requires more private expression. It is impossible for all people to love each other, but, in a small group, love helps remedy and remove harm. Under such circumstances, justice is secondary. In society as a whole, the fact that everyone desires something creates conflict, hence the need for justice. Love, on the other hand, requires and encompasses sacrifice. The lover wants his beloved's wishes to be

---

4 Ibn Miskawayh, *Tahdhib al-akhlaq*, trans. C.K. Zurayk, pp. 15-17; Dwight
  M. Donaldson, *Studies in Muslim Ethics*, pp. 126-127.
5 Ibid, pp. 127.

fulfilled more so than his own. Love is also an ideal. Justice is necessary
to counter anarchy and ensure that peace prevails in society. Ibn Mishkawayh also compares love to justice. He sees the former as a greater
virtue, because, according to him, it resembles a natural unity, whereas
justice is rationally designed. Where there is love, there is the chance to
reach Allah, the ground of all Unity; by contrast, justice serves largely
human purposes. The highest form of love is the one that human beings feel towards Allah. There are three major motivations for love:
pleasure, goodness and the benefit of society as a whole. Real friends
love each other because of the intrinsic goodness of their character.
Love that depends on pleasure and gain is as temporary as these are.
Like Aristotle, Ibn Mishkawayh points out that justice is secondary in
friendship, that the reverse is also the case, namely, that friendship will
prevail among those who are fair.[6]

Christian thought accepts justice as one of the four cardinal virtues
(temperance, justice, prudence and fortitude). All of these are moral
virtues. Thomas Aquinas comments on Aristotle's theory of virtue in
his *Summa Theologiae*. According to him, St. Ambrose interprets the
phrase "Blessed are the poor in spirit" (Luke, 6:20) as follows: "We
know that there are four cardinal virtues: temperance, justice, prudence and fortitude"[7] (virtues which are also cited in Wisdom, 8:7).
Per Aquinas,

> These four virtues can be considered in two ways. First, in regard
> to their common formal notions. In this way, they are called princi-
> pal, as being common to all virtues, so that, for instance, any virtue
> which causes good in reason's consideration is called prudence; any
> virtue which realizes the good of what is right and due in operation
> is called justice; any virtue which curbs and restrains the passions
> is called temperance; and any virtue which strengthens the soul
> against any passion whatsoever is called fortitude. In a second way,
> however, these virtues can be taken according as each is denominat-
> ed from what is primary in its respective matter, and thus they are

---

6   Ibid, pp. 123-128 and also refer to Lenn E. Goodman, *Jewish and Islamic
    Philosophy*, Edinburgh University Press, Edinburgh/Great Britain, 1999.

7   St. Thomas Aquinas, *The Summa Theologiae of St. Thomas Aquinas*, Trans.
    by Fathers of The English Dominican Province, part II (First Part), 7,
    Second Number, (QQ. XLIX-LXXXIX), p.136; St. Thomas Aquinas,
    Treatise on the Virtues, translated by John A. Oesterle, p. 108; *Introduction
    to Saint Thomas Aquinas*, edited with an Introduction by Anton C. Pegis;
    Question 61, art. 1, p. 586.

specific virtues, divided off from other virtues. Nevertheless they are still referred to as principal in comparison with other virtues because of the primacy of their matter. Thus prudence is the virtue which commands, justice the virtue which deals with due actions between equals, temperance the virtue which curbs desires for the pleasures of touch, and fortitude the virtue which strengthens one in the face of danger of death. [8]

And, "Justice is a habit whereby a man renders to each one his due by a constant and perpetual will."[9] It requires that everyone should always have the desire to be just whatever the circumstances.

> Justice governs our dealing with others; the very name justice signifies equality—to adjust something is to make it equal to some standard—and equality is a relationship to something other. Other moral virtues fit a man to himself: they aim at action right for the doer. Justice over and above that, aims at action right for someone else, adjusted to match another.[10]

Justice is, however, special and different from the other virtues. "Because justice is a virtue, it regulates human action according to a standard of right reason and so renders it good."[11] And, The mean of moral virtue must be a real mean, as it is in the case of justice.[12]

Similar to Ibn Miskawayh's Islamic interpretation of Aristotle's virtues, Augustine also interprets them in the context of Christian ethics, as Aquinas notes:

> The soul has four virtues whereby, in this life, it lives spiritually, viz. temperance, prudence, fortitude and justice; and he says that the fourth is justice, which pervades all the virtues.[13]

---

8   St. Thomas Aquinas, *Summa Theologiae*, part II, 7, p 139-140; *Treatise on the Virtues*; Ques. 61, art. 3, p. 112.

9   St. Thomas Aquinas, *Summa Theologiae*, part II, (Second Part) 10, Second Number (QQ. XLVII-LXXIX), Ques. 58, art. 1, p. 115.

10   St. Thomas Aquinas, *Summa Theologiae*, part II, 10, Ques. 58, art. , p. 115; *Summa Theologiae, A Concise Translation*, Ed. Timothy McDermott, Ques. 58, art. 1, p. 383-384.

11   St. Thomas Aquinas, *Summa Theology*, Ques. 58, art. 3, p. 115. St. Thomas Aquinas, *Summa Theologiæ, A Concise Translation*, Ques. 58, art. 3, p. 384.

12   St. Thomas Aquinas, *Summa Theologiae*, part II, 7, p.168; *Treatise on the Virtues,*; Ques. 64, art.2, p.134.

13   St. Thomas Aquinas, *Summa Theologiae*, , Ques. 58, art. 8, p.127.

Another source quotes him as follows:

> St. Augustine defines virtue as nothing else than perfect love of God
> and the four cardinal virtues of Greek moral philosophy as form of
> this love. Thus temperance is love keeping itself entire and incor-
> rupt for God; fortitude is love bearing everything readily for the
> sake of God; justice is love serving God only, and therefore ruling all
> else, as subject to man; prudence is love making a right distinction
> between what helps it towards God and what might hinder it.[14]

Aquinas expands on this as follows:

> Augustine makes clear how there is an order of love in four cardinal
> virtues. But love is charity, which is acknowledged to be a theologi-
> cal virtue. Therefore the moral virtues should not be distinguished
> from the theological virtues.[15]

And, for Augustine, the ground of all virtue is the love of God.[16]

> Christians believe that the primary purpose of a moral virtue is the
> more effective service of all men, whoever and wherever they may
> be.[17]

So the virtues should be enlarged:

> For example, the duty of justice will require of him far more than
> respect for the rights of his fellow-citizens as defined by laws of
> his own society. It will also demand that he champion the rights of
> underprivileged or persecuted groups and that he concern himself
> with the interests of other nations. Thus, the virtue of justice must
> be strengthened and broadened until it becomes a creative force
> seeking equal justice for all men.[18]

When we evaluate justice and other virtues in keeping with both
Christian and Muslim moral philosophers' understanding of them, we
can conclude that they both draw on Aristotle to develop their thinking, but also that they have interpreted his virtue theory in keeping
with their own religious precepts. However, they also enhanced and

---

14   George F. Thomas, *Christian Ethics and Moral Philosophy*, p. 506.

15   St. Thomas Aquinas, *Treatise on the Virtues*, p.120; *Introduction to Saint
      Thomas Aquinas*, Ques. 62, art. 2, 3 p. 592.

16   St. Thomas Aquinas, *Summa Theologiae, A Concise Translation*, Ques.
      57, art. 1, p. 384; *Summa Theologiae*, Ques. 57, art. 1, p. 105; George F.
      Thomas, *Christian Ethics and Moral Philosophy*, p.506.

17   George F. Thomas, *Christian Ethics and Moral Philosophy*, p. 508.

18   Ibid.

expanded on Aristotle's thought by adding new virtues and vices. For example, they removed pride from the list of Aristotle's virtues. ("Aristotle had taken it for granted that pride is a virtue." "In contrast, pride is the primary sin in Christian ethics."[19]) Pride is also forbidden by the Qur'an and is regarded as a sin in Islamic ethics. Christian ethics added new virtues of its own such as humility, meekness, willingness to forgive, forbearance, patience, mercy, kindness and, of course, charity. Generosity, forbearance, forgiveness, patience are some of important Islamic virtues that were added and ordered into the system of ethics in the Qur'an. Finally, both religions accepted the same vices, e.g. envy, anger, lust, and sloth.

There are many similarities between both religions' understanding of these virtues and vices as well as in their understanding of the relation of the various virtues to justice. Some of the virtues are referred to by different names even though their meanings are the same. "Wisdom," for instance, is called "prudence" and "courage," "fortitude." And, some of the virtues have the same names, but with slight nuances of meaning. However, as one Christian writer has noted, this does not mean that they are totally the same. "Mercy in the Qur'an is not altogether different from mercy in the Bible, but neither is it wholly the same." [20] Despite these differences in understanding in each religion, these virtues represent core values. Their names matter little, nor do slight nuances of meaning obscure this fact. But, is this not to be expected where both religions are Abrahamic and also influenced by Aristotelian philosophy? On the other hand, these core values are identified with religious symbols, and essentially owned by each of these religions. From this perspective, there do seem to be many differences between Islam and Christianity; yet, when these symbols are removed, core values and principles emerge, and it becomes clear that what is shared by both faiths is greater than that on which they differ. In other words, reason and the information retrieved from religious sources cause us to meet at this point in our inquiry. Justice as a virtue is therefore highly meaningful to adherents of both Islam and Christianity.

---

19   Ibid, 511; see also Alasdair MacIntyre, A Short History of Ethics, translated into the Turkish by Solmaz Zelyüt Hünler, Istanbul, 2001, pp.133-134.

20   H.M. Vroom, No Other God, p.146.

In the current global order, two fundamental aims tend to drive international relationships: Peace and Justice. Furthermore, globalization has caused people from different cultures, religions and races to rub shoulders, often to live next to each other in a way that was impossible fifty years ago. This change, together with the pluralism it has engendered, must be properly directed. It must lead to mutual understanding and tolerance, as opposed to religious or cultural antagonism and regional hatreds. Shared moral standards and value criteria, those upon which everybody agrees, are therefore needed all the more urgently at this point. As has been argued in this essay, these do in fact exist in both religions, even if they seem to be concealed behind religious symbolism. Succinctly stated, my claim here is that the principles that the global order needs to ensure human flourishing can be found in the core values of both religions: Our own traditions hold moral riches that are all too often ignored; we needn't search in exotic or foreign places for them. These principles are respected and obeyed by believers of each faith. Non-believers respect and obey them as well, since their powers of reason lead them to acknowledge that they are universal.

Global peace may depend on the fact that, as a race, we can agree on justice as a primary core value. People everywhere complain about injustice and seek justice, yet, oftentimes, no one is willing to give up his or her interests. Individuals often defend what they take to be their rights, all the while ignoring the rights of others. In short, selfishness itself causes injustice. Where justice is upheld, order, peace, and harmony obtain. Perhaps this is because justice both presumes other virtues such as wisdom, courage, temperance, patience, equality, moderation, love, peace, tolerance, and friendship, and also subsumes them under it. Where justice reigns, human beings are respected and treated fairly; tyranny and unfairness vanish. Peace, order and harmony rule: *"Therefore, Justice is the key to the peace that will last forever, and justice and peace can not be set apart"*[21] Justice is a virtue that has personal and social dimensions. If we can acknowledge the core values of the world religions, we may be able to solve many of the current global problems, ensure security and welfare, use science and technology ethically, i.e. for the purpose of human spiritual and moral advancement, and sustain individual personal and social happiness. Finally, this mode of

---

21   Macid Hadduri, *The Islamic Conception of Justice*, p. 220.

living also has the power to lead us to eternal happiness: Justice is the alpha and the omega of moral living.

REFERENCES

Aquinas, St. Thomas, 1948. *Introduction to Saint Thomas Aquinas*, edited with an Introduction by Anton C. Pegis, The Modern Library, New York.

———.1989. *Summa Theologiae, A Concise Translation*, Ed. Timothy Mc-Dermott, London.

———. 1942. *The Summa Theologica of St. Thomas Aquinas*, Trans. by Fathers of The English Dominican Province, part II (First Part), 7, Second Number, (QQ. XLIX-LXXXIX) Burns Oates & Washbourne Ltd. London.

———. 1942. *The Summa Theologiae of St. Thomas Aquinas*, part II, (Second Part) 10, Second Number (QQ. XLVII-LXXIX) Burns Oates & Washbourne Ltd. London.

———. 1984. *Treatise on the Virtues*, translated by John A. Oesterle, University of Notre Dame Press, Notre Dame, Indiana.

Bukhari, *Sahih, Volume 8, Book 81, Number 779.*

Çağrıcı, Mustafa, *İslam Düşüncesinde Ahlâk*, (Ethics in Islamic Thought) Istanbul, 2000. (in Turkish)

Donaldson, Dwight M., 1953. *Studies in Muslim Ethics*, S.P.C:K., London.

Goodman, Lenn E., 1999. *Jewish and Islamic Philosophy*, Edinburgh University Press, Edinburgh/Great Britain.

Hadduri, Macid, 1991. *The Islamic Conception of Justice*, Translated into the Turkish by Selahaddin Ayaz, Istanbul.

Ibn Miskawayh, 1968. *Tahdhib al-akhlaq*, Engl. Trans. by C.K. Zurayk, *The Refinement of Character*, Beirut.

MacIntyre, Alasdair, 2001. *A Short History of Ethics*, translated into the Turkish by Solmaz Zelyüt Hünler, Paradigma Publ., Istanbul.

Thomas, George F., 1955. *Christian Ethics and Moral Philosophy*, Charles Scribner's Sons, New York.

Vroom, H. M., 1996. *No Other God*, translated by Lucy Jansen, William B. Eerdmans Publ. Co., Grand Rapids, MI; Cambridge, U.K.

PERSONAL REFLECTION BY AYSE SIDIKA OKTAY

I graduated from Faculty of Theology with a Ph.D. in Islamic Philosophy. Both my undergraduate studies and my Ph.D. program made me think about religions in general and the relationships among them. For a long time, I lived in Istanbul. Muslims, Christians and Jews have been living there together happily and peacefully for centuries. It is a city where mosques, churches and synagogues stand side-by-side. People who engage in religious exercises in their respective places of worship come together in nearby cafes, talk and have tea and coffee.

Everybody respects each other's beliefs and practices, and nobody in-
terferes with anyone's religious life. People of different religions share
both grief and joy at funerals and wedding ceremonies. This situation
astounds nobody who lives in Turkey, in particular in Istanbul.

Nevertheless, I have felt the urge to do something to change the Is-
lamophobia that has been on the rise in the world since 9/11. Furthermore, I was surprised and even bewildered to learn of some people's
impressions of Turkey, Istanbul and Islam—people whom I encountered at the World Congress of Philosophy in Istanbul. They hesitated
to come there for fear of intolerance and violence. Their remarks provoked me to study in greater depth in order to be able to change their
opinions. I shifted part of my academic focus to the issues of global
ethics and the relation between ethics and justice. To this end, I attended the Parliament of The World's Religions in Barcelona (2004).
I was delighted to have the opportunity to encounter people from different religions such as Buddhism and Sikhism, all the more so since
these are not widespread in Turkey.

Since then I have come to understand ever more clearly that peace
and justice lie at the heart of all of the world's religions. It is just that
people from different religions develop negative views of others when
they do not have adequate information about them. Various political and economic tensions tend to fuel these negative responses still
further.

I am, however, of the conviction that peace and justice can flourish in the world when they are established across religions. To achieve
this, we need more joint efforts. All religions have common core values
and moral principles and the more we can familiarize ourselves with
each other's beliefs, the more we can develop mutual love, respect and
understanding. Focusing on these points of connection rather than on
differences can indeed make the world can be a better place.

PERSONAL REFLECTION BY AYSE HÜMEYRA ASLANTÜRK[22]

My deep and ever-increasing interest in peaceful co-existence has been shaped by a number of factors. First and foremost, I would note that, throughout its history, Turkey has been home to a variety of ethnic groups which have lived together peacefully. Second, few countries have suffered from terrorism as much as mine has: thousands of young lives have been sacrificed. Moreover, even a glimpse at today's world is enough to cause one to become interested in peace and justice issues.

The study of Islam and Islamic theology in general crystallized my thinking about the need to promote peace and tolerance. I hope I manage to realize this goal by appealing to my students' minds and hearts while interpreting the holy book of Islam with them. I am strongly convinced that the best way to promote these noble feelings is through dialogue and education: Peace starts at home and then spreads abroad. And, peace, justice and forgiveness should be the commitment of any individual irrespective of his or her occupation.

With regard to Islam and the work of peacemaking, some challenges do arise. People misinterpret our religion and commit crimes which harm its image. However, the Holy Koran teaches us unconditionally to "Love man for God's sake."

The Manresa Conference made a considerable contribution to this. We need such forums more often in order to resolve conflicts and foster peace. For me, it is as if the conference were taking place today. I still remember the warmth, passion and intelligence which marked the sessions. This was a moment when all of our differences were put aside and the spirit of cooperation, sharing and caring prevailed.

---

22   Manresa Conference attendee and professor of theology at Suleyman Demerel University in Isparta, Turkey. Dr. Aslantürk is a colleague of Dr. Oktay.

6. HINDUISM: SOURCE OF CONFLICT, RESOURCE FOR PEACE

BRIAN BLOCH

INTRODUCTION

In this paper I will first discuss the problem of defining Hinduism and determining who speaks on its behalf. I will then explain two ways in which Hindu thought is a cause for concern about this religion's approach to peacebuilding: The theme of war as found in the *Bhagavad-Gita* (and the *Mahabarata*, of which the *Gita* is a part), and the caste system and the role of the *ksatriya*, or ruling/ warrior class in that system. At each juncture, I will present an alternative view by asking how these aspects of Hinduism and Hindu culture can serve as a resource for peace. I conclude with some thoughts on Hinduism's subjective and individualistic approach to morality.

Putting to the page one's thoughts on the question of whether Hinduism is a source of conflict or a resource for peace is no easy task. What is Hinduism? Who speaks on its behalf? In *Ahimsa and the Bhagavad-Gita: A Gandhian Perspective*, N. Sutton writes, "Hinduism [is] a religion that is quite different from the other major religious traditions in that it has no founder, no canonical scriptures and no central authority structure. It is in reality a grouping of overlapping yet autonomous traditions that frequently propound alternative and even contradictory doctrines." (2002, p. 83) Even the word *Hindu* has little to do with the tradition it describes: "In historical terms, Hinduism is a relatively new phrase. To begin with, the word Hindu had a territorial rather than a religious connotation. It implied the Indian subcontinent. Before the start of the common era, Persians and Greeks ran into the great river Sindhu... and called the people associated with the river, Sindhus or Hindus." (Gandhi, 2004, p. 45) It is unlikely that, prior to the nineteenth century, "Hindus" considered themselves part of a particular religion; rather, they saw themselves as followers of a particular sect or guru. (Gandhi, 2004, p. 45) If asked, they would likely have identified themselves as followers of *sanatana-dharma*, eternal religion.

There is a tremendous variety of beliefs and customs found in what we call Hinduism. This is evident from not only the diversity of organizations that call themselves Hindu, but also in the most basic points of theology. Some Hindus consider the pantheon of popular gods (Ganesh, Shiva, Surya, Krishna or Vishnu and Durga) to be equally supreme, while others are strictly monotheistic—generally worshippers of Vishnu/ Krishna or Shiva. Some consider the path to spiritual perfection to be the renunciation of the desire to enjoy this world while acting dutifully in one's occupation; others hold that perfection is found by retreating from society and entering a meditative trance while contemplating the void. Some believe that such a spiritual goal is attained by practicing yoga, while still others practice devotion to a supreme being. Hindus do not even agree on the overall goal of religion. Some consider the supreme to be an ultimate but impersonal energy, and others think in terms of a supreme person. And, as is the case in many faiths, inevitably there are differences even within relatively narrow traditions. The large Swami Narayana community, for example, is subdivided into two distinct groups.

Conflicts even arise over who is really Hindu since some groups claim greater authenticity than others. But there are a few basic commonalities among all the beliefs and practices and these can help to define Hinduism at least partially: all Hindus accept the Vedas as authoritative. (Hopkins, 2000, p. 62) Most of them respect the *Bhagavad-Gita*, the *Mahabharata* and *Ramayana*, accept the tenets of karma, reincarnation, and the claim that the temporary body and eternal soul are different from one another. Most Hindus consider it religious practice to visit holy places, respect saints, give alms, and glorify the Deity, however they conceive of it, through prayer, devotional songs, or mantras.

Given this background on the word *Hindu* and its broad religious connotations, we can now turn to the question of peacebuilding in Hinduism.

THE SCRIPTURE—SOURCE OF CONFLICT

The epic *Mahabharata* includes one of the most sacred Hindu texts, the *Bhagavad-Gita*, which depicts a discussion that takes place on a battlefield at Kuruksetra. An impending war is the background of this most revered spiritual text. What does this indicate about the Hindu approach to peace? Scholars like Rajmohan Gandhi believe that it says a lot. In his view, there is no way to avoid the fact that Krishna, who is considered the Supreme Lord by many Hindus, and certainly by Arjuna in the *Bhagavad-Gita*, is telling his devotee, Arjuna, to fight in the upcoming battle. Gandhi explains at length that Krishna not only inspired Arjuna to fight, but also spurred him on by appealing to his sense of revenge and retribution. Later, during the battle, he even encouraged him to break the laws of chivalry to achieve his military goals. Furthermore, there are instances throughout the *Mahabharata*, and not just during the battle itself, in which violence is used to settle old scores.

The *Bhagavad-Gita's* narrative takes place just prior to the beginning of the battle of Kuruksetra. The armies are in position, yet the *Gita* begins with Arjuna telling Krishna that he will not fight. He offers Krishna five thoughtful reasons why he should not engage in warfare. They are based on compassion for those who might die, fear of war's social consequences, fear of sin, doubts about the righteousness of this course of action, and the perhaps less noble concern that there would be no one left with whom to share the spoils of war.

Krishna's answer: You should fight. One by one, Krishna counters Arjuna's reasons, often with the philosophy that now comprises the main body of the *Gita's* teachings. For example, Krishna tells Arjuna that one should perform one's duty under all circumstances—and, at the same time, remain unattached to the outcome of one's actions. Krishna dispenses with Arjuna's appeal to compassion by claiming that one should feel compassion for the soul, not the temporary, destructible body. He also says that one should not be falsely compassionate when dealing with wrongdoers who disrupt innocent people's lives by their behavior. (Prabhupada, 1972, pp. 56-92). He counters the fear of social breakdown by pointing out that *real* breakdown comes when leaders like Arjuna neglect their duty and act whimsically; Arjuna is, after all, a warrior-king. It is his responsibility to protect his citizens from unrighteous leadership. Moreover, his cousin Duryodhana's seizing of the throne is unrighteous. When leaders neglect their duties, others will follow and neglect theirs, and society will become corrupt. As for Arjuna's fear of sin, Krishna defines sin as neglect of duty. He counters Arjuna's indecision by telling him that He, Krishna, is God; Arjuna should surrender to His will without hesitation. Finally, He

responds to Arjuna's less noble concerns for his own peace of mind
and his desire to have someone left with whom to share the battle's
spoils by saying that one must practice tolerance and equanimity regardless of the difficulties one confronts in life. How does one do that?
Arjuna should make the performance of duty superior to any personal
concerns for happiness.

While I can imagine that Krishna's instructions would not convince
many people today of the need for war, the ultimate reason he gives
Arjuna to fight may scare many modern readers: He should fight simply because Krishna, God, tells him to. God wants the war to take
place. For the contemporary reader, this raises the specter of God-con-
doned violence throughout history: the Inquisition, the Crusades, in-
discriminate Jihad, Hindutva-inspired attacks in India, and numerous
reprehensible conflicts through which people have suffered because
someone thought God was on their side. Yet, there can be no doubt
about the message of the *Bhagavad-Gita*: Krishna wanted Arjuna to
fight as an act of surrender to the Supreme will.

Fighting and war are central themes of the *Mahabharata*. In its over-
whelmingly popular pages, this epic contains a vast variety of intrigue,
political maneuvering, bloodshed, heroism, cheating, enmity and curs-
ing and counter-cursing. A superficial reading of the work rarely leads
to discussion on peace or nonviolence. Instead, the reader wants to
know who will win the trial of arms.

Some scholars say that the fighting spirit exhibited by the characters
in the *Mahabharata* has deeply permeated the Indian psyche. Rajago-
palalachari remarks that it "discloses a ... civilization and a ... society
which, though of an older world, strangely resembles the India of our
own times, with the same values and ideals." (Gandhi, 1999, p. 30) In
response to this, Rajmohan Gandhi says, "Every bloody event, war, act
of revenge or victory by treachery witnessed on Indian soil subsequent
to the epic seems to bear some resemblance to a scene from it [the
Mahabharata]." (1999, p. 30) In India's other famous epic, the *Ramayana*, the righteous side performs less questionable deeds, but it is also
bellicose in nature.

It is therefore not difficult to see why many people believe that the
Hindu scriptures encourage violence, vengeance, and war.

THE SCRIPTURE: RESOURCE FOR PEACE

An underlying theme in the *Gita* is that, in all circumstances, one should do one's duty. These days, few Hindus know much Sanskrit, and few can quote the actual slokas (verses) in the *Bhagavad-Gita*, yet many know this one line: *karmany evadhikaras te* - "everyone has the right to perform their prescribed duty." In the case of the Battle of Kuruksetra, Krishna was speaking to a warrior; it is natural that He would ask him to fight. In *Windows into the Infinite: A Guide to the Hindu Scriptures*, B. Powell writes:

> Arjuna is a *ksatriya*, a soldier by profession, and it is his moral and spiritual imperative to attend to the duties, the *dharma*, of that profession. Were Arjuna a priest, a spice merchant, or a housewife, Krishna would have given him very different advice, for violence is never acceptable for these people. But the question of war and peace is not the issue at all .... If Krishna were talking to an exhausted mother with five screaming children all needing her attention at once, she might tell Him, "Krishna, I can't face it. There's no way I can be a mom today." His reply would be, "Yes, you can. In fact, you must. It's your duty. Get in there and fight." (2002, p. 18)

It is possible, therefore, to view Krishna's encouragement to fight as simply circumstantial. Rather than violence and war being the theme in the *Gita*, they can be understood to be the plot against which various other themes play out.

In support of this reading, I note that, while encouraging Arjuna to fight, Krishna mentions *santim* (peace) nine times in seven hundred verses. He uses *ahimsa*, nonviolence, four times. Sastri explains that *ahimsa* is not only the "negation of violence" but "the giving up of concepts of 'otherness,' 'separateness,' and 'self-centeredness,' and identifying oneself with other beings. [It] is a positive doctrine of love, friendship and equality among all living beings of the Universe."(1998, pp. 67-68). Given all of these references to peace, nonviolence and love, one is compelled to ask why Krishna is trying to inspire a war at all.

In an attempt to answer this, I will return to the *Mahabharata* and the details of the events leading to the battle. When the righteous Pandavas were returning from their exile, they asked that their kingdom be restored to them. The evil Duryodhana refused. The Pandavas took his refusal in stride. They then told Duryodhana that he should at least grant each of them a village to oversee, since they were *ksatriyas* and it was their duty to rule. What else would they do? This was their

sole occupation, by both birth and training. But Duryodhana again refused, this time saying that he would not give them even that amount
of land through which they could drive a pin. Krishna then stepped
forward to mediate. Krishna went to Duryodhana and his father and
asked them to resolve this dispute peacefully. Not only did the two refuse Krishna's overtures, but Duryodhana tried to imprison Krishna,
the messenger of peace. Thus it was only after a number of unsuccess-
ful attempts to make peace that the battle became inevitable.

That it seemed inevitable is in keeping with the standard four-step
method *ksatriyas* were trained to use in resolving conflict. Violence or
war, the last step, was considered only acceptable after the first three,
all aimed at creating peace without bloodshed, had proved unsuccess-
ful.

> In the Indic tradition, the just war doctrine is [called] the Catur-
> opayas, "the four means," which include three methods of diplo-
> macy that attempt to avoid war (the fourth and final alternative).
> If one observes the first three of these tactics and cannot find a
> peaceful solution, then war becomes inevitable and may be deemed
> righteous (*dharmaruddha*). These "four means" are: *sama* (pacifica-
> tion, or praising your opponents with pleasing words); *dana* (the
> giving of a gift, such as land, in the spirit of reconciliation); *bheda*
> (a thought-provoking threat leading to a peaceful alternative); and
> *danda* (punishment, or war, which is only engaged in if the prior
> three attempts have failed.) (Rosen, 2002, p. 24)

THE PEACE FORMULA

The *Bhagavad-Gita's* last verse in Chapter Five is often referred to as
the "peace formula":

> A person in full consciousness of Me, knowing Me to be the ulti-
> mate beneficiary of all sacrifices and austerities, the Supreme Lord
> of all planets and demigods, and the benefactor and well-wisher of
> all living entities, attains peace from the pangs of material miseries.
> (Prabhupada, 1972, p. 305)

Here, Krishna is explaining that the path to peace is God-centered.
When we acknowledge that our activities are meant for God's pleasure, that all our possessions ultimately belong to God, and that God
is everyone's closest friend, we attain peace. A closer look at this verse
reveals that, in His statements, Krishna covers the key causes of war
and conflict: the pursuit of self-centered enjoyment, the desire to pos-

sess or conquer, and the inability to see universal brotherhood (based on the understanding that we have a common Father who is a friend to all). Although only theists will accept the third cause of peace, it would be hard to deny that the other two are integral components of most conflicts. In fact, in the context of his comments on religion as the cause of conflict, Stephen L. Carter writes:

> Wars are fought by countries, for causes in which the leaders believe. Critics of religious participation in politics are fond of arguing that religion has been the cause of many wars in the past. Partly true —but only partly. The religious wars, almost always, were fought by princes and their armies for some tangible benefit, such as territory or trade routes. Religion was often a convenient excuse, but it was rarely the underlying purpose. (2000, p. 125).

If readers of the *Gita* can free themselves from selfishness by acting only for God's pleasure, and can see everything in this world as God's property, and if they can understand that God is their most intimate friend, then they will be at peace both with themselves and others. Krishna supplements His peace formula with the earlier teaching in the *Gita* that we are souls temporarily occupying bodies destined to die. It is an illusion, He states, to identify only with the body's particulars while neglecting the soul within. This illusory identity is the primary key that locks us out of the world of peace, both subjectively and objectively. By thinking of ourselves as bodies, we neglect the components on which the "peace formula" is based. We focus on our enjoyment and exploit the world around us for our personal satisfaction, often at the expense of others' needs. We think ourselves members of a particular family, gender, community, religion, and country, even though each of these forms of belonging lasts only one lifetime. Such a physicalist outlook on life, which Krishna seeks to correct in the *Gita's* second chapter, is the source of behavior that leads to conflict and away from peace and brotherhood. Krishna may want Arjuna to fight (and we have already shown that fighting was a last resort), but not because of earthly emotions such as revenge, hatred, and the desire to possess and enjoy.

THE THREE MODES OF NATURE

Later in the *Gita*, Krishna offers Arjuna an analysis of this world which aims at helping him achieve peace. He describes the three *gunas* or modes of nature. A person influenced by the mode of goodness (*sattva-guna*) is characterized by self-satisfaction, kindness, cleanliness, respect, clear thinking, and a worldview that tends to see oneness or commonalities in the world's differences. A person in the mode of passion (*raja-guna*) feels intense longings, works industriously, tends to think selfishly, craves upward mobility, and is proud and lusty. Passionate people tend to see more dualities than commonalities. Those in the mode of ignorance (*tama-guna*) tend to be indifferent by nature. They may sleep more than necessary, procrastinate, be prone to self-pity and addictions, be frustrated, thoughtless, and angry, and they have the tendency to see little beyond their own existence. (1972, pp. 687-97) Krishna encourages Arjuna to adopt the mode of goodness as that is the path toward peace and clear decision-making.

So, why, after all these instructions about peace, is Arjuna still asked to fight? Krishna says, "Do it because I am asking you to fight, and do it with devotion. Fighting is your duty, and this is a righteous war, since we have exhausted all peaceful alternatives. Know, too, that each of the warriors on the battlefield is a soul. Each one who dies in My presence will reach heaven." The *Bhagavad-Gita* tells us that with a peaceful mind and free from selfish desire, Arjuna took up his weapons and faced the opposing army.

COMMENTATORS ON THE GITA

The fact that the *Gita* can be seen both as a source of violence and a resource for peace is epitomized in the interpretations of Sri Aurobindo[1] and Mahatma Gandhi. While Aurobindo does not see the *Gita* as condoning war, he does understand it as a call to action, which can, at times, include the use of force to establish proper order (including expulsion of the British from India). He writes:

> If one is among the ... seekers of [the] Truth, one has to take sides for the Truth to stand against the forces that attack it and seek to stifle it. Arjuna wanted not to stand for either side, to refuse an action of hostility...; Krishna, who insisted so much on *samata* (equality, equanimity) strongly rebuked his attitude and insisted equally on his fighting the adversary. It is a spiritual battle inward and outward; by neutrality and compromise or even passivity one

---

1 Sri Aurobindo was an Indian Nationalist-turned–spiritual leader whose writings on passive resistance may have inspired Mahatma Gandhi. He later parted ways with Gandhi over the issue of nonviolence.

may allow this enemy force to pass and crush down the Truth and its children." (Danino, 2002, p. 57)

Aurobindo also comments on Gandhi's nonviolent (*ahimsa*) movement in light of what he considered to be the *Gita's* central teachings. He here includes a clarification of his role in the *ahimsa* movement (he is often portrayed as its forerunner and as Gandhi's inspiration):

> In some quarters there is the idea that [my] political standpoint was entirely pacifist.... It is even suggested that [I] was a forerunner of the gospel of Ahimsa. This is quite incorrect. [I am] neither an impotent moralist nor a weak pacifist. The rule of confining political action to passive resistance was adopted as the best policy for the National Movement at that stage and not as a part of a gospel of Nonviolence or pacifist idealism. (Danino, 2002, p. 51)

Gandhi had a different outlook. While he admits making different comments on the *Gita* at different stages of his life (Clough, 2002, p. 72), he consistently saw it as a text that emphasizes nonviolence: "That the overall teaching of the *Gita* is not violence but nonviolence is amply demonstrated from the argument which begins in the second chapter and is summarized in the concluding eighteenth chapter. Violence is not possible unless one is driven by anger, by ignorant passion and by hatred. The *Gita* wants us to be incapable of anger and strives to carry us to a state beyond ... a state that excludes feelings of anger, hatred, etc."(Clough, 2002, p. 76) Gandhi considered the events leading up to the Battle of Kuruksetra and Krishna's encouragement to fight as part of a great allegory: "I regard Duryodhana and his party as the baser impulses in many, and Arjuna and his party as the higher impulse. The field of battle is our own body. An eternal battle is going on between the two camps and the poet seer has vividly described it. Krishna is the Dweller within, ever whispering in a pure heart." (Clough, 2002, p. 73).

He further comments on the indirect message that all readers of the *Mahabharata* should understand: "The author of the *Mahabharata*, of which the *Gita* is a part ... has shown to the world the futility of war by giving the victors an empty glory, leaving but seven victors alive out of millions said to be engaged in the fight in which unnamable atrocities were used on either side. (Clough, 2002, p. 74)

THE CASTE SYSTEM: A SOURCE OF CONFLICT

The Hindu caste system is infamous. In its traditional form, it strati-
fied society into four main groups, *brahmanas* or intellectuals, *ksatriyas* or administrators/ military, *vaisyas*- businessmen / agricultural-
ists, and *sudras* or laborers. As time passed, these major divisions were
further divided into thousands of substrata called *jats*, and grew to
include the untouchables (*dalits*), or those considered outside the caste
system because they do unclean work (sewage disposal, leatherwork,
etc.). There are about 160,000,000 *dalits* in India today.[2]

Officially, the caste system has now been outlawed in India, but this
is not obvious to one living there. Caste distinctions are quite prevalent
in rural areas where marriages, job opportunities, social status, and the
ability to participate in religious functions are all affected. Certainly
such divisions, and the feelings they engender, provide fertile ground
for conflict, even violence. It is common for the higher castes to make
sure the lower ones acknowledge their inferiority by inflicting financial
and even physical harm on anyone who attempts to change their station.

In response to this, the Indian government has introduced a number
of measures similar to the U.S.'s affirmative action program. These ensure that "scheduled castes"[3] have places saved for them in Parliament,
education, and the job market. Though it is often praised as helpful,
especially by Westerners, this system also leads to conflict: The higher
castes resent the program and the lower castes fight one another for
the few available opportunities.

Within the caste system, the *ksatriya* class is the one which raises
concerns about Hinduism and peacebuilding. *Ksatriyas* are warriors,
kings, and high-level government administrators. Ancient texts describe their military education, which included training in weaponry
and military strategy. A section of the *Vedas*, the *Dhanurveda*, served
as a training manual for *ksatriyas* and is dedicated to the making and
use of weapons for battle.

Ksatriyas were an integral part of Indian traditional culture and are
the most prominent figures in the *Mahabharata* and *Ramayana*. They

---

2   According to the Dalit human rights website: http://www.dalits.org/
    globalcastesystems.htm
3   A term used to describe the group of "lower caste" members of Indian
    society.

are often portrayed as proud, vengeful and hot-tempered, and Hindu society has idolized them for ages. Their prevalence in Hindu scripture and culture led some to the conclusion that Hindus considered armed conflict an inevitable reality, something for which they should be prepared.

THE CASTE SYSTEM: A RESOURCE FOR PEACE

How can the caste system be a source of peace? It is important to look at the concept of the caste system as it is presented in the *Bhagavad-Gita*. In Chapter Four, verse 13, Krishna states that one's position in the *varnas* or castes is determined by *guna* and karma, nature and the work to which one is naturally attracted. *Jamna*, or birth is clearly not a criterion. By this analysis, the present system, with its concentration on birth, is a distinct departure from the *Gita's* idea. If instead the social system concentrated on an individual's real *sva-dharma*, or inclination or interest, then the *varnasrama* (caste) system would become more like a giant guidance counselor system than a system of oppression maintained by the higher castes to subjugate the lower ones.

Even if one accepts that the *Gita's* system reveals the original intention of the caste system, the question still arises: Why is such a system needed? Interestingly, the answer to this is that it necessarily increases social cooperation and decreases conflict. The *varnasrama* system, as described by Krishna, tries to acknowledge and deal with two natural forces in society, stratification and differentiation, two classical sociological principles. These principles acknowledge that "power differentials are inevitable" and that "my role is different than your role." (Brubaker, 2005) *Varnasrama* works to create a cooperative society wherein the various occupational designations bring out the best in people and allow them to work hand in hand with others who have different types of expertise. The *brahmana* is meant to live simply, study, practice religious principles, and offer advice freely to all who need or want it, especially to the *ksatriyas* or social leaders. The *ksatriyas* may be passionate, but they are trained to follow the *brahmanas'* guidance because the latter are situated in the mode of goodness and are therefore more clear-thinking. In this way, the passion of the warrior class was both contained and guided toward piety. *Ksatriyas* were trained to have the utmost respect for *brahmanas; conversely, brahmanas* were trained to value simplicity and material detachment and not to become overly dependent on the wealth of the *ksatriyas. Brahmanas* who were successful in the culture of their own values were thus able to give honest and non-prejudicial advice to the society's leaders and anyone else who approached them. Brahminical values include *sama,* peacefulness, and *ksanti,* tolerance; *brahmanas* naturally encouraged *ksatriyas* to make peaceful settlements of dispute in all but the most extreme situations.

Still, the presence of *ksatriyas* in society allowed for peace among the other castes. *Ksatriyas* kept the peace, generally ruled in peacetime, and were the only members of society who fought in wars. The *ksatriyas* spared the other castes from having to deal with violence either to themselves or their social structure. In return, they were supported by taxes paid only by the business and farming class. (*vaisyas*)

The *varnasrama* system was based on the idea that all members in society should aim at spiritual emancipation. Instead of working for upward social mobility, they were to remain dutiful and satisfied with their current occupations, and to use their life's energy for spiritual growth.

CONCLUDING REMARKS

As Rajmohan Gandhi writes, "Anything said about India is true, and so is its opposite." (1999, p. *ix*) This is the case for India as well for its main religious tradition, Hinduism. If someone asked me if Hinduism encourages or discourages peace, I would have to say that it does both. Indeed from *Mahabhrata* times until today, one would be hard-pressed to say conclusively where Hinduism lies on the subject.

In this paper, I have presented both sides of this question by briefly examining the scriptures and the Hindu caste system. After preparing this paper, however, it seems to me that the type of analysis I have offered here, one that looks at Hindu thought as both a source of violence and a resource for peace, is helpful but still not complete. Something additional needs to be said to give a more balanced understanding of this topic

Studying attitudes toward violence and peacebuilding is one of the many ways we can gain insight into the moral structure of society. By analyzing moral codes we can focus on objective, interpersonal, and subjective applications of morality. Objective and interpersonal valuations are easily observed and defined. They are evident in all the duty-based behaviors and virtues that engender social cooperation and peace within the family and in the society as a whole. In a religious society like that of Hinduism, objective moral codes are defined in scripture; interpersonal moral codes arise out of the day-to-day dealings between members of society and, over generations, they are often encoded into law. Using these valuations to assess a society's standard of morality is useful, but it does not necessarily get at the heart of a culture. For that we need also to consider subjective morality.

The Hindu scriptures are full of examples of applications of all three levels and types of moral principle. Where greater weight is given to subjective moral principles, it is assumed that the persons described have fully assimilated such a principle into their psyche. As previously mentioned, Hinduism is not easily defined, and although it has created perhaps more scripture than any other religious culture, the religion itself has never been institutionalized. There is therefore no Hindu equivalent of canon law. Traditionally, Hindus were expected to read scripture under a teacher's guidance, and then to resonate with what they had understood as its essence. Ultimately, according to the *Gita* the student of the *Vedas*[4] was meant to understand that everything was to be offered to the Supreme in devotion, including all of one's possessions and, especially, all of one's actions. The *Bhagavad-Gita* denigrates those who do not come to this realization but rather insist on thinking of religious life as simply a means to greater comfort, wealth and mundane happiness. (Prabhupada, 1972, p. 129-130) When it is lived out on this deeper and more spiritually-oriented level, morality is a matter of the individual's subjective understanding of where to search for God and how to make their actions pleasing to Him. Hence there is no uniform moral code. While the *Vedas* are full of moral formulas and religious rituals intended to guide spiritual seekers, those who wished to get at the actual purpose of the *Vedas* had to do something more than formulaically follow its dicta. They had to move beyond a simplistic and objective understanding of morality and participate personally and fully in their own spiritual lives. The *Mahabharata* provides a number of examples of individuals who were in pursuit of spiritual understanding and therefore lived out their moral lives at this level. Bhismadeva, for example, regarded filial service as part of his spiritual surrender. He took vows to renounce his kingdom (his birth-

---

4 By using the word *Vedas* here, I distinguish these four original Hindu texts from the *Bhagavad-Gita*. The former emphasize reliance on moral formulas and ritual for the purpose of achieving worldly satisfaction; the latter encourages the reader to transcend such considerations.

right) and to practice lifelong celibacy, so that his father could marry a woman to whom he had become attracted. Later, the kingdom was threatened by the fact that it lacked an heir. There was fear of ensuing social chaos. Bhismadeva, however, refused to recant his vows. Was he irresponsible?

Gandhari, who identified deeply with the religious concept of a wife's chastity, voluntarily blinded herself when she was told she would be married to the blind Dhrtarastra. There was no social obligation for her to do this, yet, she chose to live with this blindness as a yogi practices meditation. Was there something not quite right in her thinking?

And, Arjuna, who considered surrender to the will of the Supreme to be higher than any other moral or religious principle, fought the battle of Kuruksetra despite his misgivings, all of which were based on objective and interpersonal levels of morality.

Western culture and religion have a different orientation and, for the most part, tend to look down on subjectively-based morality. So it seems wise to be cautious when attempting to apply a Western moral compass, even on a broad-ranging subject like violence vs. peace building, to a culture that so much values the internal and subjective application of moral principles.

By way of conclusion, I would suggest that the characters in the *Mahabharata* and those who came after them were indeed morally literate. But to appreciate their stance on a moral issue like violence vs. peacebuilding, or even on the much denounced caste system, we need to look beyond objective and interpersonal valuations and reach into their subjective experience with its spiritual orientation.

Does Hinduism encourage or discourage violence? It does both, because while its scriptures provide Hindus with more prescriptions and aspired-for-virtues, they also strongly encourage, and even expect, that, in the search for truth as it is undertaken by each spiritual aspirant, each will adopt and apply those virtues in a very personal, and therefore, subjective way and this leaves a great deal of room for individual opinion and choice.

REFERENCES

Brubaker, D., 2005. Theoretical Overview, PAX 564: *Creating and Leading Healthy Organizations.*

Carter, S.L., 2000. *God's Name in Vain: The Wrongs and Rights of Religion and Politics.* New York. Basic Books.

Clough, B.S., 2002. "Gandhi, Nonviolence and the Bhagavad-Gita," in *Holy War: Violence and the Bhagavad-Gita*. Hampton. Deepak Heritage Books.

Danino, M., 2002. "Sri Aurobindo and the Gita," in *Holy War: Violence and the Bhagavad-Gita*. New Delhi: VIHE Publications.

Dasa, B., 1998. *Surrender Unto Me: An Overview of the Bhagavad-Gita*, New Delhi: VIHE Publications.

Gandhi, R., 1999. *Revenge & Reconciliation: Understanding South Asian History*, New Delhi: Penguin Books.

Powell, B., 1996. *Windows Into the Infinite: A Guide to the Hindu Scriptures*, Fremont: Asian Humanities Press.

Prabhupada, A.C.B., 1972. *Bhagavad-Gita As It Is* Mumbai: Bhaktivedanta Book Trust

Rosen, S.J., 2002. "Kurukshetra in Context: An Analysis of Violence in the Bhagavad-Gita," in *Holy War: Violence and the Bhagavad-Gita*. Hampton, Deepak Heritage Books.

Sastri, S.Y. and Y.S., 1998. Ahimsa and the Unity of All Things: A Hindu View of Nonviolence, *Subverting Hatred: The Challenge of Nonviolence in Religious Traditions*. Maryknoll, Orbis Books.

Sutton, N., 2002. "Ahimsa and the Bhagavad-Gita: A Gandhian Perspective," in *Holy War: Violence and the Bhagavad-Gita*. Hampton, Deepak Heritage Books.

PERSONAL REFLECTION BY BRIAN BLOCH

As I became an elder in my religious organization (the International Society for Krishna Consciousness), I witnessed the intensity of internal conflict and its effect on the group. This experience led me to study other traditions. I discovered that such conflict was not unique to my religious organization but rather pervades most of them. The very people who are often called on to bring peace to the greater society in fact lacked the ability to create it among themselves.

My work has come to be focused on helping religious communities to develop the skills, systems, and attitudes that make it possible to deal with internal conflict. I am attempting to take the work corporations have done in establishing Internal Conflict Management Systems (ICMS) and apply it in a religious context. My hope is that, as our religious communities endeavor to create peace among themselves, they will be better equipped to bring peace to the world.

7. THE NATURE OF THE ONGOING TERRORIST THREATS TO AMERICAN CITIES: SOME THOUGHTS ON THE PROBLEM OF ETHICAL LIVING POST 9/11

DEBORAH S. (NASH) PETERSON

INTRODUCTION

In the course of the years since the 9/11 incident, the problem of the threats to American cities seems to have redefined itself to such an extent that it is no longer possible to merely point a finger at a single external adversary. And, if we can no longer say that the enemy is exclusively without (i.e. geographically external to our shores), then we are forced by the disjunctive syllogism to raise the question of an enemy within. It may indeed be the case that the enemy is within in the physical and geographical sense—that the U.S. has been and continues to be infiltrated by Al-Quaeda operatives. There is also the possibility that the U.S. government itself may have been one of the contributing causes of the events of 9/11 and may be perpetuating the political and economic problems that have ensued. There is, however a third sense in which it might be said that the enemy is within, namely in the psyche of the individual citizen.

My purpose in this paper is to propose an alternative, albeit somewhat unconventional, strategy for thinking about the problem of peace making, one which centers on this latter sense of the enemy as within. I will attempt to make some observations on what I take to be the state of mind of the individual American citizen (and so by implication on our collective mindset at present) as these are evidenced in our actions in two arenas of our everyday life. These will be followed by some thoughts on how this state of mind may be contributing to overall world tensions. Concomitantly, I will argue that one path toward peace—one which seems to be often overlooked—begins with the meditative work that can be done by each of us. This may seem an oddly passive stance in the face of the recent, dramatic historical developments, but it should be understood that it does not by any means preclude social action. My aim here is a modest one. I wish only to underscore the point that, before we can begin the work of peace making on any large scale, we first need to render ourselves peaceable. As rational beings, we are at least able to question and understand the extent of our own involvement with the complex of problems that has developed—and so perhaps to exert an indirect influence on it. To my mind, the latter is a way of responding to the world situation which the morally responsible person cannot and should not ignore at this point in time.

THE PROBLEMS OF CONSUMERISM & TRUTH IN MEDIA

First, there is the all-pervasive phenomenon of commercialism and the question of our participation in the system of consumerism which we have created in the U.S.; secondly, there is the issue of truth in media and our vulnerability to the multiple levels of deception and disinformation that it propagates.

Generally speaking, Buddhist ethics, a source to which many Western thinkers would not necessarily turn to address these issues, places great emphasis on personal economy, simplicity of lifestyle, and what it terms 'mindfulness.' For this reason, and others detailed below, I take it to be an effective guide in analyzing our relation to both of these institutions. [1] As Rita M. Gross, co-editor of *Christians Talk about Buddhist Meditation, Buddhists Talk about Christian Prayer*, notes in the context of a series of comments on prayer in Buddhism, Buddhists are intensely concerned not with what in Western tradition would be identified as metaphysical questions, but rather with 'method,' with "what works to develop and transform people spiritually." [2] Such spiritual self-transformation is what I take to be fundamentally at issue when I state that the enemy may be 'within,' i.e. in the psyche of the individual citizen.

CONSUMERISM

The commercialism that we are surrounded by affects so many areas of our lives that we cannot even begin to account for them. With some exceptions, a tremendous number of the items we regularly purchase are linked to oil either directly (gas, heating oil, etc.) or indirectly, (groceries which are ferried halfway across the continent in order to make them available in chain stores). Even a quick glance around a shopping mall makes it evident that we also consume unlimited amounts of oil by-products in various forms (plastic shopping bags, plastic water bottles, picnic utensils, plates cups, take-out containers, etc.) What one family alone uses and disposes of in a single week is staggering. Moreover, as of this writing, even the expanding interest in recycling seems not to be effectively offsetting our production of these almost obscene amounts of industrially generated waste.

TRUTH IN MEDIA

As concerns our relation to the media, even the briefest reflections on past news reportage, for example, coverage of the U.S. incursion into Iraq, makes it apparent that much of it was intended to move us to acquiesce to decisions taken by the U.S. government and, above all, to glamorize war. The headline, "Shock and Awe" used by CNN in conjunction with photographs of the U.S. bombing of Baghdad is one of the more glaring cases in point.

More insidious, however, is the level of fear inspired by both media reportage of these events and subsequent and ongoing government announcements concerning shifts in the terror threat levels and supposed impending actions. Aristotle understood well the fact that, of all the human emotions to which speakers and people in positions of authority may appeal, fear is the one which is most easily provoked and has the strongest hold on us. When it is used as a means of manipulating the populace, it is guaranteed to produce a reaction. Still, there are bound to be at least some individuals who question the motives of these organizations; through research and information analysis, they come to understand the cynical mindset behind such media reportage. The level of cynicism that underlies much of what we are still now receiving—even roughly seven years after 9/11—is, I would suggest, such that it engenders intellectual and moral confusion and spawns delusion on a myriad of levels. One obvious area is information incoming on the situation in Iraq. Few, if any, of us can claim to know the real facts about it at this point—and this after several years of U.S. military involvement there.

From the Buddhist perspective, the problems associated with our involvement with these institutions are all reducible to a matter of 'desire' or 'cravings'—not in the literal, physical sense of the term, but in the larger and more general one. Alone economic data of everyday life in the present day U.S., particularly in American urban centers,

point to the conclusion that we are indeed driven by such desires to
an obscene extent: Millions of us seem to have such a need to conform
to peer pressure when it comes to possessions and all forms of material gain that we readily do whatever is necessary to "keep up with the
Jones'", e.g. invest in the latest gas-guzzling SUV, shop the malls regularly and blindly purchase goods made in, for example, Central American or Asian sweatshops, then carry them home in endless numbers of
plastic bags, bottles, containers, etc. Perhaps the underlying issue here
is our own greed—accompanied by an intense self-absorption? Similarly, as concerns the influence exerted by the media, we desire to be
free from fear in our communities, so, in response to the information
we take in, we do things like engaging in exaggerated acts of patriotism
or tacitly agreeing to legislation that limits our basic freedoms and
intrudes on our privacy. We even go so far as to agree to send our sons
and daughters off to fight in a war when neither the motivation for it
nor its tactical objectives have ever been made clear. What is driving
such choices? Fear, perhaps?

In Buddhism, both fear and greed are taken to be 'afflictive emotions',
emotions which have the power to blind us when it comes to moral
choices and which, when given free play, can undermine our spiritual
equilibrium and cause us to engage in actions which have enormous
destructive consequences.

Buddhist ethics, together with the relatively rigorous meditative
practice(s) it entails [3] provides a unique set of tools for countering
the corrosive effects of (at least) the two 'afflictive emotions' identified
here. When the mind is stilled, it is less likely to drive us to indulge in
activities which are excessive or arbitrary. Instead, we discover that a
cup of tea and an hour to meditate can suffice to ensure happiness.

In what follows, I briefly outline the basic principles of Buddhist
thought, discuss some of the conclusions to which this system of principles points as concerns our involvement with the institutions of consumerism and the media, and then attempt to bring these principles to
bear on solving the problems I have identified here.

THE FOUR NOBLE TRUTHS

The philosophical framework within which one lives and develops
spiritually in Buddhism is that of the Four Noble Truths. As the Dalai
Lama notes, "in essence, the Four Noble Truths say that we naturally
desire happiness and do not wish to suffer—and that the suffering

that we wish to avoid comes about as a result of a chain of causes and conditions...." [4].

The first of these truths is the claim that *there is no permanence in things*, or *all things are transient*. The Dalai Lama terms this the "truth of suffering". How is it to be understood? As 'conditioned', our existence is characterized not only by a natural delight in sensory experience, but also by a lack of certitude, a natural tendency to bodily decay: illness, pain and death. This instability is also an observable feature of our minds. Buddhists refer to the principle of 'dependent origination', the idea that we are all simultaneously and mutually dependent on the nexus of other created and conditioned beings for our continuing existence, and that the cumulative effect of *karma* (which in the original Sanskrit means merely 'action') can entrap us in *samsara* (conditioned existence). The Buddhist scripture, the *Dharmapada*, speaks eloquently to this:

> The iron itself createth the rust
>
> Which slowly is bound to consume it.
>
> The evil-doer by his own deeds
>
> Is led to a life full of suffering. [5]

Reflection on this state of affairs, on our distractedness of mind and dependence on other created beings, leads to the second of the Noble Truths: *the suffering which we experience as beings who are mutually subject to these conditions of dependence is a consequence of our own ignorance and delusion*, and it is incumbent upon us to recognize this fact and proceed, through the lifelong work of meditation, to remove those delusions and blockages from our vision of reality so as to be able to see it for what it truly is. [6] That is, if we observe the actions of our minds in meditation, we recognize that any distraction, whether it be in the direction of pleasure or pain, is just that—distraction. Pleasures and pains are transitory in nature; but, meditation makes it possible for us to see that we can achieve a state of - indeed various levels of - liberation from them.[7]

This second tenet of Buddhism, namely that suffering is the consequence of our own ignorance and delusion, that we are by nature unsteady of mind, is one of the things that has motivated the development of this essay. It is a radically simple insight, yet profoundly penetrating as far as human nature is concerned—and, together with the first of the Noble Truths, constitutes a powerful starting point in the process of self-transformation.

As concerns our involvement (entanglement perhaps?) with the institutions of commercialism, we need, I believe, to ask ourselves exactly what the delusions are to which we as individuals are subject on an everyday basis. What do we consume? To what degree of excess? Does our purchasing such items as plastic containers have the potential to complicate the world situation further? i.e. Are our actions creating suffering for others? And, most importantly, can we say what is motivating us to do this? Perhaps some form of 'ignorance'? Or willful denial of the possibility that our actions have any real consequences? If the answer to any of these questions is in the affirmative, then can we at least set limits for ourselves—and adhere to them?

Secondly, where the media is concerned, we may need to ask ourselves what it is that we actually fear. Are the threats real (it certainly cannot be denied that some of them are and they need to be taken seriously), or are they only apparent? i.e. Has the fear that we often act on been provoked in us by the information we regularly receive? Or, maybe such fears result from the way information is packaged by the media? In other words, can here once again sort out the real from the apparent—even to a limited extent? Can we observe and detachedly assess our own reactions to incoming information? And, can we suspend our involvement with diverse, irrational and often unnamable fears that the media provokes in us and find peace of mind in spite of them?

As noted, both the greed which seems to underlie our involvement with consumerism and the fear that we are subject to as a result of media manipulation are what Buddhists would term 'afflictive emotions'[8]. It is up to each individual to discern which of these emotions is driving him or her. There are, however, ample empirical data on consumer behavior which point to underlying and deeply troubling collective attitudes toward these institutions. Alone the annual statistics on auto sales, the mass and relentless purchase and use of large, fuel-inefficient vehicles (and all types of machinery powered by fossil fuels) suggest a prevailing *laissez-faire* view toward the consequences of such choices.

Most of the world's moral theories place considerable emphasis on the distinction between needs and wants. Buddhism is no exception to this. Shantideva, the eighth-century Indian guru and author of *The Way of the Boddhisattva*, a guide for the spiritual seeker (the individual who wishes to develop *boddhicitta* (enlightened consciousness)), warns of the dangers associated with lack of mental and spiritual discipline and emphasizes the central import and value of such discipline:

> For those who fall in a state (i.e. having a sense of entitlement to wealth and power—my note)
>
> The earth itself and all that it holds
>
> Are powerless to satisfy.
>
> For who can give them all they crave?
>
> Their hopeless craving brings them misery
>
> And evil policies invade their minds.
>
> While those with free, untrammeled hearts,
>
> Will never know the end of excellence. [9]

It is important to underscore the fact that Buddhism teaches that the nature of the 'afflictive emotions' is such that they are not forced upon us, but rather arise from within. If this is a correct assessment of human nature, then it points to a unique conclusion about human suffering—and one which must seem radically subjectivist when compared to the conclusions generally arrived at on Western moral theories about the causes of human suffering. That is, for the Buddhist, suffering - including the larger scale suffering that results from human conflict and war—is fundamentally a problem that is rooted in human consciousness (exceptions being, of course, events like natural disasters), and not in the decisions and actions of political or financial institutions, or in military action. If this assessment of the root cause of human suffering is correct, then it must ultimately have a human solution.

The third of the Four Noble Truths of Buddhism is that *we are so designed as to seek an end to the suffering which mortal life entails* and, it is in the cessation of suffering that true peace is to be found. How does one begin the process of thoroughly 'unbinding' oneself from the oppressiveness of material conditions, desires, delusion, etc.? This is the second of the Buddhist insights that is equally as unambiguous as it is powerful, and one that has also served to motivate this paper: Freedom and peace are to be obtained only if one is able to get at the very root cause of suffering and uproot or annihilate it. What is meant by "getting at the root cause of suffering"? The work of removing negative karma, or the burden of past wrong actions from our own consciousness involves thinking in clear cause and effect terms about what we have done in the past and how it has adversely affected others and ourselves. Until we see the causal connection between our past action and our present state of mind, we cannot begin the work of purification of consciousness.

The Fourth Noble Truth in Buddhism is that *there exists a correct path to the cessation of suffering. It is referred to as the Middle Way and is neither the route of asceticism nor that of self-indulgence,* but a properly calibrated, continually practiced "awareness", i.e. ongoing analysis of the state of one's own consciousness and reflection on one's actions in keeping with what one discovers within. The result of these spiritual labors is the cultivation of *compassion.* [10]

In the words of the Dalai Lama, "At a basic level, compassion (*nying je*) is understood mainly in terms of empathy—our ability to enter into and, to some extent, share others' suffering. But Buddhists—and perhaps others—believe that this can be developed to such a degree that not only does our compassion arise without any effort, but it is unconditional, undifferentiated and universal in scope." [11]

Furthermore, in Buddhism, it is held that the work that we do on ourselves, removes inner obstacles to our awareness of others and their suffering and causes us to grasp ever more clearly the rightness of the principle of non violence and embrace the discipline of nonviolent living. Violence and aggression of all sorts are unconscionable to the individual who has taken upon him-or herself the work of self-transformation. [12]

By implication, any type of indirect involvement with violence and aggression through institutions such as consumerism and the media would be as well.

Are Buddhists optimistic about our ability to achieve freedom from such 'afflictive emotions'—on either an individual or a collective basis? Optimistic, yes, but also realistic. In the context of a plea for the spiritual growth of human consciousness and the development of compassion, the Dalai Lama says:

> From my own limited experience, I am convinced that through constant training one can change one's mind; in other words, our positive attitudes, thoughts, and outlook can be enhanced, and their negative counterparts can be reduced. [13]

This finely tuned sense of ethical discretion, i.e. 'mindfulness' is some-thing that each of us as individuals has the opportunity to develop with proper direction. We can give serious consideration to the claim that, essentially, the roots of violence and all forms of aggression are in each of us merely by virtue of the fact that we are human. Then we can do the work necessary to transform those negative impulses into disciplined, compassionate and human responses to the current world situation. At a minimum, making ourselves aware of our habits of consumerism and regularly questioning the information we receive through the media, and then modifying our responses to both of these might, as I have argued here, be two effective starting points. [14]

SOME FURTHER REFLECTIONS ON BUDDHIST ETHICS: ONE-WORLD THINKING

As noted, the Buddhist strategy for peace making is somewhat differ-ent from any strategy that one would be able to extract from the work of any of the major figures in the Western philosophical tradition. From the Buddhist perspective, we need to work first on what we can actually affect, namely, our own mental state. Solutions to larger, insti-tutional problems will follow when we collectively come to understand that they are necessary. In other words, for the Buddhist, the world can perhaps be changed, but one mind at a time.

In his work, *Ethics for the New Millennium*, the Dalai Lama proposes to expand this vision of individual spiritual transformation and make it applicable to the question of the spiritual progress of humanity as a whole. He claims that, at this point in history,

> A spiritual revolution is called for, certainly. But not a political, an economic or even a technical revolution. We have had enough expe-rience of these during the past century to know that a purely exter-nal approach will not suffice. [15]

He also observes that, given the rapid and relentless changes that are taking place in the world at present, we may be forced to extend our definition of moral responsibility, to adopt a pattern of what is often loosely termed 'one-world' thinking. For him, this is based in a notion of *universal responsibility*, or the idea that each of our actions almost invariably has some consequence(s). The commonly heard phrase 'when a butterfly flaps its wings in South America, the effects are felt in China' appropriately illustrates this idea. That is to say, on the Buddhist view, we are all mutually interdependent (to a far greater degree than Western philosophers would claim), i.e. dependent on the nexus of living things for our continued existence. Wrongdoing, anywhere and in any form, particularly violence, rends the fabric of these connections and so adversely impacts upon the entire network. If our habits of consumption are as problematic as I have suggested they are, and if our largely unquestioning relation to the media is indeed the cause of much moral confusion about the political and military developments of the last years, then our (individual and collective) choices and actions vis-à-vis these institutions may indeed have deeply problematic consequences. We may be rending the fabric of life on the planet, or at least contributing significantly to the process.

Opponents of such a holistic ethics as is being proposed here often argue that it leads to absurd conclusions. They claim, for example, that it presents us with an exaggerated or even superfluous set of responsibilities, responsibilities to individuals and situations that we do not and cannot know. I would concede that it can conduce to such awkwardness when taken at face value and when the indirect strategy behind it—that of creating a sort of synergy of compassion—is overlooked. Buddhists are, however, less concerned about such this sort of thing than they are with the practical matter of bringing about individual and collective enlightenment. Moreover, the meditative methods developed in Buddhism, together with its foundational principles, the Four Noble Truths (and the Eightfold Noble Path) [16] have, over the centuries, proven to be an effective antidote to the human phenomenon of 'afflictive emotions' and hence also to the destructive actions which flow from these.

As noted, from the Buddhist perspective, the problem of peace making turns on the fact that we, as individuals, are obligated to labor continually on ourselves, to strive for ever greater awareness of the ways in which our actions (and equally as much, our intentions) can and do impact the world as a whole. Such mental discipline, which, when 'globalized' to something like a notion of universal 'mindfulness', and taken together with a commitment to nonviolent living, constitutes an ethical mode of living that has the potential to unburden us of a great deal of negative karma both individually and collectively. At very least, it could make it less likely that our choices would further aggravate existing world tensions.

In *Ethics for the New Millennium,* the Dalai Lama also revises and expands what is in most of the world's religious and philosophical traditions the concept of *justice* and just action. His thinking on this derives from his notion of *universal responsibility* and also takes into account his reflections on the current state of relations between first and third world, particularly as they have evolved over the last decades with the intrusion of multi-national corporations into the economies and societies of the latter.

He construes just action in terms of a conjunction: We ought both to do no harm *and* to correct injustice where it occurs. In other words, we are responsible for ourselves, our thoughts and actions, and generally our own progress toward enlightenment—but we are also responsible (both singly and collectively) for intervening in and actively working to ameliorate situations in which anyone or any group is wronged by another. Such a statement has considerably greater logical force than any of the more straightforward injunctions against wrongdoing taught in many of the world's moral traditions. I take to also presume reflection on our own contribution, direct or otherwise, to any and all of the present day, larger scale, institutionally driven forms of injustice.

POSTSCRIPT

The French philosopher, Descartes, found himself in a unique historical predicament when he sat down to write his *Discours.* He realized that the traditional training he had received in both metaphysics and ethics no longer sufficed to answer the questions he was confronted with and that it needed to be temporarily set aside so that an entirely new system of thought could be developed. In his case, that new system had to account for science.

We as moderns may now be in an analogous situation with regard to ethical theory. We may be in need of a new paradigm for thinking about the problem of ethical living, a paradigm that allows us to construe it in global terms. The events of 9/11 and the ensuing political and economic developments may be forcing us to revise our current models and make a shift toward one-world thinking. If so, Buddhist ethics constitutes one such paradigm to which we might turn.

The Buddhist meditative tradition, combined with its ethical principles, provides us with a highly potent spiritual medicine, an effective antidote to much, if not all, that ails us ethically, including the greed and fear I have here suggested may be driving many of our choices in everyday life. This tradition may, therefore, provide us with a means of countering our internal enemies—at very least these two—and so help us place ourselves on a path toward greater enlightenment, both singly and collectively. [17]

NOTES

1. This essay constitutes an exploratory study only. Additional analyses could, no doubt, be worked out on the basis of other moral theories, analyses which might prove equally insightful or more so. My purpose here is to outline and discuss some of the uniquely practical Buddhist insights as they apply to these two areas of present day American life, and then to offer some critical observations on this for readers' consideration.
2. Gross, p. 96.
3. Attempting to study the Buddhist tradition by focusing on either its moral theory or its meditative practices alone is a common error among Western scholars and something to be avoided if one is to fully understand the power this tradition holds for transforming the individual. However, it is also fair to say that the close conformity of theory and practice does raise issues of subjectivism and religious esotericism. Gross' response to this, one with which I concur, is to note that "Religious esotericism is criticized in many quarters, but in this case at least, there is no alternative. The psychological and spiritual energies being tapped into are too subtle and to powerful for it to be any other way." (Gross, p. 100)
4. *The Essence of the Heart Sutra*, p. 25.
5. The *Dharmapada* (Buddhist Scriptures), Ch. 4 (On Karma)
6. "... our most basic problem and the root of all suffering is ignorance of what is really the case", Gross, p. 98.
7. As noted, from a Buddhist perspective, the fundamental problem of life is that of 'attachment.' We are all caught up in the 'cycle(s) of desire', driven by our own ignorance to believe that the material things we 'crave' are somehow permanent or of ultimate value. In the words of the Dalai Lama, "At the root of all suffering lie two powerful forces: self-grasping—the deluded grasping at an intrinsically self- and self-centered thought that cherishes only one's own welfare. These two attitudes reside deep within the innermost recesses of our hearts and there join forces and hold unchallenged dominion over our lives." (EHS, p. 145)
   And, as he elsewhere notes, "Destructive acts are motivated by ... a mind dominated by the afflictions. In the entire history of human society, it is these mental afflictions, these undisciplined states of mind that underlie all of humanity's destructive acts—from the smallest acts of killing to the greatest atrocities of war. We must remember that ignorance itself is an affliction: for example, when we fail to grasp the negative long-term consequences of an action and instead act out of short-sighted thoughts of gain." (EHS, p. 35)

8. As the Dalai Lama also states, "In Tibetan, we call such negative and emotional events *nyong mong*, literally "that which afflicts from within" or, as
the term is usually translated, "afflictive emotion." On this view, generally
speaking, all those thoughts, emotions, and mental events which reflect a
negative or uncompassionate state of mind (*kun long*) inevitably undermine our experience of inner peace. All negative thoughts and emotions—
such as hatred, anger, pride, lust, greed, envy and so on—are considered
to be afflictions in this sense. We find that these afflictive emotions are so
strong that if we do nothing to counter them, though there is no one who
does not value their life, they can lead us to the point of madness and even
suicide itself. But because such extremes are unusual, we tend to see negative emotions as an integral part of our mind about which we can do very
little. And, in failing to recognize their destructive potential, we do not see
the need to challenge them. Indeed, far from doing so, we have a tendency
to nurture and reinforce them. This provides them the ground in which
to grow. Yet, as we shall see, their nature is wholly destructive. They are
the very source of unethical conduct. They are also the basis for anxiety,
depression, confusion and stress, which are a feature of our lives today."
(*Ethics for the New Millennium*, p. 86-87)
9. *The Way of the Boddhisattva*, Shantideva. Ch. 8, p. 135, ll. 174-76.
10. "But this sense of equanimity toward all others is not seen as an end in
itself. Rather, it is seen as the springboard to a love still greater. Because
our capacity for empathy is innate, and because the ability to reason is also
an innate faculty, compassion shares the characteristics of consciousness
itself. The potential we have to develop it is therefore stable and continuous. It is not a resource which can be used up—as water is used up when
we boil it. And, though it can be described in terms of activity, it is not like
a physical activity which we train for, like jumping, where once we reach a
certain height we can go no further. On the contrary, when we enhance our
sensitivity toward others' suffering through deliberately opening ourselves
up to it, it is believed that we can gradually extend our compassion to the
point where the individual feels so moved by even the subtlest suffering
of others that they come to have an overwhelming sense of responsibility
toward those others." (ENM, p. 124)
11. ENM, Ch. 8, p. 123.
12. The Dalai Lama provides a general observation on the work of meditation and levels and types of self-awareness it can bring about, a remark that
indicates that this is not an easy path: "By looking into our own minds, we
can discover that the stronger our grasping is, the more forcefully it gener-
ates negative and destructive emotions …" (EHS, p. 35)
13. *The World of Tibetan Buddhism*, p. 64.
14. The fact that one often has access to entirely different sets of facts about
the world situation via the foreign media is noteworthy in itself. Buddhist
epistemology is both strongly empirical and realistic, and so encourages

examination and critical comparison of any such competing informational claims.

15. ENM, Ch. 1, pp. 16-17.

16. Logically and methodologically, the Eightfold Noble Path follows from the Four Noble Truths. Where the Four Noble Truths answer the question "What is the case?" i.e., "What is the human predicament?", the Eightfold Noble Path provides guidelines on how one ought to proceed in life given this predicament. Discussion of the details of Buddhist practice in keeping with the Eightfold Noble Path exceeds the scope of this paper, however, I note that it consists of the following precepts:

1. Right view

2. Right thinking

3. Right speech

4. Right action

5. Right livelihood

6. Right effort

7. Right mindfulness, and

8. Right concentration.

17. This essay constitutes only a brief exercise in the application of Buddhist principles to two present day problems associated with peace making, However, it is important to understand that on the level of the metaphysical, Buddhist meditative practice pursues the notion of 'non-attachment' still further — to the point at which it is claimed that the ego and our attachment to it are the most fundamental obstacles to the achievement of enlightenment. In the words of the Dalai Lama, "By understanding emptiness, by clearly perceiving the empty nature of all phenomena, including ourselves, we can liberate ourselves from negative emotions, and thus from the creation of unwholesome karma and the power of the internal enemy. Through this process, we can begin to undo the harm we've caused by our grasping, and the derivative strong emotions to which it gives rise. The moment we begin to develop insight into the empty nature of self and all reality, the process of releasing our deluded grasp begins. At the moment of our first insight into the empty nature of self and reality, we start to break free of the enslavement of ignorance and the attack of the internal enemy. By reducing our grasp, we start to undo the causal chain of unenlightened existence. By undermining self-grasping ignorance, the first link of dependent origination, you prevent the arising of the second link, and ultimately become free from the endless cycle of suffering lifetimes." (EHS, p.37)

WORKS CITED

PRIMARY SOURCES

Conzee, E., (trans.) *Buddhist Scriptures*. 1959. Penguin Books, London, UK.
The Dalai Lama.1999. *Ethics for the New Millennium*, Riverhead Books/ Penguin, New York, NY.
The Dalai Lama. 1995. *The World of Tibetan Buddhism*, trans. & ed. Geshe Thupten Jinpa, Wisdom Publications, Boston, MA.
Shantideva. 1997. *The Way of Bodhisattva*. Shambala Publications, Boston, MA.

SECONDARY SOURCES

The Dalai Lama. 2002. *The Essence of the Heart Sutra*. Wisdom Publications. Sommerville, MA.
Gross, Rita M., 2003. *Christians Talk about Buddhist Meditation, Buddhists Talk about Christian Prayer*, Continuum Publications, NY, NY.

PERSONAL REFLECTION BY DEBORAH (NASH) PETERSON

A number of work and travel experiences have come together to move me to commit to peace and justice work. In the 1980s, I was involved in political activities as a student in Germany and worked briefly for Amnesty International as a translator on a volunteer basis. Working for third world executives at the International Monetary Fund in the 1990s in Washington, D.C. as a writer/editor gave me direct insight into some of this institution's economic decisions and policies via-à-vis the third world: Their horrible implications were hidden beneath piles of economic data, but hardly difficult to discern. Further work with *Concerned Philosophers for Peace* as an M.A. student and first-hand experience of the events of 9/11 catalyzed my thinking about war completely. I became thoroughly dissatisfied with all that I had previously learned about its root causes. The conduct of the Gulf War in 1991, and the various types of information incoming to Washington, D.C. on this conflict only further confirmed my rejection of it as a means of solving human problems. It seemed utterly abhorrent and to be resisted at all costs.

At the same time, however, I observed that a single, well-meaning individual, or even well-organized and committed groups of people, were able to effect very little in this regard—particularly in 1991. This caused me to re-focus my efforts rather drastically. Instead of asking how I might work on the world, I found it necessary to ask myself in what respect I might be contributing to any sort of conflict, including larger scale incidents. My search for an answer led me to Eastern thought, Buddhism in particular.

On the surface, there is little or no solace to be found in the Buddhist claim that, ultimately, the roots of violence are in us as individuals, not in the world. But, if this analysis is correct, then the solution must also lie within us, both individually and collectively and there is reason for renewed optimism about the project of peace making. Meditation, as I learned, is key to ridding oneself of one's negative emotions, including the appetite for conflict and violence. After having been introduced to this discipline, I began to grasp one of the main assumptions underlying Buddhist peacemaking efforts: The world is changed one mind at a time.

This journey of exploration has led me to conclude that, if we can gain a better understanding of the nature of human consciousness and so of our spiritual purpose here on earth, and if we can learn to value nonviolent living more highly and educate people to it more thoroughly, then there is at least the possibility that the lives of future generations will not have to be marred by tragedy.

PART 2
TWENTIETH-CENTURY PEACEMAKERS

8. NONVIOLENCE AND JUSTICE AS INSEPARABLE PRINCIPLES: A GANDHIAN PERSPECTIVE

VEENA RANI HOWARD

The *Mahābhārata*, the Grand Hindu epic, celebrates the virtue of *ahimsā* (nonviolence):

Ahimsa (nonviolence) is the highest dharma (law, sacred duty). Ahimsa is the best tapas. Ahimsa is the greatest gift. Ahimsa is the highest self-control. Ahimsa is the highest sacrifice. Ahimsa is the highest power. Ahimsa is the highest friend. Ahimsa is the highest truth. Ahimsa is the highest teaching. (*Mahābhārata* XIII: 116:38-39)[1]

Ahimsā, of course, is one of the most fundamental concepts associated with Gandhi's life and work. But, interestingly it is also this which is most likely to be misconstrued. Gandhi's understanding and use of *ahimsā* is broader, more active, and less immediately intuitive than the word suggests. It is as complex as Gandhi's character, that of both an aspiring saint and rebellious political leader.

The *Mahābhārata* glorifies *ahimsā* (nonviolence) as the highest dharma. This notion became one of the central axioms of Hindu ethics and yogic philosophy.[2] *Ahimsā* is fundamental to Gandhi's political and personal philosophy. To understand his *ahimsā* and its founda- tions in Hindu philosophy it is essential to know the etymological meanings of the word *ahimsā* and *dharma*. The Sanskrit word *ahimsā* is literally a negation of the word *himsā*, "killing" or "injury" and hence is translated as "not-harming" or "non-injury." [3] Traditionally, however, the principle of *ahimsā* is much broader: it includes abstaining from harming others not only in actions but also in thought and speech. It is difficult, if not impossible, to practice *ahimsā* in the true sense of the word. The *Mahābharata* recognizes *ahimsā* as the highest form of self-control and sacrifice.

The word *dharma*, literally "that which sustains," has no English equivalent and is generally translated as law, duty, virtue and justice.[4] Rendered as justice, it implies sustenance of law and righteousness; it is the universal principle of harmony. It mandates that we seek equilibrium and balance. But, understood in this way, it is different from the system of legal judgment as it aims at fairness and equity. For the latter, the word *nyayā* is used.[5] The concept of *nyāya* is comparable to the modern judicial system in which legal justice is sought on the grounds of argumentation and evidence.

Thus the Sanskrit phrase—*ahimsā parmodharma*—can be translated as "nonviolence is the greatest duty or virtue" or "nonviolence is the highest law," i.e. it is the greatest duty of human beings to harm no living being. Abstaining from any form of violence requires extreme discipline and vigilance. Gandhi was aware of the "impossibility" of practicing absolute nonviolence: "Perfect nonviolence is impossible so long as we exist physically. . ."[6] Therefore, often the customary understanding of *ahimsā* equates it with passivity—abstention from action, especially that which involves conflict. *Ahimsā* represents the highest level of self-control. Understood merely as self-control or self-limitation, it leads one to conquer the seductions of ego, but can also translate into complete passivity and therefore indifference to, and even deliberate avoidance of, socio-political issues.

In his philosophy and practice, however, Gandhi, unequivocally inverts the traditional understanding of *ahimsā* (as passivity, acquiescence or withdrawal) into an active notion. For him it is not merely abstention from injury, but the highest justice: real *ahimsā*, according to Gandhi, requires resisting the structures of violence. "The principle of nonviolence necessitates complete abstention from exploitation in any form," emphasizes Gandhi.[7] This may seem only superficially opposed to *ahimsā* construed as passivity (in performance of apparently aggressive actions), but this is where Gandhi is often misunderstood. To clarify what it came to mean for him, we must look at the very beginning of his career.

Gandhi's political life as well as his spiritual journey began in South Africa. Mohandas Gandhi, a young lawyer trained in England and dressed in western clothes, was neither acquainted with the politics of nonviolent activism, nor was he grounded in spirituality.

One evening, while he was on a South African train, a white man objected to his traveling first-class because he was "colored." In spite of the conductor's threat to "push" him out of the compartment, Gandhi refused to get off the train, noting that he carried a first-class ticket. He asserted that it was his right to travel first class. In spite of his resistance, the constable pushed him and his luggage off the train at one of the stations. Obstinate in asserting his rights, he had refused to move to the third class compartment and the train steamed away. Feeling shocked and humiliated, the barrister spent the entire night in the "cold, bleak and windswept waiting room" at the train station reflecting on the incident. This direct encounter with prejudice had awakened him to the darker side of humanity: social injustice manifested in forms of colonial suppression and racism. In the grave silence and bitter cold of that dark night, Gandhi, the lawyer, must have considered seeking retribution for the humiliating and discriminatory action carried out against him. He records the incident in his autobiography.

> I began to think of my duty. Should I fight for my rights or go back to India…? It would be cowardice to run back to India without fulfilling my obligation. The hardship to which I was subjected was superficial—only a symptom of the deep disease of colour prejudice. I should try, if possible, to root out the disease and suffer hardships in the process. [8]

Gandhi decided to fight for the rights of Indians and social justice (which he later extended to a fight for India's independence), but not with arms; and he decided to seek justice, but not retribution. This form of justice consists of mercy and forgiveness—"not returning two slaps for one," nor retaliation— "tit for tat"—as demanded by modern judicial systems. This decision in favor of non-retributive justice would seem quixotic and impractical to those who even remotely understood the titanic power of the British Empire as well as the shrewdness that goes with Gandhi's profession, namely the practice of western law. But Gandhi had deep insight into the power of the "Mighty Empire" as well as into the strengths and weaknesses of the native people. Perhaps this is precisely why he wanted to fight the situation by utilizing a weapon mightier than, and also unfamiliar to, his opponent: nonviolence. He states:

> The British want to put the struggle on the plane of machine guns where they have the weapons and we do not. Our only assurance of beating them is putting the struggle on a plane where we have weapons they do not. [9]

Gandhi had realized as a result of both his professional training and his knowledge of the Hindu metaphysical Law of Karma, that sustainable justice cannot be achieved by violent means. The concept of karma or "action" is central to Hindu ethics and is understood as the

universal principle of cause and effect. Every action and thought produces "moral reverberations" which spill over into not only this life but
our next lives as well. S. Radhakrishnan, a prominent scholar of Indian philosophy, summarizes the law of karma: "All acts produce their
effects which are recorded in both organism and environment... Good
produces good, evil, evil. Love increases our power of love, hatred, our
power of hatred."[10] Justice is not served in one lifetime, but may take
eons. It flows from our actions. The Law of Karma makes justice so
comprehensive and mysterious that it is impossible to think that using violent means can lead to sustainable justice. A violent response to
almost any circumstance only perpetuates the cycle of retribution.

It is not, however, immediately clear how *ahimsā* can be used as a
weapon; nor is it obvious how justice mandates nonviolence. There
are numerous apparent contradictions in Gandhi's approach to justice,
war, and nonviolence. Clarification of some of them is attempted below.

Ahimsā, the principle of Hindu ethics understood as a private virtue and a retreat from socio-political action, paradoxically, presents an
ethical problem: What to do about the structures of social violence—
the kind Gandhi experienced in the train? These generally accepted
and institutionalized inequities automatically inflict suffering on many
every day. Should an individual who is committed to nonviolence simply ignore them? Or tolerate them? Is silence in the face of this to be
interpreted as consent? Gandhi transforms the traditional principle
of withdrawal from harmful action into an innovative ideology: One
should not retreat from such actions, but actively engage in a fight
against evil by using nonviolent methods: "*Ahimsā* without action is
an impossibility" because virtues such as *ahimsā* can only be practiced
in the domain of action.[11] Gandhi's interpretation of it is thus contrary
to the commonplace understanding of *ahimsā* within the tradition.

Gandhi naturalized the ethical principle *ahimsā* for the political
arena. He transformed this spiritual virtue into a political device—"a
celestial weapon"—in order to resist the structures of violence. For
this passive yet powerful form of resistance, he had to develop a new
term, *satyāgraha*, literally, "*soul-force* as opposed to armed strength."[12]
Satyāgraha is often translated as passive resistance, which is quite
the opposite of Gandhi's definition. As he explained it, "submit not
to evil, and take the consequences." For him, this kind of nonviolent
confrontation "is a more active and real fight against wickedness than

retaliation whose very nature is to increase wickedness."[13] Such active resistance to evil, however, does not logically arise out of conventional forms of *ahimsā* as it is portrayed in ancient Hindu texts. This leap from the non-active, privately spiritual idea to the active, "public" spirituality of *satyāgraha* is one of Gandhi's most original insights. As he says, *ahimsā* "does not mean meek submission to the will of the evildoer, but it means the pitting of one's whole soul against the will of the tyrant. Working under this law of our being, it is possible for a single individual to defy the whole might of an unjust empire..."[14]

This form of *ahimsā* is directly grounded in active compassion. Gandhi explains the connection when he says, "There is as much difference between *ahimsa* and compassion as there is between gold and the shape given to it, between a root and the tree which sprouts from it. Where there is no compassion, there is no *ahimsa*. The test of *ahimsā* is compassion. The concrete form of *ahimsa* is compassion."[15] *Ahimsā* brimming with compassion seeks not merely reaction, but moral conversion. In his biography of Gandhi, D.G. Tendulkar writes, "Gandhi's ambition was nothing less than the conversion of the British Empire through nonviolence, so as to make them see the wrong they have done."[16]

Gandhi's *ahimsā*—suffering for others—necessitates fighting against social injustice. "Resistance of violence by self-suffering"— *satyāgraha*—by its very nature, according to Gandhi, results in sustainable justice. In his rendition of *ahimsā* as "resistance to social injustice by nonviolent means" Gandhi seems to be interpreting the phrase *ahimsā parmodharma* as "nonviolence is the highest justice." As he says, "no man could be actively nonviolent and not rise against social injustice no matter where it occurred."[17] However, his pursuit of justice seems convoluted, too, insofar as he would actively seek social justice, but not against those who commit evil. Where he shows no shyness in destroying structures of violence, he is infinitely patient with and compassionate toward the evildoer. Consider the following rather startling proclamation:

> The purest way of seeking justice against the murderers is not to seek it... Their punishment cannot recall the dead to life. I would ask those whose hearts are lacerated to forgive them, not out of their weakness—for they are able every way to have them punished—but out of their immeasurable strength. Only the strong can forgive.[18]

Does this not contradict the conventional principles of justice, i.e. most any system of reward and punishment? And, is it even practical? Gandhi's idea of justice might seem absurd, but it is clear that, on his theory as it is related to *ahimsā*, he seeks resolution without revenge. This stands in sharp contrast to the modern legal system. Of this higher form of justice, he says, "In undiluted justice is mercy."[19] The practitioner of *ahimsā* seeks a permanent solution: justice not in retribution but in conversion of the soul of the evildoer by the power of mercy and compassion. In his words, "'Tit for tat' is a wrong principle. It is certainly not based on forgiveness. What can we gain by being wicked with the wicked? The good lies in our showing love and compassion even for such persons."[20]

As noted, Gandhi's *ahimsā* as the highest form of justice, *ahimsā parmodharma*, might seem to contradict the traditional understanding of it as mere withdrawal from violent actions for the purpose of personal spiritual fulfillment. But, the foundations for Gandhi's interpretations of it go much deeper than one might initially think. They lie in the Hindu notion of ontological identity, the unity of the self and other. *Ātman* (literally Self or Spirit) dictates that within each one of us there resides a divine reality. The other is none other than our very own self and none other than the Divine Reality. This is also a central claim of the *Bhagavad-Gītā*. This apparently war-affirming narrative was Gandhi's favorite text. He interpreted it allegorically and looked to it for metaphysical and ethical insights. It affirms the need for an ethical engagement and does so by reference to foundational metaphysical principles of Hinduism. It sets a standard for wisdom and was therefore for Gandhi a sort of guiding light: "The man equipped with discipline looks on all with an impartial eye, seeing *Ātman* in all beings and all beings in *Ātman*." [21] Realization of the unity of self and other renders meaningless the issue of retribution and violence; at the same time, it affirms the need for self-sacrifice, for resisting social violence. The other is one's very own self. Traditional Hindu metaphysics and modern altruistic social concern meet in Gandhi's interpretation of *ahimsā* as *dharma* (the highest justice).

Mahatma Gandhi was also aware of the moral dilemmas associated with prohibiting violence in all situations. The *Bhagavad-Gītā* presents the reader with what is perhaps the direst of all predicaments, the choice between violence and nonviolence in a time of war. Gandhi's trust in the power of nonviolence caused him, however, to deliberate further on this:

> Suppose a man runs amuck and goes furiously about sword in hand, and killing anyone that comes his way, and no one dares to capture him alive. Any one who dispatches this lunatic will earn the gratitude of the community and be regarded as a benevolent man. From the point of view of *ahimsa* it is the plain duty of everyone to kill such a man. [22]

Ahimsā for Gandhi is an active force, *himsa* is only for sustaining justice and ensuring the well being of others when all options have been exhausted. The latter is like a "surgeon's knife" [23] and is actually a form of *ahimsā*. Gandhi warns against passivity in the name of practicing ahimsā.

> He who refrains from killing a murderer who is about to kill his ward (when he cannot prevent him otherwise) earns no merit, but commits a sin, he practices no *ahimsa* but *himsa* out of a fatuous sense of *ahimsa*. [24]

Ahimsā does not "simply mean non-killing" but compassion and justice.[25] In his commentary on the *Bhagavad-Gītā*, Gandhi claims that "Compassion contrary to the just action is not compassion, but hostility." [26] His rendering of *ahimsā* as justice and mercy is in full agreement with praise of *ahimsā* in the *Mahābhārata* as the "highest justice" and the "greatest sacrifice." Self-sacrifice for the other is *ahimsā*—one's highest duty. Gandhi's justice is not blindfolded, but proceeds with the open eyes of wisdom overflowing with mercy. His political and moral journey began with the direct experience of social injustice in South Africa, and he subsequently experimented with, and successfully utilized, both existing ethical principles of Hindu tradition and Western activist ideas. [27] He also drew on legal reasoning in his efforts to guarantee human dignity by confronting social evils. Perhaps such experimentation in synthesis of principles is necessary once again given the quandaries we are now facing as regards terrorism and retribution.

By redefining the ethic of *ahimsā* in the light of the Hindu notion of ontological identity—the unity of the self and the other—Gandhi shows us the full power of this principle, one which juxtaposes in *ahimsā*, both justice and mercy.

NOTES

[1] In the translation of *Mahābhārata* by M.N. Dutt the word *ahimsā* is translated as "abstention from cruelty." The *Mahābhārata* (Anushasana Parva: 116. 38-39), translated by M.N. Dutt, Delhi: Parimal Publications, 1994, p. 256. *Ahimsā parmodharma* (Nonviolence is the greatest of all virtues or duties) became the axiom of Gandhi's political movement.

[2] In the *Mahābhārata*, *ahimsā* is the highest of al ethical virtues: "As the feet of all beings having feet fit in an elephant's foot, so is all virtues (dharma) and worldly pursuit (artha) sustained in nonviolence." The *Mahābhārata* (Śanti Parva: 245. 18-19), translated by M.N. Dutt. In the *Yoga Sūtras* of Patnajali, *ahimsā* is first of the five restraints, including truth, not stealing, self-restraint, and non-possessiveness, essential for liberation.

[3] "There is violence at the root in the very act of living and hence arose the negative word *ahimsā* indicating of the dharma to be observed by embodied beings." In *The Collected Works of Mahatma Gandhi*, Vol. 45, p. 286.

[4] The word *dharma* is not easily translated into English. It has several meanings: Cosmic Law, ethical law, virtue, sacred duty, right justice, religion, and righteousness. *Dharma* is the cosmic principle of balance, harmony and justice.

[5] The Sanskrit word *nyāya* means, standard, method, axiom, in the right manner, logical or syllogistic argument or inference, lawsuit, judicial sentence, etc. In Hindi and Gujurati languages (in which Gandhi spoke and wrote) the word *nyāya* is used for justice and legal proceedings similar to those of the western judicial system.

[6] Gandhi, Mahatma, 1990. *All Men are Brothers: Autobiographical Reflections,* compiled and edited by Krishna Kriplani, New York: Continuum, p. 83.

[7] Ibid., p. 83.

[8] Gandhi, Mohandas K., 1957. *An Autobiography, The Story of my Experiments with Truth.* Translated from the original Gujurati by Mahadev Desai. Boston: Beacon Press, pp. 111-112.

[9] Collins, Larry and Lapierre, Dominque, *Freedom at Midnight.* New York: Simon and Schuster, 1975. p. 64.

[10] Radhakrishnan, S., 1980. *An Idealist View of Life.* London: Unwin Paperbacks, p. 218.

[11] Gandhi, M.K., *The Collected Work of Mahatma Gandhi.* Vol. 45, p. 285.

[12] Gandhi, M.K., *The Collected Works of Mahatma Gandhi,* Vol. 16, pp. 6-7.

[13] Gandhi writes for *Young India* (1925). Gandhi, Mahatma, 1990. *All Men are Brothers: Autobiographical Reflections,* compiled and edited by Krishna Kriplani, New York: Continuum, p. 85.

[14] Quoted in Barash, David P., 1999. *Approaches to Peace: A Reader in Peace Studies.* New York: Oxford University Press, p. 184.

[15] Gandhi, M.K., *The Collected Works of Mahatma Gandhi,* "ahimsa vs. compassion," Vol. 45, p. 285.

[16] Clough, Bradley S., Gandhi, 2001. "Nonviolence and the Bhagavad-Gita," in *Holy War, Violence And The Bhagavad-Gita*, ed. Rosen, Steven J., Virginia: Deepak Publishing, p. 67.

[17] Gandhi, Mahatma, 1990. *All Men are Brothers, Autobiographical Reflections*. Compiled and edited by Krishna Kriplani. New York: Continuum, p. 81.

[18] Gandhi, M.K., *The Collected Works of Mahatma Gandhi*, Vol. 22, pp. 412-413.

[19] Gandhi, M.K., 2001. *The Bhagavad-Gita According to Gandhi*, ed. John Strohmeir. Berkeley, California: Berkeley Hills Books, p. 107.

[20] Ibid, p. 180.

[21] Gandhi, M.K., *The Bhagavad-Gita According to Gandhi*, p. 123.

[22] Gandhi, M.K. *The Collected Works of Mahatma Gandhi*, Vol. 36, p. 449.

[23] Gandhi writes: "The surgeon who, from fear of causing pain to his patient, hesitates to amputate a rotten limb is guilty of himsa." In *The Collected Works of Mahatma Gandhi*, Vol. 36, p. 449.

[24] Gandhi, M.K., *The Collected Works of Mahatma Gandhi*, Vol. 36, p. 449.

[25] Ibid, p. 449.

[26] Gandhi, M.K., 1995. *Gītā Mātā* (in Hindi) Delhi: Sasta Sahitya Mandal, p. 142.

[27] *Indian Opinion* reported in June, 1990, a lecture by Gandhi on "The Ethics of Passive Resistance," wherein he was reported as saying that: Jesus Christ, Daniel and Socrates represented the purest form of resistance or soul force (*atmabal*). Resist not evil meant that evil was not to be repelled by evil but by good; in other words, physical force was to be opposed not by its like, but by soul force. The same idea was expressed in Indian philosophy by the expression "freedom from injury to every living thing." In Jordens, J.T.F., 1998. *Gandhi's Religion, A Homespun Shawl*. New York. Palgrave, p. 220.

9. JESUS AND GANDHI

TERRENCE RYNNE & MICHAEL DUFFEY

Some of Mohandas Gandhi's Christian contemporaries believed that he was among the most exemplary disciples of Jesus they had ever known. Reflecting on what Gandhi, a confirmed Hindu, took from the life and teachings of Jesus is very illuminating for us as Christians. In Part I, we will highlight two important influences on Gandhi, namely, Jesus' teaching in the Sermon on the Mount and the symbol of the Cross. In Part II, we will describe two important ways in which Gandhi has influenced contemporary Christian witness: his emphasis on changing social structures nonviolently and his advocacy on behalf of the poor.

PART I ⸱ TERRENCE RYNNE

Gandhi did not always value Christianity. During his childhood, advocates of India's various religions, such as Zoroastrians, Sikhs, Muslims, and Jains, were all welcome in his father's house. As a child, he was, however, put off by Christianity, and seemingly by it alone. Christian missionaries stood on the corner of his grade school loudly deriding the gods and beliefs of Hinduism. Converts to Christianity were "denationalized" and "British-ized." During Gandhi's youth, Christianity was the religion of "beef and brandy" and the religion of the "sahib."

As a young adult, he began to study various religions including his own, Hinduism. He was studying for the bar exams in London when he was given the New Testament to read. He later wrote: "the Sermon on the Mount went straight to my heart…the verses, 'But I say to you, resist not evil; but whosoever strikes you on the right cheek, turn to him the other also. And, if any man take away your coat, let him have your cloak as well,' delighted me beyond measure." [1] This text inspired him for the rest of his life.

How did he understand it? First, it is important to realize that he heard it with Hindu ears. At a young age, he had learned a Gujurati

---

1 Mohandas Gandhi, *An Autobiography Or The Story Of My Experiments with Truth* (Ahmedabad: Navijavan Publishing, 1927), 4.

poem that echoed the "turn the other cheek" message. It concluded, "But the truly noble know all men as one, and return with gladness good for evil done," [2] i.e., overcome evil with good. Secondly, he heard it as a son of the soil of India. Until one visits that country, one has no idea how thoroughly religion can permeate the daily lives of people. The culture's overall sense of reverence for life strikes one immediately: a town elephant wanders through a business district and is given breakfast offerings by each shop owner; or, first thing in the morning at the front doors of their simple dwellings, people put out bread crumbs in an elaborate mandala design as an offering, one which is then consumed by the ants. In Indian culture, all of life is not only regarded as sacred, but also as a unified whole. The basic spirit of *ahimsa*, "do no harm to life," is evident everywhere. It was this intense religious sensibility that Gandhi brought to his reading of the New Testament.

He understood the message of the Sermon on the Mount, the return of good for evil, love for hate, nonviolence for violence in much the same way as contemporary exegetes do. For him, as well as for modern scholars, its words are not just the expression of a lofty moral ideal. One scholar, for example, explains that they are "focal instances:[3] cameo descriptions of situations of conflict that are so narrowly drawn that they invite the listener to enter into them through their imaginations. Jesus is confronting his listeners with situations of oppression that are very recognizable to them: a master striking his slave with the back of his right hand; an occupying Roman soldier pressing a Jew into service to carry his pack; a poor person sued for his last stitch of clothing. He is asking them to imagine how they might creatively and nonviolently respond in such situations in ways that might take their oppressors by surprise, and challenge them to change their attitudes and behaviors. 'Turning the other cheek' signifies to the master that the one who is struck is not cowed. It challenges the master to reconsider his behavior. Voluntarily going the extra mile will surprise the Roman soldier. It invites him to see the pack carrier as a human being. Giving your cloak to the one who has sued you for your shirt might bring the opponent up short and reveal to him the inhumanity of his actions.

---

2 Gandhi, *Autobiography*, 32.

3 Robert Tannehill, "The 'Focal Instance' as a Form of New Testament Speech: A Study of Matthew 5:39b-42," *Journal of Religion* 50 (1970): 372-85.

For Gandhi as well, the message of "turn the other cheek" was the opposite of "passivism"; it was instead one of heroic and creative action, the only way to break the circle of violence that kept people oppressed and to bring about a moral conversion in the oppressor. He later coined the word *satyagraha*, which allowed him to distinguish what he had learned in the Sermon on the Mount from "passive resistance," "pacifism" or mere "civil disobedience." *Satyagraha* applies the message of Jesus (and Hinduism), as Gandhi understood these, to politics and relations between masses of people. That is, he sought to develop not just a personal ethic, but a *way* for people to fight nonviolently against oppression and evil in this world.

Gandhi was disturbed when he heard Christians putting aside the teaching of the Sermon on the Mount as impracticable, dreamy idealism or restricted to being the personal ethic of only a very few—the typical ways both Catholics and Protestants dismiss it as irrelevant to daily life and *realpolitik*:

> For many of them contend that the Sermon on the Mount does not apply to mundane things, and that it was only meant for the twelve disciples. Well, I do not believe this. I think that it has no meaning if it is not of vital use in everyday life to everyone.[1]

For Gandhi, nonviolence was at the center of what Jesus taught and lived and died for. Gandhi could therefore not understand how one could be a disciple of Jesus and not be fundamentally committed to nonviolent living:

> Christianity is no Christianity in which a vast number of Christians believe in governments based on brute force and are denying Christ every day of their lives [5]

Just now Christianity comes to a yearning humankind in a tainted form.[6]

Gandhi spent the whole of his life demonstrating that the Sermon on the Mount could be a guide to eminently practical politics, as he nonviolently opposed a ruthless and globe-spanning Empire and the thousand-year old systematic injustice of untouchability. He labored endlessly and nonviolently to raise up his cherished "dumb millions" in the villages of India. He continued to hope that Christianity would

---

4   *Harijan*, March 23, 1940.
5   *Young India*, Oct. 27, 1927.
6   *Harijan*, March 6, 1937.

some day be authentically lived, that the West would come to the message of the Sermon on the Mount afresh. Through his "experiments with truth," he aimed to demonstrate its workability in a whole range of situations.

The second of the many lessons Gandhi took from Christianity concerned the symbol of the Cross. In a famous scene captured on film, he had stopped at the Vatican on his way back from the 1931 Roundtable Conference in London and happened to see a rough-hewn crucifix. His reaction was immediate and emotional:

> Chance threw Rome in my way. And I was able to see something of that great and ancient city... And what would not I have given to bow my head before the living image at the Vatican of Christ crucified. It was not without a wrench that I could tear myself away from that scene of living tragedy. I saw there at once that nations, like individuals, could only be made through the agony of the Cross and in no other way. Joy comes not out of infliction of pain on others, but out of pain voluntarily borne by oneself.[7]

Gandhi's understanding of the cross was that if one lived a Christian life, he would probably end up in conflict with the powers that be. He saw that Jesus befriended the poor and stood with the disenfranchised. Furthermore, he tried to move those responsible for oppression, in both religious and civil leadership, to change their behaviors. They rejected his efforts and found him to be a threat. Why did Jesus die? Because of the way he lived. The cross was the result of his living in keeping with these principles to the end.

The theology of atonement that has held sway for a thousand years, the "penal substitution theory" which has the Father offering up his Son in a bloody sacrifice for forgiveness of humanity's sins, was revolting to Gandhi. He understood the Cross not in metaphysical terms, but in more immediate political and historical ones. It was for him, the final step and consequence of a life spent befriending those in need and resisting oppression and violence. As American missionary, Stanley Jones, writes:

> Never in human history has so much light been shed on the Cross as has been shed through this one man, and that man was not even a Christian. Had not our Christianity been so vitiated and overlain by our identification with unchristian attitudes and policies in pub-

---

7   *Young India*, Dec. 31, 1931.

lic and private life, we would have seen at once the kinship between Gandhi's method and the cross.[8]

PART II ~ MICHAEL DUFFEY

Gandhi was a Karma Yogi who struggled to find the truth through act-ing in service to others. And, like Jesus, the Son of Man who came not to be served but to serve, Gandhi's life was one of service. His service often took the form of opposing evil social structures. Gandhi force-fully demonstrated that religious belief required political engagement to support human dignity. True religion is not an individual search for enlightenment and salvation, but the organized effort to reform social structures in order that they serve the common good. As Dashrath Singh notes, it was Gandhi's "profound structuralism, [that put] blame on the wrong structure rather than the evil actor." [9] And, Martin Lu-ther King, Jr. credited Gandhi with bringing the Christian principle of *agape*, or self-sacrificing love, to bear on social relations by creating social movements aimed at changing existing social structures.

Gandhi demonstrated in both South Africa and India the possibil-ity of organizing successful mass movements to reform sinful struc-tures. Christian Churches are aware of the sinfulness of certain social structures—and of the fact that they themselves often create, main-tain and legitimate them. Throughout the past century Catholic social teaching has called for socio-political and economic structural reform. It must, however, be noted that Christianity still remains entrenched in the deepest and most enduring social sin, patriarchy.

Gandhi called attention to the structural violence in which West-ern culture was deeply implicated. He argued that Christianity in the West has been militant, aggressive, and imperialist in its ambitions. As Singh states,

> In the history of human culture and civilization it was perhaps Ma-hatma Gandhi who for the first time could see the ocean of violence inherent in present social structures of different societies of the world and above all in Western civilization.[10]

---

8 E. Stanley Jones, *Mahatma Gandhi: An Interpretation* (New York: Abing-don-Cokesbury Press, 1948), 105.

9 Dashrath Singh, "Gandhi and the Concept of Structural Violence," in *Gandhi Marg*, July-September, 1998, Vol. 20. np.

10 Singh, op. cit.

Often, with the intent of defending their religious values and saving innocent lives (usually those who are on "our side"), Christians have justified killing others with an easy conscience. Now, at least in part on account of Gandhi's devotion to nonviolence, reformers within Christian churches are asking as never before: "Can we kill in the name of Jesus, whose mission of salvation was accomplished by suffering without retaliation and by accepting death?" They recognize that early Christianity grew by leaps and bounds not by militancy or through conquest but by the example set by the followers of Jesus, people who impressed others by the quality of their brotherly love.

Gandhi emphasized the contradiction underlying the use violent means in pursuit of justice. His insistence on integrity of means and ends challenged the exceptionalism of the Christian worldview that so often permits violent means to attain justice and peace. Gandhi insisted that Jesus' nonviolence must be lived unconditionally. He demonstrated its utility in his struggle against race, caste, and religious discrimination.

Jesus' constructive idealism aimed at realizing justice and bringing about forgiveness by means of love and mercy. Like Jesus, Gandhi was a champion of the poor. In Gandhi, we witnessed the living out of what the Catholic Church would, half a century later, call the "preferential option for the poor." Like Gandhi, the U.S. Bishops declared two decades ago that all public policy must be judged first of all on the basis of whether it helps the poor (*Economic Justice for All*, 1986).

Gandhi frequently quoted the Gospel of Mark, "It is not enough to say, 'Lord, Lord.'" It is not what we profess, but what we do that counts. It should be clear just how much Gandhi treasured the life, death and teaching of Jesus, and perhaps still clearer just how much we, as Christians, owe to him.

PERSONAL REFLECTION BY TERRY RYNNE

Many years ago as a young adult during the height of the Vietnam War, I happened upon the book *The Nonviolent Cross* by James Douglass. As a Catholic Christian I was bowled over by it. It calmly reflected on the ways Gandhi and his disciples such as Danilo Dolci in Sicily and Vinoba Bhave in India effectively practiced nonviolent resistance to evil and oppression. Moreover, it suggested that at the heart of the Christian gospel was the call to nonviolent, loving action. This forever changed my reading of the New Testament and my understanding of the meaning of Jesus' life and death on the cross.

All through the subsequent years of my working life, from the time I received an M.B.A. in marketing and health care administration from Northwestern University, through ten years as a hospital administrator and then twenty years running my own health care marketing firm, this vision of active peacemaking, inspired by the New Testament and Gandhi, stayed with me. Finally, after selling my firm I was able to turn towards peacemaking in a more dedicated way. I completed a doctorate in theology at Marquette University, researching the topic *Rethinking Christian Salvation in the Light of Gandhi's Satyagraha*. It served as the basis for the book *Gandhi and Jesus: The Saving Power of Nonviolence*, published by Orbis Books in March of 2008. After selling our respective companies, my wife Sally and I started the Sally and Terry Rynne Foundation dedicated to peace and the empowerment of women. One of our first grants was to help launch the Marquette University Center for Peacemaking in September, 2007. The mustard seed took root long ago.

PERSONAL REFLECTION BY MICHAEL DUFFEY

In the late 1960s, two friends were killed in Vietnam and I saw the devastation that their deaths brought to their families. Shortly thereafter, I was a college student, reading Gandhi and Thomas Merton on violence. My teachers, James Douglass, Charles McCarthy, and other prophetic people like Dan Berrigan challenged me personally to take a stand on the issue of war. Thousands of lives were being extinguished as a result of the hubris of American political leaders. By my senior year, I was deeply troubled, but still grateful for a faith in the good Creator and the sacrificing love of Jesus that grounded in me a redeeming vision of the world. Two years in the Peace Corps in Nepal deepened my appreciation of Gandhi and Buddhism—and the conviction that the war and poverty were the real enemies to be resisted. Whenever I have seen the tragedy of violent death—Asia, the U.S., or Central America—I have found myself committed to a nonviolent path. It seems to be the only way for human beings to realize their full humanity. This commitment anchors my teaching, writing, and community involvement.

10. MAHATMA GANDHI AND WAHIDUDDIN KHAN ON NONVIOLENCE AND JIHAD

IRFAN A. OMAR

ON RELIGION AND THE NONVIOLENT PATH TO PEACE

Mohandas Gandhi (d. 1948) is widely held to be one of the twentieth-century's foremost champions of *ahimsa*, non-injury or nonviolence. He is credited with having inspired scores of intellectuals, activists, and civilians to reflect on alternative modalities of being. Hence many political and social movements and peace and justice oriented organizations continue to move toward adopting a nonviolent ethic. Religious intellectuals and communities as well are drawn to nonviolence as a viable means of achieving peace and resolving conflict. Since religions have often been viewed as part of the problem of violence, it is fitting therefore that they are now expected to reflect on the possibility of becoming *active* agents of non-violence.[1]

Since Gandhi, numerous other noted religious and secular activists and intellectuals have made strides in advancing those ideas which were both propounded and implemented by Gandhi. Dr. Martin Luther King, Jr. was among the most celebrated of his Western followers. Through his own theoretical and practical work, King tried to address the problems of racism and prejudice against African Americans. He did so by advocating what Gandhi termed *satyagraha*, or "soul-force," the power of nonviolent resistance that is sustained deep within one's soul. The civil rights struggles in the United States aimed to overcome what seemed to many an insurmountable obstacle, one which anyone concerned with human rights and justice necessarily had to confront. King not only utilized some of Gandhi's proposed principles and applied these in his activism, but he also acknowledged his debt to the Mahatma as a revivalist of nonviolent ethics in our times. He rightly said of Gandhi that he "lived, thought, and acted, inspired by the vision of humanity evolving toward a world of peace and harmony. We may ignore him at our own risk."[2] King of course was also deeply touched

by Gandhi's reference to the teachings of Jesus and their relevance in
the civil rights struggle.

Gandhi has also inspired thinkers and activists in other religious
traditions, including Islam. Khan Abdul Ghaffar ("Badshah") Khan
and Abu'l Kalam Azad were two among many Indian Muslims who
were deeply moved by the combination of religious (read "moral") and
social grounds which Gandhi drew on to develop his unique methodology. Both adopted nonviolence as a means to "struggle" (*jihad*)
for justice, albeit with their own respective nuances. Badshah Khan
later became known for a major achievement, namely, for showcasing
the spirit of nonviolence by creating the so-called nonviolent army or
"Servants of God" (Khudai Khidmatgars).[3]

Gandhi was quite well-versed in his study of other religions. In particular, he drew a great deal from his readings in Western humanism
and Christianity. For example, he added the notion of "agape" to his
notion of nonviolence, but gave it a weightier meaning than *ahimsa*
would entail.[4] He was intensely drawn to the moral and spiritual
teachings of the great world religions because, for him, religious life
was synonymous with the righteous and harmonious co-living with
all others. If rituals help us get there, that is well and good, but they
should not be regarded as central to religion. He often referred to the
teachings of Jesus and quoted from the Bible to draw Christians' attention to the gap between teaching and practice in their religion. Gandhi
did the same to Hindus. He reminded them that their scriptures seek
to promote tolerance despite the intolerant actions of some Hindus
who opposed Gandhi's approach of seeking truth in all religions. As
a devout Hindu himself, he reserved his severest criticism for his co-
religionists—a fact which attests to his greatness as a statesman. He
also knew a great deal about other religions such as Zoroastrianism
and Sikhism. Jainism exerted perhaps the greatest influence on him
because of its dominance in his home state of Gujarat.[5] Finally, he had
a great deal of advice and sympathy for Muslims. He was perhaps a
more emphatic defender of spiritual Islam than many Muslims were.
He often reminded them of the "true" meaning of jihad which he understood to be that of struggle against injustice and inequity. What
follows is a brief discussion of Gandhi's thinking on Islam as juxtaposed to the thought of a contemporary Muslim theologian, Maulana
Wahiduddin Khan. The latter calls for the adoption of nonviolence as
a universally applicable methodology.

WAHIDUDDIN KHAN'S AL-RISĀLA MOVEMENT

Maulana Wahiduddin Khan (b. 1925) is an internationally known Islamic scholar and founder of the Al-Risāla Movement. Over the years, he has published numerous books, essays and other audio-visual materials. His books have been translated into many of the world's languages. Since 1976, he has also been editor-in-chief of the monthly journal, *al-Risāla*, which is published in Urdu.[6] One of Wahiduddin Khan's many aims is to bridge the gap between traditional Islamic learning and modern knowledge. Thus, he started his movement with the intention of producing Islamic literature that addresses the minds and hearts of the contemporary age. His own interest in modern knowledge and his mode of thinking has resulted in a distinct interpretation of Islamic teachings. Khan's audience includes both Hindus and Muslims, secular people as well as graduates of the Islamic seminary system and other reform-oriented individuals. Among the many themes found in Khan's writings, two stand out due to their relevance to modern life: peace and nonviolence in Islam. Through his analysis of Islamic teachings, Khan essentially attempts to redefine and reclaim the notion of jihad for peaceful religious activism. This he supports by systematic treatment of Islamic textual and historical sources.

Khan's Al-Risāla Movement advances the idea that peace is achievable through non-confrontational, non-idealistic and, above all, non-political means. When he says that the way to peace is through non-political actions he is identifying with radical apolitical pacifism, a direction of thought not widely accepted among Muslim thinkers today. In fact, on this point Khan, who has great admiration for Mahatma Gandhi, differs even with Gandhi and judges him to be incorrectly advocating political activism instead of educational and moral reform. In other words, he shares with Gandhi the claim that peace and justice-oriented activism should be nonviolent, but disagrees that such activism should take on political authorities by challenging the status quo and disrupting the rule of law, even if that rule of law happens to derive from an unjust and oppressive social system.

WAHIDUDDIN KHAN'S CRITIQUE OF GANDHI

Khan admires Gandhi, but he is also critical of his thinking about how peace can be attained. That is, for Khan, Gandhi's approach to nonviolence poses a problem. This difference itself can be a starting

point for the modern reader in understanding their thought more
thoroughly; specifically, it can clarify how each of them defines the
notions of peace, nonviolence, and, above all, jihad. Khan is close to
Gandhi's thought in certain respects, but he is also distant from him in
his approach to achieving social and religious reform. He reserves the
right to criticize the man and his political actions, but is nevertheless
deeply grateful to him, especially for the latter's principle of nonviolence (ahimsa). Indeed, this is where he resonates with Gandhi most.
But even here there is a moderate distinction between Gandhian nonviolence and Khan's vision of nonviolent struggle.

Khan's major objections to Gandhi's thinking are two: The first has
to do with his view of nonviolence. Gandhi took it to be a tool for
actively seeking justice by way of protest, demonstration and boycott
without resort to physical force. It implies active resistance to things
that are deemed unjust and so inevitably involves political activism.
Khan, on the other hand, is opposed to political activities such as
demonstrations and rallies. He argues that because Gandhi's nonviolent struggles amounted to political activism, they distracted people
from availing themselves of the moral and educational opportunities
at hand. By challenging the British Raj, even nonviolently, Gandhi in-
stantly aroused the emotions and political hopes of the masses, and he
did so without providing tools for developing the basic moral framework necessary for carrying out nonviolent resistance without showing his followers how to base their work on nonviolence as an ethical
principle. Nonviolence has to be adopted as part of personal morality
by individuals if it is to function in the context of social movements.
In Khan's view, nonviolent struggle implies "accepting the status quo"
and remaining apolitical, i.e. a struggle to achieve peace on the basis of
what is given rather than what is desired. He is therefore advocating
radical pacifism in response to externally imposed violence and injustice. At the same time, he is proposing that those who would engage in
this sort of resistance remain actively focused on potentially positive
ways out of seemingly hopeless situations.

Based on views held by Gandhi, Nehru and other Congress Party
leaders around 1930, it is believed that such leaders were bent on em-
barking on what later became known as a program of "civil disobedience" against the "evil British power." They began to mobilize people
against the British Raj rather than attending to an even greater problem, namely, the rise of Hindu-Muslim differences which were causing

regional conflicts. Gandhi himself was, however, very serious about Hindu-Muslim unity. His intention from the very beginning was to achieve a consensus of both Muslim and Hindu leaders along with the masses from both communities, to unite them in a common struggle against the British. Unlike some other Muslim leaders, he knew that British policy in general towards the Congress party was divisive and that the British abetted (or perhaps even devised) the politics of communalism between Hindus and Muslims.[7]

Khan also considers another of Gandhi's movements, the famous "Salt March," also referred to as "Dandi March" to be problematic. The slogan given to the average person at the time was *namak banāo, āzādī lāo* ("make salt, bring independence"). Khan believes that this and other similar movements inculcated into the masses an attitude of "rebellion." The act of resisting lawful behavior came to be glorified by this movement; it was even thought to be heroic. But when such an attitude is instilled in the mind, it is essentially impossible to control its effects on people. Hence Wahiduddin Khan contends that Hindus and Muslims would have been expected to retain such rebellious attitudes even after they achieved their immediate goal of an independent India. Once the British left, as history has shown, Indians continued to reflect a general tendency to resist law and order.[8]

Another criticism launched by Khan against Gandhi is that the latter believed that all religions are in essence "one." Khan insists that religions are different and that these differences are a natural way of leading one to the Truth. Unity cannot be brought about by claiming that there are no differences, but rather acknowledging those differences and then cultivating what he calls the "spirit of tolerance" and mutual respect among people. This is true unity: knowing the differences, yet respecting and accepting them as a fact of life for the purpose of ensuring peaceful co-existence. To bring about social harmony one must not attempt to *end* differences, but rather focus on ways to achieve harmony *in spite of* them. Differences, Khan says, are natural and they will always be there. In fact, in this world, differences are not the manifestation of evil; rather, they are the very key to human achievement. It is by becoming aware of them that human beings can cultivate a greater appreciation of, and respect for, others.[9] However in Gandhi's defense, it should be noted that he was merely referring to the moral apparatus of the religions when he said that, after examining the major religions of the world, he "... came to the conclusion that all religions were right, and every one of them imperfect, because they were interpreted with our poor intellects, sometimes with our poor hearts, and more often misinterpreted." [10]

ON JIHAD AND THE SELF

The term "jihad" is primarily used in the Qur'an to mean "struggle"— personal spiritual struggle, but never to mean "holy war." In the post-Crusades literature produced in the Muslim world, some have undoubtedly used the word " jihad" to justify wars that were seen as holy. However, this was done largely in response to usage of the same sort of notion by the crusaders. Insofar as the Qur'an is concerned, in most of the Makkan verses (revealed in the first 12 years of Muhammad's ministry) in which the term "jihad" appears, the Qur'an simply seeks to inculcate a sense of personal effort (jahada). Thus one can conclude that the term "jihad" was used definitively, and in a personal and religious sense, before any fighting between Muslims and their Makkan opponents took place. Once Muhammad left Makkah (to avoid being harmed) and moved to Madinah (known as the hijrah), the Qur'an notes that Muslims had permission to fight in order to defend themselves from invasion and aggression. The word that is used in the Qur'an to refer to this "fighting" in self–defense, or what might be termed a "necessary war," is qitāl.

In popular Muslim literature, however, the word "jihad" continued to evoke an emotional response even though the notion is primarily associated with one's inner spiritual struggle to do the common good and to give oneself to God by way of repentance and prayer, practicing patience, and by putting others before oneself. The latter, is according to the Prophet Muhammad, the "greater jihad" (jihad al-akbar), while the act of participating in a necessary war, one which is only conditional and must only be fought as a last resort is called the "lesser jihad" (jihad al-asghar).

When Gandhi uses the term "jihad," he seems to be placing it somewhere in between these two meanings, influenced as he must have been by the various sources at his disposal. His experience in South Africa, made him familiar with the terminology and symbolism needed to appeal to the Muslim mind. However, this experience was restricted to certain kinds of Muslims, mainly those from Gujarat with whom he also shared some cultural and linguistic characteristics. Addressing Muslims in India was an entirely different and perhaps more difficult experience; yet Gandhi worked relentlessly for Hindu-Muslim unity, just as he spoke out against social ills such as caste discrimination, poverty and mistreatment of women.[11]

JIHAD AS 'SATYAGRAHA'

The word *satyagraha* is often translated as "soul-force" or the power of truth, love and nonviolence.[12] It includes actions that represent nonviolent resistance to injustice. These actions vary but primarily include challenging injustice and those who are instruments of such injustice without demonizing them or denigrating their humanity. In fact, this is a way of appealing to the humanity of the oppressors. *Satyagraha* uses fasting and other self-sacrificing activities for the purpose of dissolving, as it were, self-interest or selfishness on the part of the oppressor. Jihad is defined in similar terms as a means of achieving justice. It is true that the method of the sword has been suggested for this as well. But the "greater jihad" starts long before one is even able to pick up the sword; it begins deep within one's soul and involves, first and foremost, 'cleansing the heart' of all selfishness. Jihad is primarily self-effacing, and it aims—once again—to dissolve both one's own ego and that of the oppressor.

Gandhi challenged Muslims' readiness to deal with their religious and spiritual heritage. For example, he states that the word "jihad" in the Qur'an means qualified violence—a method of last resort. At the same time, however, he argued that jihad, when it is understood as applying violent means, requires that the agent be free of any flaw before picking up the sword to attack another. In this he uses the Christic paradigm to make it impossible to justify jihad as violence. Gandhi could not completely purge the notion of jihad of its connection to violence, so he tried to frame its overall meaning in the ethos of religion in general, i.e. contextualizing it as part of a larger struggle with conditions that may be impossible for anyone to fulfill. Thus those who are themselves not free from sin should refrain from judging others and advocating jihad against them. The status of being sinless or blameless as a human being is only reserved for infants since they have not yet had a chance to err. For all practical purposes, therefore, it may be said that no human being is allowed to wage jihad of the sword since no one is really free from sin. As Gandhi states:

> . . .where is the unerring general to order Jihad? Where is the suffering and love and purification that much precede the very idea of

drawing the sword? We are too imperfect and impure and selfish to
resort to an armed conflict in the name of God.[13]

In the 1920s and '30s, Gandhi asked Muslims to join the independence movement and claimed that it was incumbent upon them to do
so, required by their faith. In some ways, he did equate "fighting" (i.e.
resisting) the British with the Islamic notion of jihad. As McDonough
points out "this was an audacious claim which elicited both response
and rejection" from the Muslim masses as well as leaders.[14] Khan
would also disagree with Gandhi's assumptions about the Muslims'
role in the freedom struggle in India.

In critiquing Gandhi's invocation of jihad as a means to political
ends, Wahiduddin Khan is restating his interpretation of jihad as
nonviolent spiritual (non-political) struggle. If the matter were pressed
further, it could be argued that, if Muslims were to implement jihad to
"fight" the British, by which Gandhi meant nonviolent political struggle, then, in the minds of many Muslims, this would translate into *fight
by all possible means*—and so eventually by violent means. But Gandhi approached other scriptures in the same way, drawing inspiration
from them actively to recruit followers for his nonviolent non-cooperation movement.[15] Nevertheless, in using the notion of jihad to recruit
Muslims in what Gandhi believed to be the nonviolent struggle, he
was playing with fire. For Muslims, *jihad* has become a highly charged
idea and often invokes the image of armed struggle. Thus Wahiduddin
Khan's critique has to be viewed within the framework of his attempts
to de-link the notion of *jihad* from any form of violence.

COLLECTIVE SELF-CRITICISM AS A MEANS TO PEACE

Gandhi maintained the view that Islam was a "liberal" religion much
like his own Hindu tradition. He was speaking of the Islam he had
discovered through the writings of Ameer Ali, Shibli Nu'mani and his
friends and colleagues, Abul Kalam Azad and Khan Abdul Ghaffar
Khan.[16] Gandhi defended Islam by contending that the intolerant ver-
sions of Islam that had surfaced were not just a liability to Muslims,
but rather that Hindus were equally to be blamed for them. The growing animosity and conflicts that occurred at this time were the result
of negative actions on the part of members of both communities. In
Gandhi's view, Hindus had a greater responsibility to diffuse the situation since they were the majority community, and they could do so

by developing trust in their Muslim neighbors and treating them with respect.[17]

Wahiduddin Khan takes this same path; he implicates his own community in the misfortunes that resulted from the communal riots, even though they often experienced much greater losses in these situations than did their Hindu neighbors. Khan takes the risk of becoming unpopular among Muslims in so far as he undertakes the task of collective self-criticism. He shows remorse for Muslim behavior, and, at the same time, ignores majority Muslim sentiment and diminishes the importance of their view of themselves as victims. He places much harsher blame on Muslim religious, secular and political leadership than on the larger community when it comes to inciting violence and creating tensions between Hindus and Muslims.[18] Khan rejects the dichotomous notion that Hindus are aggressors and Muslims are victims. In fact he blames Muslims for these tensions even though they have almost always suffered greater loss of life and property, because, in Khan's view, they did nothing to prevent the other party from becoming hostile and ultimately violent. For example, he argues that Muslims should have reached out to Hindus in an effort to diffuse tensions, long before these tensions developed into full-fledged violent actions against Muslim communities. His conclusion is that many of the problems that Muslims have faced as a minority in India since independence from the British are primarily due to their own attitudes towards, and mistrust of, Hindus.

CONCLUSION

Both Gandhi and Khan are moral idealists; both see violence as a fact of life and would permit the use of violent means if certain (albeit difficult to conceive) conditions are met. However both see the teachings of their respective religions as promoting nonviolence as a primary means of achieving resolution in human conflicts. Violence is, in their view, fundamentally a moral evil. Both are also in agreement as to the superiority of the method of nonviolence. Where they differ is in their understanding of, and involvement in, political life. Gandhi saw politics as "energy" to be turned against the very people who use political systems to oppress and impose an unjust order upon the masses. He was confident that politics could be a means for realizing the common good. By contrast to this, Wahiduddin Khan sees Islam as a religion which primarily seeks to cultivate a *moral* rather than a political ethos.

He builds a case for such an ethos through his methodical interpretation of Islamic textual sources. In this he challenges several dominant
views dealing with political and cultural traditions, both historic and
contemporary. Khan advocates the path of spirituality to address both
external and worldly problems as well as spiritual concerns. He wants
to separate religious and political domains of struggle. Gandhi combines religious and the political aspects of activism into a one unified
whole, acting more like a Muslim apologist who would deny that there
is any separation between the "church" and "state." Khan, by contrast,
seems to uphold the view similar to the Hindu notion of spiritual excellence, i.e. individual moral excellence to be attained at the expense
of worldly gains, manifested in the belief that one's existence in this
world is only temporary and thus not worth so much attention. That
attention should instead be entirely reserved for the "realization" of
one's soul (*atman*).

NOTES

1 This is, of course, a complicated issue since religions have largely been used
   in the service of political ends. This itself has apparently required violence,
   rather than being understood as the very source of it. A more nuanced
   discussion of this is beyond the scope of the present paper.

2 Martin Luther King, Jr., 1983. *The Words of Martin Luther King, Jr.* New
   York: New Market Press, 71.

3 There are many works on the life and achievements of Badshah Khan. One
   that seeks to present him in proper historical and social context and is, at
   the same time, not unnecessarily dense is Eknath Easwaran's, *Nonviolent
   Soldier of Islam: Badshah Khan, A Man to Match his Mountains.* Petaluma,
   CA: Nilgiri Press, 1984, 1999.

4 Bhikhu Parekh, 1997. *Gandhi.* London: Oxford University Press.

5 See M. K. Gandhi, 1997. *Hind Swaraj and Other Writings*, ed. Anthony J.
   Parel. Cambridge: Cambridge University Press.

6 The journal, *al-Risāla* was also published in English for some years under
   the same name. The English edition has recently resumed publication under the title *The Spiritual Message*, and is being published from Mumbai
   through an independent outlet.

7 Mark Tully states that the British policy of separate electorates, initiated
   in 1909, contributed to Hindu-Muslim tensions in its earlier phase. See
   his "India: The British Legacy Fifty Years On," in *Asian Affairs* 29, 2 (June
   1998): 134ff.

8 Maulana Wahiduddin Khan, 1988. *Tā'mīr kī taraf* [Towards progress]
   (Urdu) New Delhi: Maktaba al-Risāla.

9 *Al-Risāla* (Urdu), July 2000, 14.

10   Sachin Agarwal, "Gandhi and Faith," *Communalism Combat*, July 1998, 36.

11   Manojkumar Jha, 1990. *Hindū Muslim Ektā aur Gāndhī* [Hindu-Muslim Unity and Gandhi] (Hindi) Delhi: Sanmarg Prakashan.

12   Dennis Dalton, 1993. *Mahatma Gandhi: Nonviolent Power in Action* New York: Columbia University Press, 249.

13   M. K. Gandhi, *Young India*, 10 July 1924.

14   Sheila McDonough, 1994. *Gandhi's Responses to Islam* New Delhi: D. K. Printworld, 37.

15   McDonough, *Gandhi's Responses to Islam*, 47-8.

16   Ibid., 52-3.

17   M. K. Gandhi, 1967. *The Collected Works of Mahatma Gandhi*, vol. 19, New Delhi: Ministry of Information and Broadcasting, Government of India, 153.

18   Maulana Whiduddin Khan, "Nonviolence and Islam," unpublished paper, 12.

II. THE JESUITS AS PEACE MAKERS: NEGOTIATING WITH IVAN THE TERRIBLE, PETER THE GREAT AND SITTING BULL[1]

JOHN PATRICK DONNELLY, S.J.

Let us begin with two quotations. "Blessed are the peacemakers, for they shall be called sons of God" [Mt 5:9]. Less familiar is the statement of the Jesuit Constitutions that Jesuits are "to travel through the world and live in any part of it whatsoever where there is hope of greater service to God and of the help of souls."[2] The still earlier *Formula*, or first draft of the *Constitutions*, urged the Jesuits to be peacemakers and reconcilers for different factions within society.[3] This paper will look at three case studies of Jesuits as peacemakers. I confess that I have chosen these three cases because of their exotic locations and personalities no less than their importance.

ANTONIO POSSEVINO AND IVAN THE TERRIBLE[4]

Our first case study began on February 24, 1581, when a Russian envoy, Istoma Sevrigin, arrived unexpectedly at Rome. Papal-Russian contacts had been rare but not unprecedented. Ivan the Terrible sent Sevrigin because he was losing the Livonian War against Poland, which Ivan had started in 1563 by taking over much of Livonia—mostly today's Latvia and Estonia—from Poland. But then things

---

1 A longer version of this paper was presented at Fordham University, in March of 1995.

2 Jesuit *Constitutions*, #304.

3 *Formula*, #3.

4 The main sources for this part are Antonio Possevino, *The Moscovia*, translated and introduced by Hugh Graham (Pittsburgh: University of Pittsburgh Center for International Studies, 1977); A. M. Amann, editor, "Ioannis Pauli Campani S.I. relatio de itinere Moscovitica" *Antemurale* VI (1960-61), 1-85; Stanislas Polcin, *Une tentative d'Union au XVI siècle: La mission religieuse du pere Antoine Possevin S.J. en Moscovie (1581-1582)* (Rome: Istituto orientale, 1957); Norman Davies, *God's Playground: A History of Poland* (New York: Columbia University Press, 1982).

went sour. In 1571 the Crimean Tartars sacked Moscow. In 1578 the Swedes defeated Ivan's army. Still worse, in 1575 the Poles elected a new king, Stephan Bathory, a dedicated Catholic famous for skilled generalship. In his coronation oath Bathory promised to recover the lands that Ivan had invaded. He made good his promise. The war climaxed in 1581 when a Polish army of one hundred seventy thousand men besieged fifty-seven thousand Russians in Pskov, which lies some three hundred thirty miles south, southwest of modern St. Petersburg. The siege lasted six months until the Peace Treaty of Jam Zapolski was signed and the war ended, largely through the efforts of the Jesuit Antonio Possevino.[5]

In 1581, Ivan needed peace and tried to enlist Pope Gregory XIII's help by making vague promises to enter a Holy League against the Turks. Gregory had long dreamed of uniting Emperor Rudolf II, Venice, Bathory and Ivan against the still dangerous Ottomans. He also hoped that the Catholic faith might penetrate Ivan's Iron Curtain. It was a forlorn hope. As the Cardinal Secretary of State observed, Ivan's letter asking for papal intervention contained not a hint of religious concessions. Gregory chose as papal legate Antonio Possevino. He was to accompany Sevrigin back to Moscow and was charged with fostering religious reunion between Moscovia and Rome by mediating peace between Bathory and the Czar. He was also to seek the Czar's permission to build a few Catholic churches for the Catholic merchants trading in Moscovia.

On his way north, Possevino tried to enlist the support of Venice and of Emperor Rudolf in Prague. He then conferred several times with Bathory before heading toward Moscovia.[6] Meanwhile Possevino was studying books on Moscovia and Russian Orthodoxy and searching the Greek Church Fathers for arguments to blunt Russian charges against Catholicism.[7] On the final leg of his trip to Moscovia, Possevino was accompanied by four other Jesuits. On August 20, Ivan greeted Possevino and his companions at Staritsa on the Volga with elaborate ceremonies, but he kept the Jesuits under virtual house arrest, treating them like spies.[8] Possevino tried to open the religious question with Ivan, but the Czar only made a vague promise to discuss this after

5   Davies, 426-31.
6   Polein. 4, 9.
7   Ibid. 5-7.
8   Ibid, 13-14.

peace with the Poles was concluded. Ivan did promise to allow Latin Masses for Catholic merchants in private homes, but no Muscovite could attend these services.[9]

Meanwhile the siege of Pskov continued; sickness and a spirited Russian defense were taking a toll on the huge Polish army. Ivan wrote Bathory a long letter dated June 29 which offered terms which he claimed were advantageous, but the letter called Bathory a liar, thirsty for Christian blood, and ended with an ultimatum: if Bathory did not accept his terms Ivan would drop all diplomatic relations between Poland and Muscovy. Bathory's answer, which reached Ivan on August 2 identified Ivan with Cain, Pharaoh, Nero, Herod and even Satan. Bathory proposed that the two monarchs fight a duel: that would decide their war and spare Christian blood. If Ivan refused to duel, he deserved to be called a woman and not a man.[10] In sixteenth century diplomacy, royal egos were often more important than political or economic considerations. Both Ivan and Bathory had giant egos. Possevino, the peacemaker, had his work cut out for him.

When Ivan and Possevino met again on September 12, the Czar officially charged him with negotiating a treaty with Bathory. The final treaty should include a ten-year armistice. Possevino was then to return to the Czar, who had kept two of his Jesuit companions as hostages. Possevino sent the third Jesuit to Rome with dispatches.[11]

After five meetings with Ivan at Staritsa,[12] Possevino returned to the Polish camp. There in October he discussed Ivan's proposals with Bathory and Jan Zamoiski, the Polish Grand Chancellor. The Polish leaders decided to continue the siege of Pskov to keep pressure on Ivan, but they agreed to negotiate. Possevino informed Ivan of this, and Ivan sent delegates to meet Polish representatives near Jam Zapolski, neutral territory close to Pskov. The deliberations lasted from December 13, 1581 to January 15, 1582. Both also used various ploys to strengthen their bargaining position. Both sides threatened to leave the conference. Another ploy was to introduce irrelevant issues, then try to trade them for points on the major issues.[13] Several

---

9   Ibid,16.
10   Ibid. 10-11, 16-17.
11   Ibid., 17-22.
12   Ibid, 14-17.
13   Possevino, xxiii-xxv—Graham's Introduction.

168 JOHN PATRICK DONNELLY, S.J.

times Possevino adroitly intervened to prevent breakdowns. Even on the last day, negotiations were so fragile that the Poles threatened to walk out.[14] Possevino's book *Moscovia* gives a detailed account of the twenty-one sessions of negotiations.[15] News from the siege, now Russian successes, now Polish, affected the bargaining.

Was Possevino an honest broker, was he impartial? Yes and no. He despised Ivan as a cruel tyrant and admired Bathory.[16] Still, Possevino had strong reasons to help Ivan's representatives. They wanted peace because their country was prostrate; he wanted peace both on principle and because without a favorable peace, there was no hope of an anti-Turkish alliance, no hope of fostering religious union with the Russian church or even of establishing a tiny foothold for Catholic worship. At one point Possevino offered to forfeit his own life to Ivan rather than see the negotiations fail.[17] In the end, the Russians got the best of the bargaining. Soon after the Peace of Jam Zapolski was signed on January 15, 1582, the Poles lifted the siege of Pskov and retreated to the borders the treaty assigned them. Ivan gave up nothing that his armies had not already lost.[18]

After the treaty, Possevino went to Moscow to discuss religious issues with Ivan. Now that he had peace, Ivan was willing to yield nothing—indeed he became so angry while debating theology with Possevino that he raised his iron-tipped staff to bash in the Jesuit's brains.[19]

THE TREATY OF NERCHINSK, 1689

The month of August 1689 was a landmark in Russian history for two reasons. In Moscow Peter the Great's supporters overthrew the Regent Sophia and made young Peter the Great effective ruler. On August 27 [old style] thousands of miles to the east at Nerchinsk, Russian and Chinese diplomats concluded a treaty which determined a border between Russia and China which, with minor adjustments, lasted for nearly one hundred seventy years. By the Treaty of Nerchinsk the

---

14 Ibid, 139.
15 Ibid, 106-39.
16 Ibid, xiv, xix, xxiv—Graham's Introduction.
17 Ibid, 123, 125.
18 Ibid, xxv.
19 Ibid, 72.

Russians ceded to the Chinese land almost equivalent to Germany and France combined.

Nerchinsk was the first treaty made by China with a European powerer and the first to be worked out according to European patterns of diplomacy. Earlier the Chinese had viewed foreign countries, whether Asian or European, not as sovereign equals but as mere tributaries.

Ivan the Terrible had encouraged Russian expansion eastward, and Cossack pioneers had begun to explore and conquer the vast reaches of Siberia. This brought the Russians up against lands that the Chinese had long regarded as their own. Although local peoples had accepted a vague Chinese suzerainty as far back as the fifteenth century, the Chinese had never effectively ruled the region. Gradually Russian traders moved south to the Amur River, the Russian-Chinese border today. Russian soldiers built forts, notably at Albazin.

In 1680, the great Chinese Emperor Kang Xi was determined to stop these encroachments and sent troops to build forts in the disputed territory. He consolidated the new Manchu dynasty which ruled China until the early twentieth century. In 1685 he sent a large Chinese army to assault Albazin, the most forward Russian outpost. The Russians surrendered and retreated north to Nerchinsk. The Chinese army destroyed the fort and returned home. The next year the Russians returned and rebuilt their fort at Albazin. Kang Xi ordered his army to retake it. The second siege lasted thirteen months. The Russians started with eight hundred twenty-six men; less than seventy were still alive when the Chinese lifted the siege after Peter decided to negotiate the border between the world's two largest countries.[20]

---

20 The most important source for this section on the treaty of Nerchinsk is Joseph Sebes, *The Jesuits and the Sino-Russian Treaty of Nerchinsk* (1689) (Rome: IHSI, 1961), 67-70. I have also used John J. Stephan, *The Russian Far East: A History* (Stanford: Stanford University Press 1994), 26-49, 278; Yuri Semyonov, *Siberia: Its Conquest and Development* (Montreal: International Publishers, 1963), translated by J.R. Foster, 113-23, 274-75; George V. Lantzeff and Richard A. Pierce, *Eastward to Empire: Exploration and Conquest on the Russian Open Frontier to 1750* (Montreal McGill-Queen's University Press, 1973), 178-82, and Benson Bobrick, *East of the Sun: The Epic Conquest and Tragic History of Siberia* (NY: Poseidon Press, 1992), 88-90. The text of the treaty is printed in *Russia's Conquest of Siberia: 1558-1700* (N.P.: Western Imprints, Oregon Historical Society, 1985) edited by Basil Dmytryshyn et al., Vol. I, #133. On Chinese attitudes in dealing with foreigners, see Sebes, 114. Also useful are Carl Bickford

The Chinese would be negotiating from strength, but they wanted a settlement badly so they deal could with Mongol tribes. The Russians too needed peace in Siberia since they had to face the Ottomans, the Poles and the Swedes in the West, and their treasury was depleted. Both China and Russia hoped that peace would foster trade between Russian and China. Both were at the limits of their reach along the Amur River. These economic, geographic and strategic factors were more important than the Jesuit contribution to the final peace.

The Chinese delegation arrived first on July 20 at Nerchinsk and included some fifteen thousand men, mainly troops. The Russian garrison at Nerchinsk numbered a mere five hundred men. On August 9, the Russian chief negotiator, Fyodor Golovin, arrived with fifteen hundred troops and the Polish translator Andrei Belbotskii, who was as fluent in Latin. The final treaty was concluded August 27, 1685.

The lead Chinese negotiator was Prince Songgotu, commander of the Emperor's bodyguard and an old friend of the Beijing Jesuits. He was helped by Sabsu, the governor of northern Manchuria, who had commanded the Chinese army during both attacks on Albazin.[21] The negotiations were to be conducted in Latin; the official text of the treaty was in Latin, with a Chinese translation for the Chinese and a Russian translation for the Russians. The text was the work of two Beijing Jesuits, but they were far more than mere translators. They informed the Chinese delegation about the outside world and about European negotiating procedures. The two Jesuits were the Frenchman François Gerbillon and the Portuguese Thomas Pereira. Pereira had long been the Emperor's personal music teacher; Gerbillon later became his official geographer. As Pereira was departing, Kang Xi gave him his own gown and told Songgotu to treat the two Jesuits as the Emperor himself—no doubt a bit of hyperbole, but significant. He told the Jesuits, "I am treating you with the honor and distinction that I accord to my grandees, whom you shall accompany...." The Jesuits

---

O'Brien, *Russia under Two Tsars, 1682-1689: The Regency of Sophia Alek-seeva* (Berkeley: University of California Press, 1952), 105 ff. and Fred W. Bergholz, *The Partition of the Steppes: the Struggle of the Russians, Manchus and the Zunghar Mongols for Empire in Central Asia, 1619-1758: A Study in Power Politics* (New York: Peter Lang, 1994).

21   Semyonov, 115-16.

did not fit into any regular Chinese category of officials, but influence often escapes fixed categories.[22]

Jesuit influence in Beijing had grown since Matteo Ricci arrived there in 1601. The Jesuits quickly established themselves as the emperors' main geographers and calendar makers. They served as the key conduit for western science, mathematics, geography, philosophy, art and religion to the Chinese, and of Chinese culture to the West. The Jesuit hope of finding a Chinese Constantine failed. Still, the favor the Jesuits enjoyed at court secured a measure of toleration for Christian missionary work anywhere in China.

There are three main accounts of the Nerchinsk negotiations. Both Jesuits wrote diaries of them. There is also Golovin's official report to Peter the Great. Because Emperor Kang Xi did not want his negotiating with Western barbarians as equals to set a precedent, it seems there were no comparable Chinese accounts.

The Jesuits' motives for participating in the negotiations were mixed. Ending the Russian-Chinese hostilities was important, but Nerchinsk also offered an opportunity to earn the Emperor's favor. This the Jesuits achieved. Three years later, Kang Xi issued a decree which permitted any Chinese to become Christian.[23]

The Jesuits also tried to win the favor of the Russians. The Jesuits needed a new route to China through Russia and Siberia. Since Matteo Ricci's days, the Jesuits had come east under the patronage of the Portuguese crown, but the Portuguese empire in the Orient was crumbling under Dutch assaults. Increasingly the Italian, Portuguese and Spanish Jesuits in China were being replaced by French Jesuits. Louis XIV did not want Frenchmen to be subject to the Portuguese patronage and urged finding a new route.[24] French-Portuguese rivalry among the Jesuits in China, represented at Nerchinsk by Gerbillon and Pereira, does not seem to have hurt their work.

The Portuguese route was long, dangerous and unhealthy. Of the six hundred Jesuits sent to China before the Treaty of Nerchinsk, only one hundred arrived. "All the rest," we are told, "had been destroyed by shipwreck, illness, murder, or capture by pirates or other robbers." [25]

---

22   Sebes, 110, 119.

23   Semyonov, 122; Sebes, 78, 109. In 1717 Kang Xi cancelled the decree in the aftermath of the Chinese Rites controversy.

24   Sebes, 87, 88.

25   Sebes, 96. Semyonov, 114.

Both sides at Nerchinsk wanted peace, but a final agreement did not come easily. Hard bargaining was required to make them accept compromises. Here the Jesuits were the necessary catalyst. At the first session the Chinese demanded that the Russians surrender all the land between Lake Baikal and the Pacific—an area equivalent to the land from Boston to Denver. The Russians refused, and the Chinese dropped that opening ploy the next day. Pereira worked hard to get the Chinese to accept the Russians as equals, not barbarians.[26] As the negotiations continued, the Chinese turned more to the Jesuits for advice, rather to the annoyance of the Russians, who felt that they might otherwise have gained an advantage. It is impossible to trace all the rough spots in the negotiations. Some items from the section headings in Pereira's diary include:

Second meeting ends in an impasse.

Chinese distrust so great that war is imminent.

Russians refuse Chinese demand that Albazin be the border.

Russian intransigence, Chinese counter measures.

Most of Chinese give up hope.

Russians ask for new meeting but delay making proposals.

Russians ask for Jesuits to go to their camp—Chinese allow only Gerbillon to go.

Belbotskii brings new proposals for protocols in future negotiations.

Difficulties over having the Noz mountain as a border.

Russians send protest letter to Chinese.

Jesuits visit Russian camp to urge concessions.

New Russian proposals, Chinese counter proposals.

Jesuits urge Russians to come to a decision; urge Chinese to be patient.

Celebration following the signing of the treaty.[27]

Clearly, without the Jesuit brokers, the Nerchinsk negotiations would probably have been aborted. Two recent scholars have said that the treaty "may be considered one of the most successful ever made, in-

26   Sebes, 108.

27   Sebes, 172-73. I have rephrased, shortened and dropped many of these entries for the sake of brevity.

augurating a period of peace which lasted for one hundred seventy years." [28]

SITTING BULL AND FATHER PIERRE-JEAN DE [29]

For our last Jesuit peacemaker, we must leap almost two hundred years forward and across the Pacific to the mid-western United States. By 1867, the Civil War was over. But what of the Indians? In 1867 Congress set up a Peace Commission, which has been termed "a reasonable mixture of military firmness and humanitarian leniency." [30] The Commission, admitting that past wars were mainly due to the white man, said, "But it is said our wars with them have been nearly constant. Have we been uniformly unjust? We answer unhesitatingly, yes." [31] The Commission had a new "hitherto untried policy... to conquer by kindness" [32]—to settle the Indians on reservations which would be off-limits to all white men except Indian agents and missionaries, give them personal possession of plots, if they wanted them, up to three hundred twenty acres for a family, farming implements, seed, and training for the men in how to farm, for the women in how to make clothes. The army pulled back and burned its forts. Both humanitarians and the military were convinced that the treaties were the Indians' last chance to survive. [33]

---

28   Lantzeff, 181.

29   For this part of the paper I have used the following sources: Robert M. Utley, *The Lance and the Shield: The Life and Times of Sitting Bull* (New York: Henry Holt, 1993); Stanley Vestal, *Sitting Bull: Champion of the Sioux, A Biography* (Norman: University of Oklahoma Press 1932/ reprint 1956); H.M. Chittenden and A. T. Richardson, *The Life, Letters and Travels of Father Pierre-Jean De Smet, 1801-1878* (New York: Francis P. Harper, 1905) Vol. III; John J. Killoren, *"Come Blackrobe"* (Norman: University of Oklahoma Press, 1993); John Upton Terrell, *Black Robe: The Life of Pierre-Jean De Smet, Missionary, Explorer & Pioneer* (Garden City, N.Y.: Doubleday, 1964); Gilbert J. Garraghan, *The Jesuits of the Middle United States* (New York: America Press, 1938) Vol. III; Francis Paul Prucha, *The Great Father: The United States Government and the American Indians* (Lincoln: University of Nebraska Press, 1989) 2 vols.

30   Prucha, I, 490.

31   Ibid I, 491.

32   Ibid.

33   Killoren, 315

But how to convince the tribes to sign the treaties? Secretary of
the Interior, H. O. Browning, appointed as "envoy extraordinary" the
famous Belgian Jesuit, Pierre-Jean De Smet to this task. The native
Americans esteemed De Smet the Black Robe more than any other
white man. General William Harney, a member of the Peace Commission, claimed that De Smet "has almost unbounded influence over the
Indians."[34] Starting in 1844, De Smet had made five major journeys
among the tribes securing peace. Late in 1867, he traveled from St.
Louis to Fort Buford near the borders of North Dakota, Montana,
and Canada. He sat in council with tribe after tribe, an estimated fifteen thousand Indians, and urged them to accept the treaties. Later
that year, the land being offered the Indians was reduced to less than
half his own recommendations.[35] He returned to St. Louis to prepare
for a second trip but his health collapsed—he was 68.

By April 1868 his health had been sufficiently restored for him to
join five generals, including William T. Sherman and Phil Sheridan, in
a special train across Nebraska. Enroute they held a successful meeting with leaders of the Brûlés tribe.[36] Sherman promised adequate
hunting grounds and protection from white intruders and distributed
presents to the Indians.

But what of the hostile Hunkpapa Sioux who were hiding somewhere in the upper reaches of the Missouri and Yellowstone Rivers?
Sherman proposed that De Smet go and find them. De Smet's boat
trip up the Missouri took thirty-three days and included many stops
to discuss the treaty with tribes along the way. Many chiefs warned him
against going to the Sioux, saying that it would cost him his scalp. But
when he insisted on going forward, eighty Indians from seven tribes
accompanied De Smet, his old friend and interpreter, C.E. Galpin,
and Galpin's famous Sioux wife, Eagle Woman. De Smet had warned
Galpin, "I know the danger of such a trip. I have no other motives than
the welfare of the Indians and will trust to the kind providence of
God."[37]

The expedition set out on June 3, 1868. Thirteen days later their
scouts made contact with eighteen Hunkpapa Sioux. The next day as
the Sioux and De Smet advanced down the Powder River valley, sud-

34   Terrell, 348; Utley, 77; for Harney's quote: Killoren, 310.
35   Terrell, 349-56; Killoren, 309.
36   Killoren, 313-16.
37   Chittenden, 896.

denly five hundred warriors came racing toward them. De Smet unfurled a banner of the Blessed Virgin he had carried for the occasion. The Sioux were intrigued by the strange flag and came up to shake De Smet's hand and led him into Sitting Bull's vast camp of some five thousand warriors.[38]

De Smet exhausted, asked for food, then fell asleep. When he awoke he was face to face with Sitting Bull and three other chiefs. Just days earlier, Sitting Bull had led raids near Forts Buford and Stevenson which killed two white men and captured two mail riders of mixed blood. Sitting Bull stripped the riders and sent them back to the army with the message that he and his chiefs would not meet with the Peace Commissioners and would go on killing white men till they all cleared out of Indian country.[39] Sitting Bull now addressed De Smet: "Blackrobe, I hardly sustain myself beneath the weight of white man's blood that I have shed. The whites provoked the war" with a massacre of some seven hundred "women, children and old men.... I rose, tomahawk in hand, and I have done all the hurt to the whites that I could. Today thou art amongst us and ... I will listen to thy good words, and bad as I have been to the whites, just so good am I ready to become toward them."[40] Sitting Bull promised to convene a Great Council.

The Great Council met on June 21, 1868 and drew some five thousand Indians. After passing the peace pipe with leading chiefs, De Smet spoke and urged the Indians to renounce war and embrace the Great Father's offer of land, farming implements, domestic animals and training. Otherwise the sheer power of the white man and his armies and the dying off of the buffalo and other game meant inevitable death. The four chiefs spoke and agreed. De Smet wrote a summary of Black Moon's speech, who concluded, "We have been forced to hate the whites; let them treat us like brothers and the war will cease. Let them stay home; we will never go to trouble them.... Let us throw a veil over the past, and let it be forgotten."[41]

De Smet left the Indian camp and traveled three hundred fifty miles to Fort Rice, where, together with three generals and the representatives of some fifty thousand Indians, he signed the peace treaty on July 2. Eight speakers from among the twenty tribes represented paid

38 Terrell, 369-70; Chittenden, 909-11; Killoren, 319.
39 Utley, 78; Chittenden, 912.
40 Chittenden, 912; Terrell, 371.
41 Chittenden 916-17; Killoren 320-21; Terrell 372-74.

special tribute to De Smet and his work. The next day the generals wrote De Smet: "You will find your true reward for your labors and for the dangers and privations you have encountered in the consciousness that you have done much to promote peace on earth and good will to men."[42] On July 4, the army distributed presents and De Smet left for St. Louis University. When he got home, he was so sick that the doctors despaired of his life. Again he recovered and lived until 1873.[43] The peace did not last so long.

The sequel to this story is well known. In August 1868, roving bands of Indians raided and killed in Kansas and Colorado. On November 27, Lieutenant Colonel George Custer's men raided a sleeping village of Cheyennes and killed more than one hundred Indians. Eight years later, Sitting Bull avenged that at the Little Big Horn. In 1871, Congress gave up making treaties with native American groups as if they were foreign nations.[44] De Smet was therefore the least successful of our Jesuit peacemakers, but through no fault of his own.

CONCLUSIONS: JESUITS AS PEACEMAKERS

Let us try to draw some tentative generalizations from these three test cases of Jesuits as peacemakers. In no case did they cause the peace; rather the warring nations saw peace as more desirable than war for military, economic, and political reasons. But this realization is often not enough to secure peace. In earlier times, the ego of monarchs and, in modern times the rage of nationalism have kept nations fighting to the point of either total defeat or total victory. Would not all the nations of Europe have profited if they had embraced Benedict XV's peace proposals in 1917? Yet, the slaughter continued until empires crumbled.

In all three of our cases, the Jesuits acted as catalysts. They were able to play this role because they enjoyed a degree of trust from both sides. Why trust? Ironically, because they were outsiders, persons who had little to gain from victory and much to gain from peace. Possevino was an Italian mediating between Poles and Russians. Gerbillon and Pereira were western Europeans in a dispute between Chinese and Russians. De Smet was a Belgian—Sitting Bull and the Sioux may

---

42   Chittenden, 922.
43   Chittenden, 919-21; Terrell, 375; Killoren, 322-27.
44   Prucha, II 495-96; Killoren, 297-329.

not have known this, but he did not fit their usual categories for white men. He was a Black Robe, a special category, certainly neither army nor government agent nor settler, rather a man who had long enjoyed charismatic relations with Indians. Peace is built on trust, and the Indians trusted De Smet when he told them that their only alternative to the hated reservation was extermination, for they knew he had their interests at heart.

At Jam Zapolski, the Russians knew that Possevino preferred the Poles, yet they could trust his basic neutrality because he in principle wanted peace and because his other goals—the alliance against the Turks, opening Russia to Catholicism and eventual church reunion—could not grow out of a treaty which hurt Moscovia. Likewise at Nerchinsk, the Jesuits were in the employ of the Chinese emperor, but the Russians knew that the Jesuits wanted that alternative route to China across Siberia, and for that they needed peace and Russian benevolence.

What did the Jesuits as such gain from their peace making? Possevino's work gained nothing from Ivan but it did increase Bathory's favor toward the Jesuits. Nerchinsk was followed by a short-lived edict of toleration in China. De Smet's work was undone within months. These three Jesuit peace efforts have generally been praised by historians—for all that's worth—but not always: several nineteenth century Russian historians blamed the Jesuits for the loss of the Amur River Valley and, ironically, a Soviet historian praised them.[45] What did the Jesuits really gain? Christ's commendation: "Blessed are the peacemakers."

---

45 Stephan, 32, Sebes, 77; Semyonov, 118, 122.

12. THE ROLE OF THE CHURCH IN CONFLICT MANAGEMENT IN NORTHERN IRELAND

HIDEYUKI KOYAMA, S.J.

"**R**eligion as it relates to conflict is a double-edged sword; it can cause conflict or it can reduce it," [1] as Johnston and Sampson say. The Catholic Church, for example, supported an oppressive elite during much of Filipino history; similarly, the South African Dutch Reformed Church provided the theological justification for apartheid. But, as far as religion and society are concerned, there is the other side to the coin—a positive one that comes into play in varying degrees in each of these cases. [2]

In this paper, I will argue first that the Catholic Church could be an instrument of peace in Northern Ireland. Secondly, most of the research carried out thus far on conflict management in Northern Ireland has been done at the macro-political level. David Bloomfield [3] has dealt with the cultural-community level, but has only minimally discussed the role of the churches. I will therefore attempt to fill this gap. This paper will not, however, be a full case study of the activities of the Church there, but only an attempt to highlight those which seem most relevant. My main purpose is to show what is possible, what the Church could do to lessen the conflict. [4] To begin with, I will provide a brief sketch of background of the conflict in Northern Ireland.

---

1 Douglas Johnston and Cynthia Sampson, eds, 1994. *Religion, The Missing Dimension of Statecraft*. Oxford: Oxford University Press, p. 269.

2 Ibid., p. 269.

3 David Bloomfield, 1997. *Peacemaking Strategy in Northern Ireland:Building Complementarity in Conflict Management Theory*. London: Macmillan Press Ltd.

4 A more comprehensive discussion of peacemaking in Northern Ireland can be found in 'Grassroots Peacemaking in Northern Ireland: A Typology' (John D Brewer, 'Northern Ireland: Peacemaking among Protestants and Catholics', Mary Ann Cejka and Thomas Bamat, eds, 2003. *Artisans of Peace: Grassroots Peacemaking among Christian Communities*. New York: Orbis Books, pp.74-90).

180   HIDEYUKI KOYAMA, S.J.

BACKGROUND OF THE NORTHERN IRELAND CONFLICT[5]

The Northern Ireland conflict is one which divides Catholics (43.76% of the population) and Protestants (53.13%). [6] It is supposedly a religious war, one which has been fought over doctrinal principles between people for whom religion is the primary source of identity. Yet, religion disguises the conflict's inherently political character. The terms 'Catholic' and 'Protestant' do not have the same meaning in Northern Ireland as in most parts of the world. That is, generally speaking, they indicate a purely religious difference, between two kinds of Christians. However, in Northern Ireland, where religion is so closely linked to other differences, they involve a combination of ethnic, social, economic and other differences, all subsumed under the heading of religious allegiance. [7] The conflict there may be over the legitimacy of the state and access to its political, economic, and cultural resources, but religious affiliation defines the boundaries of the groups that are in competition. Religion has an indirect influence on the conflict. And, it seems to have been instigated by both parties—by the Catholics because of either their subordinate political and economic position or their aspiration for a united Ireland, and by the Protestants who fear being taken over by the Republic of Ireland. It is not as intense as many others in the world, for example, that in Aceh, Indonesia. However, the fact that it is played out in the First World has caused it to draw massive amounts of world attention.

The current situation in Northern Ireland is the legacy of the sixteenth century social structure created by what is termed a process of "Plantation," or voluntary migration of English and Scottish Protestants to that country. The planters in Ulster came predominantly from Scotland as opposed to from England. They brought with them Presbyterianism and its tendency to separatism. From the beginning of the venture, the Presbyterians had experienced exclusion at the hands of

5 John D Brewer, 'Northern Ireland: Peacemaking among Protestants and Catholics' in Mary Ann Cejka and Thomas Bamat, eds, 2003. *Artisans of Peace: Grassroots Peacemaking among Christian Communities.* New York: Orbis Books.

6 April 2001, Northern Ireland Census, *Background Information on Northern Ireland Society-Population and Vital Statistics* (http://cain.ulst.ac.uk/ni/popul.htm)

7 John Whyte, 1990. *Interpreting Northern Ireland.* Oxford: Oxford University Press, p. 105.

the Anglicans. Scots outnumbered the English in Ulster by a ratio of five to one in 1640.

Throughout the eighteenth and nineteenth centuries, Ireland essentially remained a Plantation society. That is, the social structure created at the time of this process of plantation became fixed in place. Its lines of differentiation produced Protestant-Catholic divisions, and these came to represent all other lines of cleavage. The economy of the Protestant-dominated East Coast developed more rapidly than the rest of Ireland because of the linen factories and shipbuilding activities that centered around the port of Belfast. Economic developments in the nineteenth century reinforced the division of the island into two identity groups, mutually sculpted in opposition to each other. And, it became increasingly difficult to contain both in one territory. Social-structural strains eventually developed to the point that the colonial society 'planted' there in the sixteenth century was overturned in 1921, at least in twenty-six of the country's counties, with the partition of the island into a Catholic dominated Irish Republic and a Protestant dominated Northern Ireland.

Catholics in Northern Ireland felt like second-class citizens compared to Protestants when it came to privileges, rights, and opportunities. A sustained period of civil unrest occurred after 1968, when Catholic demands for civil rights were initially rejected and dealt with forcefully by both the police and Protestant organizations. The violence that has occurred since 1968 has intensified long-standing traditional hatreds. Everyone involved seems justified in assuming the status of victim, with Catholics being victims of four centuries of social exclusion, and Protestants, of thirty years of terrorism. And, both view the other as the perpetrator. Reciprocal acts of blame and mutually exclusive claims to victimhood complicate peacemaking, since victims' demands for justice can be divisive unless they are extended to all who have suffered. Thus peacemaking needs to be broadly understood as doing more than merely bringing an end to violence. Issues of equality, justice and political and civil rights also resonate through the ages.

While a peace process had been under way since 1997 with the various ceasefires declared by the paramilitary groups, the main political parties reached an historic accord, the Belfast Agreement or Good Friday Agreement, on April 10, 1998. On July 29, 2005 the Provisional IRA, the main paramilitary group on the Catholic side, issued a statement confirming that its armed struggle would end and that all IRA

units had been ordered to lay down their arms. On September 26, the
IRA declared that it had put its formidable armory out of commission, an assertion which was supported by the Canadian decommis-
sioning expert General John de Chastelain, together with a Catholic
priest and a Protestant minister.

THE ROLE OF THE CHURCH IN CONFLICT MANAGEMENT IN NORTHERN IRELAND[8] CONFLICT RESOLUTION AND CONFLICT SETTLEMENT

In the absence of a generally accepted term for this area of study, "conflict management" is used to denote no particular type or theoretical approach to conflict, but merely provides a general context within
which Bloomfield frames his argument. There are the two poles of
current thinking in conflict management theory: that which favors
power-bargaining, negotiation and compromise to achieve resolution,
and that which promotes non-negotiated, cooperative problem-solving
to achieve a deep and integrative solution. For the sake of convenience,
the two approaches can be styled respectively 'conflict settlement' and
'conflict resolution.'

The resolution approach prescribes an outcome derived through
mutual problem sharing, a format in which the parties cooperate with
each other to redefine both their conflict and their relationship. Far
from compromising or bargaining away any of their goals, they engage
in a process of information sharing, relationship building, joint analysis and cooperation. For this to be possible, they must be able, as it
were, to delve into the issues which are driving their conflict and find
a deeper level on which to build a new relationship. That is, they must
find shared values that transcend the issues that caused the conflict to
erupt in the first place.

Underlying this approach is the assumption that the roots of conflict lie in the subjective relationships between the disputants. This
implies that transformation of the conflict is possible through transformation of the disputants' perceptions of it, and of each other. Out
of the seedbed of the existing relationship grow the issues that spark
a conflict—and, in fact, the conflict is really about something deeper.
Feelings and perceptions must be shared and acknowledged, and mutual trust and understanding developed. Only then can the issues be

8 Hideyuki Koyama, 2005. *Ethnic Conflict and Religion: A Study of the Church in Northern Ireland*. Kyoto: Horitsubunka-sha (ISBN 4-589-02843-3)

cooperatively addressed within the context of a new relationship between the partners. Conflict resolution aims to remove not only the current manifestation of the conflict, but its underlying cause insofar as it redefines and reconciles the parties' relationship with each other. The work of redefining this inter-disputant relationship is given priority over all other tasks.

All human beings share the same basic needs. But, cultural variation among our different identity groups gives us different means of satisfying them. In this sense we are in competition with other groups. Human needs may be the basis of conflict, but they are also, in an indirect sense, the means for solving it. Identical, shared needs are the transcendent common elements of the parties in a conflict. It is when people have a grasp of these that they can allow them to transform their relationships into a cooperative one. Needs are the deeper stratum of commonality below the surface level of incompatible interests. They are the common ground out of which cooperative efforts towards integrative solutions can be forged. And, it is here that we must speak of the facilitative role of the third party as envisaged by the resolution theorists, namely, that of creating the opportunity for communication and discussion and providing information, while, at the same time, allowing the conflicting parties to keep to their own initiatives in the search for solution.

In contrast to conflict resolution, conflict settlement prescribes an outcome that is built on agreement reached by the conflicting parties through negotiation and bargaining. By this definition, a settlement means an agreement over the issue(s) of the conflict, one that often involves a compromise, or some concessions from both sides. It can be the case that neither achieves all of their desired goals, but this disappointment is offset by the mutuality of the compromise. Formal negotiation and political bargaining are examples of this approach. If politics is the art of the possible, then settlement is simply the art of the practical. Underlying this approach is a particular view of the nature, form and roots of conflict. It takes it to be generated in response to objective, power-related issues. Since 1969, the main agents involved in attempts to settle the conflict in Northern Ireland have been the British and Irish governments and the Irish political parties.

THE ROLE OF THE CHURCH

The resolution approach is the mode of engagement of the Church in Northern Ireland. It is well recognized that the Primate of the Church of Ireland, Archbishop Robin Eames, Presbyterian minister Roy Magee and Redemptorist priests were influential in brokering the paramilitary cease-fires and facilitating political agreements. These are the examples of the types of work the churches engaged in, work that affected change at the macro-political level. For Fr. Alex Reid and Fr. Gerry Reynolds, Redemptorists who also influenced the political process, the important factor is "dialogue and contact." They accepted paramilitaries as fellow human beings and built relationships with them. They delved deep into their psyches and asked why they resorted to violence. Bloomfield says that "(Conflict) resolution aims to remove not only the current manifestations of the conflict but its underlying causes, by addressing, redesigning and reconciling the parties' relationships with each other." [9] The Redemptorists tried to grasp the underlying causes of the conflict. And they succeeded in persuading the paramilitaries to partake in a democratic way eventually to produce a just society. In other words, this was not just a political conflict but a human one.

There are numerous other examples of such work conducted at the grassroots level, many of which seem more modest in scope. The difficulties which prevent the Catholic Church as an institution from playing a positive role in the peace process arise from its lack of interaction with the working-class people and paramilitaries on the one hand, and with Protestants on the other. The initiatives presented here as case studies have attempted to facilitate contact and dialogue among these groups.

The Jesuits set up a community in Portadown in County Armagh in 1980. Portadown is the most sectarian town in Northern Ireland and is close to where the Orange Order[10] was founded. In Portadown, Protestants are in the great majority and Catholics have suffered as second class citizens since the town came into existence. The Jesuits in Portadown do not have a parish church. They have chosen to live in

9 Bloomfield, p. 69.

10 The Orange Order is a Protestant political society dedicated to sustaining the 'glorious and immortal memory' of William of Orange and of his victory over James II at the Boyne in 1690, a victory which confirmed the Protestant ascendancy in Ireland.

a public housing complex in a Catholic area and to have a part in the ordinary struggles of the ordinary people, to be involved in the work of community development and building bridges. And, they have chosen to share the pain of working class Catholics as second-class citizens, to become the voice of the voiceless.

Mrs Norma McConville, a member of the Church of Ireland, was an officer of the Housing Executive and developed a good working relationship with the Jesuits at Iona Community in Portadown. She made great efforts to improve the housing situation in Churchill Park and was awarded the M.B.E. [Member of the British Empire] for her cross-community work in January 1996. She says:

> Declan and Brian Lennon were running a Women's Group, Guided Prayer Group, etc. They invited me. I went out anyway. It was a great learning experience for me. I was learning about myself. Listening to others…there must be equal rights of people. I started off with friendship. I found Iona at ease. I had the freedom to speak until I understood better. They challenged me gently. They opened me to different things. I have a great respect for them. We worked out a relationship. There was mistrust of Jesuits among Protestants. I was prepared to meet them as friends. I have grown, listening to them. They accepted me. They listened to my point of view. They allowed me to grow all the time. They never excluded me. We worshipped together. By attending the Women's Group I could get insights about the life of the Catholics from the women's point of view.

According to Jim Borsey, a local leader of Community Centre, Churchill Park was built in the 1960s and 1970s. Protestants were also living there. Priority was given to young couples and ex-servicemen. When the Jesuits arrived in 1980-81, Churchill Park was a slum. The houses were empty and it looked like a drinking club. Borsey said: "We moved there as a newly-married couple. Many people abused alcohol. We could hear shots being fired. It was very depressing. My wife was almost close to a nervous breakdown." Jesuits lived among them and taught them how to organize themselves, take responsibility for themselves and generally have more self-respect.

The Jesuits responded to their developmental needs while at the same time building relationships with Protestant people. Building bridges from Churchill Park was inevitably a difficult task, and many things were done to achieve this such as the race which was held in the town attended by young Protestants and Catholics, the conjoint meetings of clergy of different denominations, the cross-community Passion drama, the history conference, etc. Brian Lennon, S.J. recounted the following story:

> Recently a group of Catholics and Protestants from Portadown met in our community centre with representatives from Catholic and Protestant Churches in England, Scotland and Wales. A local lay Catholic spoke about his feelings as a Catholic. A local Protestant minister felt it portrayed him as an oppressor. A heated discussion took place. But no one walked out. People were still talking to each other at the end of the meeting. More encounters are planned. Reconciliation work, if it is to be real, needs to explore feelings, to help people speak the truth in charity, to move beyond politeness.

Rev. David Chillingworth, Rector of Seagoe Parish Church (Church of Ireland) emphasizes the grassroots character of the acts of reconciliation in Portadown:

> Firstly, what has been attempted here has been almost entirely 'grassroots' in character. It comes out of local working-class communities, both Protestant and Catholic. It hasn't been a 'top-down' development in any way. Secondly, the movement that is developing has a very broad base. It has involved churches, community activists, Craigavon Council, external funding agencies and local business. People have given each other enormous encouragement. None of us knows what the future holds in terms of the 'big picture.' But I remain firmly convinced that the future big picture and the small picture are inextricably linked. If anything will give the politicians courage to create an imaginative settlement of our problems, it must be what they see happening on the ground in local communities. I hope that they will take a look at Portadown.

After the Jesuits' extensive involvement in the Orange Parade issue, [11] the work of building bridges has become much more difficult. Still, it is generally acknowledged that reconciliation is a long process and

---

11   The parade of the Orange Order. For the Catholics the Orange Parade issue is basically a matter of equal citizenship. For the Protestants it is mainly a cultural issue: they fear that their cultural tradition may be undermined. Confrontation between the Orange order and Catholic residents had become acute by the mid 1990s for two reasons. The population had become segregated during the 25 years of war. Both sides had projected their fears and aspirations onto disputes over parades routes, giving the parades enormous symbolic importance. The most significant dispute was over the route of an Orange Order parade, on the Sunday before the

happens only over time. Reconciliation and better community relations require greater self-confidence and self-esteem among members of the Catholic community as well. In my view, this is a necessary prerequisite for reconciliation and better intra-community relations. As stated in *Violence in Ireland: A Report to the Churches*:

> For too long society maintained some sort of order by restraining the energies of the underprivileged or canalizing them solely into physical work. Reconciliation means accepting those energies, developing them and seeking to integrate them constructively into the building of a just social order with which all can identify.[12]

The Jesuits played an important part in this process, as can be seen in the interviews and their struggles in the Orange Parade issue. And the work they have done is certainly perceptible when one enters into the community centre and attends meetings that are taking place there.

Building up the confidence and self-esteem of one community in this conflict-ridden situation, however, may have adverse consequences for members of the other. As Catholics become more self-confident, working class Protestants feel more threatened and hence become aggressive. This is especially obvious when the Protestants refuse to recognize that the Catholics have been put down. There needs to be a similar program of community development for marginalized Protestants.

In Northern Ireland people see things differently, depending on which community they come from. For most of the middle-class Protestants, the conflict in Northern Ireland is equated with the existence of the IRA. They cannot see the sufferings which most of the Catholics have gone through. The RUC (Royal Ulster Constabulary) was the best police force in Western Europe for most of the Protestants, while it was viewed as a disgrace by working class Catholics. Thus both parties to the conflict assumed the status of victim—Catholics being victims of four centuries of social exclusion, Protestants, of thirty years of terrorism. As Bloomfield notes, the roots of the conflict often lie in the subjective relationships between the disputants. Transformation of the conflict is possible only through transformation of the disputants' perceptions of it, and of each other. Feelings and perceptions

12th of July, from the Church of Ireland Church of Drumcree through the Catholic Garvaghy Road area.

12   *Violence in Ireland: A Report to the Churches*. Revised edition, 1977. Dublin: Gill and Macmillan.

must be shared and acknowledged, and mutual trust and understanding developed. In this context, the value of Protestants and Catholics living together is immense. The Clonard/Fitzroy Fellowship, "Unity Pilgrims" (Redemptorists), Cornerstone Community, the Irish School of Ecumenics and the Columbanus Community of Reconciliation (Catholics and Protestants living, praying and studying together) have fostered an empathy, and a strong yearning for unity, both religious and political. Empathy has enabled them to see things from the other's point of view. Becoming a peacemaker has been a challenge to be received anew in every relationship. Inter-community work does not by any means amount to appeasement of Protestants. It is rather an essential ingredient for achieving peace.

The members of Cornerstone Community visit people who have suffered through violence. Whenever possible they do this in twos, a Catholic and Protestant together. This has proved to be a powerful healing symbol and form of witnessing. Gerry Reynolds talks about this experience:

> One summer's day in the mid-eighties the IRA shot a member of the UDR (Ulster Defense Regiment), who lived at the other side of the Wall from us in the Shankill, as he returned home from work. Next day I went with Sam Burch, a Methodist minister, to sympathize with his family. It was the first of many such visits Sam and I made to bereaved families on both sides of the conflict. Sharing the heartbreak together made these visits very painful and emotionally draining. But we were always made welcome. Some months later I visited again the mother of that Shankill UDR man. She spoke to me about her son as we shared a cup of tea in the kitchen. If only they had known him, as she said, they could never have killed him. If only they had known him as his mother knew him. Her words sum up the absurdity, the outrage, the loss, and the tragedy of every violent conflict.

Shelagh Livingstone is a Methodist and a member of Corrymeela and Cornerstone Community. She works with ex-prisoners, on the healing of memories, as well as at the pensioners' lunch club and a parent and toddler club. She talks about her experience of the cross-community lunch club.

> Older people, Protestants and Catholics, find it easier to get together because they remember the time when they lived together before

the troubles started. What is important is to take whatever step we can, even if it is a small step. That is important. [13]

Sr. Anne Kilroy belongs to a Catholic religious congregation (Sisters of Loreto) and is a member of Cornerstone Community. She has taken up the full-time post of Catholic Chaplain in Lagan Integrated College. She speaks about her experience.

> The mere fact of bringing Protestant and Catholic children together is not enough. Divisive issues need to be tackled and faced throughout the curriculum, and at all levels of the school community. This gets increasingly difficult as the school gets bigger. Yet in spite of the difficulties, I believe that the friendships formed among students and staff, some of them lifelong, is bound to make a positive, if not quantifiable, contribution to the achievement of lasting peace. At the end of the day, it is the forming of human relationships that makes the real difference. It is for this reason that I consider myself privileged to be a Chaplain in Lagan. [14]

These good works at the individual and community level are however undermined by some of the general policies of the Catholic Church. The traditional insistence, for example, that children of mixed marriages must be brought up as Catholics has a number of consequences. It tells Protestants that their branch of Christianity is regarded as inferior and that Catholics are interested in conversion, not ecumenics. It can also be viewed as a strategy on the part of Catholics to reduce the size of the Protestant community.

CONCLUSION

These case studies provide ample evidence of the fact that the Catholic Church has made positive contributions to peace in Northern Ireland. In order to do this, they needed to be free from the constraints of the Church structure and increase the level and intensity of their interaction at the grassroots level with those Catholics alienated from the Catholic Church and with Protestants as well. Such work properly reflects *the church as servant* in Avery Dulles's *Models of the Church*. Dietrich Bonhoeffer calls for a humble servant church: "The church

---

13   Talk by Shelagh Livingstone at Corrymeela (Ballycastle), 29 March 1998.

14   *Cornerstone Contact* Spring 1999. Belfast: Cornerstone Community.

must share in the secular problems of ordinary human life, not dominating, but helping and serving".[15]

Bloomfield also examines practical conflict management efforts in
Northern Ireland and identifies two distinct approaches to this, namely, the cultural and the structural. He takes it to be the case that the
cultural approach corresponds to the community level. It appears to
deal with matters related to cultural identity, to relationship, to perceptions of self and other, threat and security, and of needs related to
the communal identities of groups in conflict: In the protagonist's own
words, matters concerning cultural heritage, cultural identity, and the
relationship between two groups caught up in a conflict over identities
and aspirations. By contrast to this, the structural approach appears
to be concerned more with political arrangements, with structures for
governing, with territorial control, and with needs related to community security and political participation, i.e. with essentially objective
matters more directly based on the components of the conflict.

Bloomfield claims that the cultural and structural approaches mirror the resolution and settlement models respectively. The structural
approach mirrors the settlement model, which prescribes an outcome
that is built on agreement reached by the conflicting parties through
negotiation and bargaining. The cultural approach mirrors the resolution model insofar as the latter prescribes an outcome derived through
mutual problem sharing between the two parties, one in which people
cooperate to redefine their conflict and their relationship. This has
been the mode of engagement of the Catholic Church in Northern
Ireland.

It is, however, not entirely obvious that "conflict settlement" and
"conflict resolution" are independent arenas. There can be some interactions between the two. As the example of Fr. Alex Reid shows, the
work of the Church at the grassroots community level can sometimes
affect the macro-political level as well. But, as the work of the Jesuits
in the Orange Parade campaign also shows, the Church should not be
too much involved in the area of conflict settlement. There are limits
as to what it can achieve in a divided community. In order for it to
play a role in the peace process, the Church needs to maintain a position of neutrality. This may be easier for ecumenical communities and

---

15   Avery Dulles, 1988. *Models of the Church*. Dublin: Gill and Macmillan.
     pp. 94-95.

communities of religious orders like the Jesuits than it is for parish priests.

As Bloomfield said in 1997:

> If all the involved politicians completely settled their dispute to-morrow, by developing a comprehensive settlement over agreed structures for the future political landscape of the entire region, the settlement would still stand or fall on the presence or absence of 'widespread acceptance.' For it to flourish in a sustained and durable form, it would depend on the existence of the atmosphere of trust, respect, cooperation and optimism within and between the Catholic and Protestant communities that the cultural approach aims to develop.

The Good Friday Agreement (April 10, 1998) received overwhelming support in a referendum voted on by the people in both Northern Ireland and the Republic of Ireland. People working together at the grassroots level have certainly produced and sustained a strong commitment to peace. This widespread acceptance of the Good Friday Agreement is still fragile and needs to be reinforced by goodwill on both sides. And the Church needs to play its part in this process.

This paper does not attempt to show that the Church has done great things but rather that the efforts of the politicians in conflict settlement and those of the Church in conflict resolution need to complement each other. It is my hope that a study of the initiatives on the part of the Catholic Church will be of help to other Churches in Northern Ireland and other parts of the world where people have struggled with ethnic difference.

PERSONAL REFLECTION BY HIDEYUKI KOYAMA, S.J. :

In the summer of 1995, I was a M.A. student in British Cultural Studies (Irish Studies was one of the modules) at the University of Warwick, England. Then I was asked to preach in Coventry Cathedral (Anglican) at the Cathedral Eucharist on Sunday, August 6, the 50th anniversary of the destruction of Hiroshima. That service, at which the Bishop of Coventry presided, concluded with the unveiling and dedication of a sculpture depicting reconciliation in the wartime ruin of Coventry Cathedral. Identical sculptures were placed in Hiroshima, Belfast and Berlin. I received a Cross of Nails symbolizing peace and reconciliation. I was privileged to play a small role in the reconciliation between Britain and Japan. In a sense, this occasion triggered in me the need to study the role played by the Church in the Northern Ireland conflict. I knew that the Irish were a lovely people and, for a Japanese Catholic like me, it had been difficult to understand why there had been conflicts in Northern Ireland for ages. There I was able to witness the work of many impressive peacemakers first-hand.

ABOUT THE AUTHOR

Hideyuki Koyama is a Jesuit priest, and a lecturer in peace studies, ethnic relations and Irish studies at Sophia University, Tokyo. He graduated from Sophia University, Heythrop College in London, and earned his Ph D. in Ethnic Relations at the University of Warwick, England.

13. THE VOCATION OF PEACEMAKING IN THE VICTORIAN ERA: SOCIAL TRANSFORMATION, BREAD, AND PEACE

ANGELA HURLEY

Every gun that is made, every warship launched, every rocket fired signifies, in the final sense, a theft from those who hunger and are not fed, those who are cold and are not clothed. This world in arms is not spending money alone. It is spending the sweat of its laborers, the genius of its scientists, the hope of its children. (from "A Theft from Those Who Hunger..." by Dwight D. Eisenhower)[1]

Although pacifism constitutes a recurring part of the mosaic of history, the dominant images of history are traditionally those of war. In fact, as writers such as Howard Zinn,[2] remind us, history is largely written from the perspective of powerful rulers and battles. Sifting through the thoughts and stories of people from every century reveals, however, that pacifism and pacific movements have always developed, even if in marginal form. If more historians were to take on the task of reviewing such evidence, collecting the pieces of the pacifist puzzle and identifying the features common to various peace movements and the individuals involved in them, then perhaps a more coherent picture of pacifism would emerge. And, it might inform both our present and our future.

Sadly, at present, war dominates the world agenda. According to theologian Karen Armstrong, the twentieth century was the bloodiest in world history. War escalated to global proportions and the techniques of war-making became unthinkable—and unconscionable. The twentieth-century was the first to experience two world wars, and, since World War II, there have been two hundred wars of a lesser

---

1 Quoted in Joseph J. Fahey and Richard Armstrong, eds. *A Peace Reader* (New York: Paulist Press, 1992), 455.

2 Howard Zinn, *A People's History of the United States*. New York: Harper-Collins, 2003).

scale. Weapons became means of mass destruction. Military expenditures came to consume national budgets, competing continually for funds that could otherwise be used for humanitarian projects.[3]

Reason would seem to dictate that now that the world's nations find themselves on the cusp of mutual annihilation, and now that humanitarian crises are proliferating, the outcry against war would be more audible. But, in fact, many continue to support it.

For the past two thousand years, Western culture has "depended" upon war as a necessity. It has been and continues to be viewed as an acceptable answer to major economic, social and political problems. These cultures may therefore fairly be described as pugnacious in their political behaviors, as placing value on being the "toughest" kid on the block. This fact is reflected in the policies of the majority of their social and political groups. Such interest in aggression and toughness manifests itself in many ways in American culture. Competition is not only encouraged, but also emphasized in every aspect of human life. Rankings, such as those used by No Child Left Behind polices to rate public schools or those utilized by US News and World Report to rank hospitals and colleges, and accountability measures are highly valued and greatly relied upon. There is a pronounced tendency to assert the correctness of one group, idea, or practice over another and, in so doing, to radically simplify what are often complex political issues. Tough punishments for criminals are advocated and applauded. Many childrearing practices and educational discipline policies aim, for the most part, at control and stringency. Sporting events are highly esteemed, especially those that are violent in nature. Entire sections of newspapers are devoted exclusively to sports. And, our language includes a wealth of combative terms, even where the situations being described do not actually involve conflict. For example, we "wage wars" on cancer or poverty or crime; we "marshal our facts for academic arguments" which we then delight in "shooting down."[4] These elements neatly fit into and feed the notion of aggression and tend to be accepted without question. Such practices are all deemed acceptable because

---

3 See especially Ronald J. Glossop, *Confronting War*. (Jefferson, NC: McFarland Publishers, 2001) for statistics on national budgets.

4 In the western tradition, discrediting academic theories seems to have been a trend from at least fifth century (BCE) Greece onward. (G.E.R. Lloyd, *The Ambitions of Curiosity*. Cambridge: Cambridge University Press, 2002).

a warrior mentality is a vital part of the reality we have constructed for ourselves. Furthermore, they seem to reinforce and strengthen the prevailing, collective mind-set.

If peace is to become a dominant cultural image, then a transformation of cultural and individual thinking must occur. How to effect such a change? Extracting a coherent theory of pacifism from the work of peacemakers of the past (or present) is not easy, for they hardly speak with one voice. In fact, they speak from widely differing perspectives and with diverse philosophic commitments. And, this task is further complicated by the fact that they have varying levels of conviction about their work.

It is with this diversity of views in mind that I will undertake here to examine the thoughts and actions of two quite different individuals, W.R. Inge and Jane Addams. Each of them worked for peace even in the midst of war, and each can therefore be called a pacifist. They may have disagreed on many points, but, nevertheless, taken together, the thought of these two individuals forms a remarkable unity. And, I would submit that it can provide a working model for a transformation to a more peaceful culture.

Both Inge and Addams were reared in the Victorian Age, though they came from somewhat different backgrounds socially, geographically, religiously, and vocationally. Jane Addams, a well-educated American and cultural icon of the early twentieth century,[5] founded and worked at Hull House in Chicago. She devoted her energies to interacting with, helping, and learning from immigrants. An avowed pacifist, Ms. Addams refused to alter her position, even during World War I when she was reviled for her commitment to it. Englishman W.R. Inge, born the same year as Addams (1860), was Eaton/Cambridge educated. He was an upper class Anglican clergyman and academic who served at both Cambridge and Oxford, and later became Dean of St. Paul's Cathedral in London. In addition, he was a well-known but controversial speaker, writer, and newspaper columnist. Dean Inge spent an entire lifetime coming to terms with his anti-war thoughts. He did not attach to himself the appellation of pacificist until the last years of his life.

Other than the fact that they were born in the same year, these two individuals seem to share little in common. What is important, how-

---

5　See especially Allen Davis, American Heroine, *The Life and Legend of Jane Addams* (New York: Oxford Press, 1973).

ever, is that they both wrote about and worked for peace. They were also both well-known figures in their time—and people who had access to their countries' leaders.

In this paper, I first analyze Dean Inge's thought. He draws from the Neo-platonic, mystical tradition and argues that inner peace is a first priority. Subsequently, I discuss the work of Jane Addams. It is developed around the concept of compassionate action. Lastly, I discuss the ideas of these two thinkers as they relate to both the literal and figurative meanings of bread for peace.

DEAN W.R. INGE

Born to an upper class family of Anglican clergymen and academics, W.R. Inge was a Victorian gentleman; still, he is difficult to analyze or categorize. He had a strong sense of class loyalty, for example, but did not feel entirely bound by it. Even as Dean of St. Paul's, he disliked "high church." Nevertheless, he valued orderliness and seemliness in the services. During most of his life he wrote against war, but was reluctant to be called a pacifist. In some of his early writing, he even termed absolute pacifists "naïve." Pessimistic on many issues, yet optimistic on others, Inge was referred to as the "Gloomy Dean" by his biographer Adam Fox as well as by others. Perhaps Lord Oxford and Asquith's opinion best summed up his personage: "he is a strange, isolated figure, with all the culture in the world, and a curiously developed gift of expression, but with kinks and twists both intellectual and temperamental." [6]

That Inge had a keen mind is, however, undisputed. His thoughts found clear expression in his writing and speaking. It also cannot be denied that he was outspoken. He was clearly not afraid to say what he firmly believed. His religious beliefs were based upon Platonic idealism. He was also a classics scholar and valued the mystical tradition [7] in religion. One of his works analyzes the thought of Plotinus. Looking back at his work from our current perspective, many of his predictions about world affairs seem almost prophetic in nature.

---

6 Quoted in Adam Fox, Dean Inge (London: John Murray, 1960), 267.

7 Inge defines mysticism as "an immediate communion, real or supposed, between the human soul and the Soul of the World or the Divine Sprit." As found in W.R. Inge. Outspoken Essays. (London: Longman's, Green, and Company, 1919), 230.

Since he lived a long life, Inge watched his native England move from the Victorian Age of stability and hopefulness, in which there was a great outpouring of literary, philosophical, and political ideas, to the misery of World War I. He was also an observer of the numerous social changes that took place in the early twentieth century, including having his own church services at St. Paul's interrupted by "pesky suffragists." [8] He watched as the class structure in England continued to transform itself, and he railed against socialists and the Labor Party. His idealism led him to believe that a second world war was impossible, yet he lived long enough to see its cataclysmic reality—and the death of his son, Richard, in that war. Until his own death in 1954, Inge continued to observe and write about the many changes that occurred in his lifetime of nearly 100 years.

Inge's sermons were well attended; he also filled lecture halls. His books were best-sellers, and, in later life, his editorials were published in church and secular newspapers. Inge's thinking was thus well known to the English people. Both he and his wife kept diaries, and his life has been the subject of several biographies.

Inge's theology and cultural beliefs are the main keys to his antiwar position. In his early writings, one finds statements concerning the atrocious, barbaric nature of war. That he clearly opposed war as a social institution, is evident from such statements as, "...the whole world looks to find some remedy for the worst disease of civilization—war and the ever-present danger of war." [9] However, like all of his thinking, his anti-war stance proves difficult to analyze in full or to categorize. Indeed it does not even seem to be pacifistic on all accounts. His pacifism did, however, become more pronounced as he grew older.

Given his idealist convictions, it is not difficult to understand that Inge felt that the values of this world were but shadowy copies of the eternal one and to be grasped only over against the absoluteness of God. He states, "Earth is a shadow of the spiritual eternal." [10] And even though he thought that sometimes the institution of the church goes wrong, he was of the conviction that the Spirit always remains:

---

8   W.R. Inge, *Diary of a Dean.* (New York: The Macmillan Company, 1950).

9   W.R. Inge. *The Gate of Life* (New York: Longmans, 1935), 99.

10   W.R. Inge. *Social Teachings of the Church* (New York: Abingdon Press, 1930), p. 110.

"Nevertheless, the gift of Pentecost has never been withdrawn..." [11] Inge constantly urged individuals to live in the Spirit and be like the saints, to be "the bearers of the light which, once kindled, shall never be put out."[12]

The main aspect of God or the Spirit that Inge constantly referenced was Love. He also claimed that God gave "principles, not rules."[13] He felt these principles were absolute and unchanging; and, in applying them to human beings, he concluded that man's worth was not determined by what he has, but by what he is.[14] In his view, the New Testament conveyed such an ethic based on Love, and, for him, God was ever-loving. As he stated, "The law of love is only a part of the law of inwardness. There can be no substitute for a genuine and unselfish affection toward our fellow men, nor for a love of God which seldom thinks of reward and punishment."[15] Inge viewed hypocrisy, hard-heartedness, and calculated worldliness as sins against the law of Love.[16] He stated that "Christianity always appeals directly to individuals; and its influence radiates out naturally from its focus in the individual soul."[17] He therefore held that peace came into the world through human beings, *from the inside, out.* His clear sense of the inner life as privileged is evident from such remarks as, "From within, out of the heart of man, proceeds all that can defile, and all that can exalt, the character."[18]

Inge was, however, reluctant to connect to social movements that were based solely on political positions or claims. He was ever-confident that Divine Love would work to "leaven the lump" that is humankind, and that it was up to each person to live in keeping with the principle of love in their worldly relationships.

Such an idea can only be implemented if one takes a long view of history and of the church, a view of the sort that Inge advocated. He felt the church was in its infancy, and had yet to work the great chang-

11   W.R. Inge. *The Church and the Age* (New York: Longmans, 1912), p. 53.

12   Ibid, p. 53.

13   W.R. Inge. *Social Teachings of the Church*, p. 32.

14   Ibid, p. 91.

15   Ibid, p. 23.

16   Ibid, p. 23.

17   W.R. Inge. *The Church and the Age*, p. 77

18   W.R. Inge. *The Social Teachings of the Church*, p. 22.

es in humanity that its theology portends. He constantly argued that God's time was not ours; God takes the long view.[19]

Both Inge's religious mysticism and his idealism informed his view of life, in general, and, of war, in particular. He thought that in order to prevent war, its causes needed to be explored and explained. These were many, including the memory of past injustices that some groups of people hold. He also felt that labeling groups of individuals led, in effect, to libel. As he noted, categorizing entire groups encouraged the use of propaganda against them, fanned the flames of hatred, and led to war. Along the same lines, he warned of the dangers of nationalism and patriotism, and of the fact that, in their extreme forms, these lead to war. Inge called people to put "hatred and vindictiveness out of our hearts"[20] in order to work for peace. As he states:

> The difference between pre-Christian and Christian moral ideas is nevertheless greater than the schoolmen realized. Christ rejects all ethical systems which accept, as right and necessary, strife and warfare as conditions of social life; He lays very little stress on honor, pride, self-respect, and patriotism; for Him, love is the fulfilling of the law.[21]

Inge faulted the Church of England for the fact that it seemed not to respect "anything but organized force." [22] Elsewhere he stated, "Lovers of peace have not much to hope for from organized religion...." [23] Indeed, the history of the Anglican Church during World War I is such that there was a good deal of support from clergy and bishops for the war. [24]

But, Inge identified the main source of war as the emotion of fear. For him, truly paying attention to the value system of Christ had the power to diminish fear and give people courage. He wrote, "The Gospel, if it were accepted, would pull up by the roots not only militarism but its analogue in civil life, the desire to exploit other people for pri-

---

19   Ibid. p. 108.

20   W.R. Inge. *The Gate of Life*, p. 106.

21   W.R. Inge. *The Social Teaching of the Church*, p. 60.

22   W.R. Inge. *Outspoken Essays*, p. 30.

23   Ibid. p. 253.

24   See Alan Wilkinson. *The Church of England and the First World War* (London: SCM Press, 1978).

vate gain." [25] Although such acceptance was not yet a reality, Inge was hopeful that, in time, it would be.

Since he considered arguments for war to be ridiculous, Inge stated, "it would be the height of pessimistic fatalism to hold that men must always go on doing that which they hate, and which brings them to misery and ruin." [26] And further: "The truth seems to be that Nature presents to us not a categorical imperative, but a choice. Do we prefer to pay our way in the world, or to be parasites? War, with very few exceptions, is a mode of parasitism. War is a parasitic industry; and Christianity forbids parasitism." [27]

He spent his lifetime attempting to analyze the causes of war and to find his own rationale for pacifism. Turning to the New Testament gospels of love, Inge took the view that eventually, as more individuals accept them, the roots of militarism would be removed. Love and forgiveness would neutralize them. This certainly does not yield immediate results, but it does give every person a sense of agency. The next thinker whom I will discuss shows how to use this personal agency to "do the work needed for peace."

JANE ADDAMS

Ms. Addams' Victorian life also included access to the heady nineteenth century ideas of evolution, progress, and socialism. The belief that the world was definitely improving, or was at least improvable through science and the application of rationality, brought optimism to the age. Although it was the case that women were not yet enfranchised, and also that educational opportunities were limited and mass immigration posed problems, and although the United States had just experienced a devastating Civil War, there was nonetheless an air of optimism in society. Life conditions were improving overall, and the world was becoming a better place. For example, Ms. Addams believed (that) in her lifetime, society was moving from a "period of industrialism to a period of humanitarianism." [28]

She was especially optimistic as concerns the human capacity for compassion: "This genius for goodness has in the past largely ex-

25   W.R. Inge. *Outspoken Essays*, p. 264.
26   Ibid. p. 260.
27   Ibid. *Outspoken Essays*, p. 260.
28   Jane Adams. *Newer Ideals of Peace*. (New York: The Macmillan Company, 1907), p. 15.

pressed itself through individuals and groups, but it may be that we are approaching a period which shall give it collective expression, and shall unite into one all those private and parochial efforts." [29] Peace groups were organized and conferences took place, in Western societies prior to World War I. They aimed at the improvement of world conditions overall. In fact, many of the leaders of the American suffragist movement were also pacifists. At least prior to World War I, Ms. Addams had reason to support her hope for the development of collective compassion.

Jane Addams exerted a tremendous influence on the lives of the poor and immigrants through the Hull House she founded with her friend, Ellen Gates Starr, in 1889. [30] It was intended as a cooperative social settlement, originally patterned after a similar settlement in London. Gradually, however, Ms. Addams' thinking about it changed. As she worked with the people, she began to think of the process as one of reciprocal learning instead of imposition of values and ideals. That is, she became increasingly aware of the need to conduct her work with a sense of care and respect, not a sense of pity. Ms. Addams claimed to have learned greatly from her interactions with people in the Hull House and in the neighborhood.

In Chicago, she helped found the first kindergarten and juvenile court system. She was active in other civil rights organizations, working for women's rights and serving on the executive committee of the National Association of the Advancement of Colored People.[31] She was also instrumental in the development of the American Civil Liberties Union. Even before World War I, she was a leader in international as well as national peace organizations. In a word, Addams was an effective social activist. She felt that personal values always needed to be put to the test of action. A contemporary of hers is known to have said, "Her compassion for the world takes a curiously practical and immediate form."[32]

Addams saw the need for a sound theoretical basis for her thinking and writing. She understood the role of ideas in informing action: "All

29   Ibid. p. 21-22.

30   Charlene Haddock Seigfried, "Introduction to the Illinois Edition" of Jane Addams. *The Long Road of Women's Memory.* (Urbana and New York City: University of Illinois Press, 2002).

31   Ibid. IX.

32   Quoted in Davis, p. 202.

the activities of life can be changed in no other way than by changing the current ideas upon which it is conducted." [33] In proposing a path to peace, then she theorized that war has not always been a part of human life. Surely, as primitive societies developed, cooperation must have ensured survival. Looking back at the symbols left by early peoples, she pointed to the value assigned to their nurturers, the ones who could grow food (usually women). She thought that the "gregarious instinct" was "older and more human than the motives of war." [34]

In her view, human life was too valuable to be deliberately destroyed. As her biographer, John Farrell, observed, early in her life she connected pacifism and internationalism to the social welfare interests for which she labored. She believed that war destroyed democracy and culture and that all of human life is sacred. [35] She is also quoted as having said, "When we once surround human life with the same kind of heroism and admiration that we surround war, we can say that...war will become impossible." [36]

Addams thought that the warrior mindset could be transformed into a compassionate one, one which aimed at nourishing life. From her perspective, the people of her time lacked moral fiber, and she called them to work: "We must be willing to surrender ourselves to those ideals of the humble, which all religious teachers unite in declaring to be the foundations of a sincere moral life." [37] She attempted to use this idea as a basis for nurturing life and thereby change existing wrong-headed practices. She asked, "How far are we responsible when we allow custom to blind our eyes to the things that are wrong?" [38]

In sum, it can be said that Addams advocated the dissolution of the roots of war in so far as she worked toward a new way of being in the world—one that would make the concept of war invalid. In *Newer Ideals of Peace*, she stated that we must "extinguish the possibility of battle at its very source by recreating the way we live and interact with one

---

33   Jane Addams, *Peace and Bread in Time of War*, (Urbana; University of Illinois Press-reprint of 1922 edition), p. 243.

34   Jane Addams, *Peace and Bread*, p. 82.

35   John Farrell, *Beloved Lady: A History of Jane Addams' Ideas on Reform and Peace* (Baltimore: Johns Hopkins Press, 1967), 18.

36   *Ibid.* 18.

37   Jane Addams, *Newer Ideals of Peace*, 27.

38   Ibid. 156.

another." [39] Human thought and energy needs to be redirected toward life-giving activities rather than life-taking ones. We need to stop giving credence to outdated myths. She felt that dependence upon the military model for government and social institutions rests upon beliefs such as "war is inevitable," or, "democracy is to be secured through war," or, "we can wage a war that will end all wars." However, she asked "Was not war in the interest of democracy for the salvation of civilization a contradiction of terms, whoever said it or however often it was repeated?" [40] Resting her concept of democracy upon the idea of the value of all the peoples of a country interacting in a manner that promotes true dialogue, Ms. Addams stressed the importance of trust and respect, *with trust outweighing the impulse to control and to proscribe.*

As biographer John Farrell interpreted Ms. Addams' thinking, "Instead of solving problems, she believed, armed conflict created new problems and made solving of the old ones more difficult. War was the very antithesis of that justice and righteousness which formed the only sure foundation for international order." [41] Ever seeking to ensure justice for all and to put forward institutions through which democracy could flourish, Jane Addams lived her plan for peace.

Instead of using war as the model for cultural heroism and courage, Ms. Addams suggested locating heroism in life nurturing activities. Within her plan, she realized the necessity of providing an outlet for human energy and excitement and the need to both perform and value heroic deeds. Energy and excitement, she felt, could be found through participating in humanitarian acts, especially in teaching starving people how to grow and prepare food. In a speech to a peace conference, she stated:

> If the race once discovered the excitement and the pleasure and the infinite moral stimulus and the gratification of the spirit of adventure to be found in the nourishing of human life, in the bringing of all the world into some sort of general order and decent relationship one with another, men would no longer think of war as their only joy and pleasure. [42]

---

39   Addams, *Newer Ideals of Peace.*
40   Addams, *Peace and Bread*, 142.
41   Farrell, 17.
42   Quoted in Farrell, 262.

Ms. Addams' peace plan, then, involved including all people in the nourishing, life-giving opportunities present in the world. By calling for a new path, or way of living, Jane Addams understood that the existing mode of reality couldn't respond to appeals for peace: a new way must be found. She realized peace would not fit into the existing order, for she viewed peace as a result of the whole: that is, peace will result from transforming all practices of our culture away from those that harm and disrespect life to those that nurture life. Peace, then, is not an action set apart, but is the result of all of our actions and of the cultural mindset in which we are embedded. The work of compassion must come to be viewed as heroic; the human longing to be courageous and active must be converted into the work of nurturing others. Peace is a total way of life, not merely an action that can be tacked onto an existing mindset.

BREAD

The notion of bread, in both its literal and figurative senses, fits neatly with the thoughts and actions of both Dean Inge and Jane Addams. Inge felt that peace is only possible when individual souls find the nourishment of the "bread of life," the Love that is God.[43] He spoke of "leavening the lump"; meaning, I think, that in the slowness of God's time, as more and more individuals realize the meaning of Love, fears will diminish and compassionate actions will result. The result will be a "lump" of humankind that will walk in the ways of peace. Jane Addams called for the literal growing of grain, as well as for making and feeding bread to others. When one does the compassionate work of helping the poor, tending the sick, and feeding the hungry, the Love of which Inge spoke can indeed enter the world.

Christ's "Bread of Life" metaphor is a powerful one with which people can readily identify. Bread does many things: it nourishes and sustains life (both physically and spiritually), it brings us into communion (making us one body), and it provides an outward and visible sign of our inward thoughts. The relational aspect of taking bread together is of utmost importance in working toward peace.

---

43   I am using Bread (Love) from the Christian perspective because that is the tradition with which I am familiar and the one in which Inge and Addams operated; however, similar concepts exist in other world religions as well.

Often we are at table with those whom we already love and the act of eating and talking together reminds us of our bonds of friendship; but, sometimes we find ourselves eating with either strangers or those for whom we do not have feelings of affection. During the process of being placed in close physical proximity and making eye contact as we talk, we break down barriers that separate us. Eating together gives "the other" a face and when faces can be put on strangers or those less well known, the walls of separation are often removed.

Even at the communion rail, we sometimes find ourselves next to a person with whom we have had words or from whom we are estranged. The physical and spiritual closeness of that moment often heals the rift, reminding us of the importance of being in positive relationships with others. Eating together, then, breaks down barriers and allows for intimacy. When barriers, both visible and invisible, dissolve, true dialogue occurs; thorny issues can be resolved amicably rather than forcefully. When we truly see the other, we can learn from them; much as Jane Addams learned from the immigrants with whom she interacted.

The giving of bread is an outward sign of our respect for the other because we know that personal energy has been expended to grow the grain and to prepare the bread. To feed the other requires selfless work, individuals must move beyond self-centeredness toward awareness of others. The act of preparing the bread and that of teaching others to grow the grain and make the bread enables us to move out of our personal sphere, to extend ourselves and to use our energy to provide nourishment to another. In addition, we put on our best "faces and manners" when we dine together.

Just as the bread one prepares physically nourishes the other for whom it is prepared, the act of preparing and sharing the bread with others nourishes the Love that is within us. Souls need to reconnect and to be refreshed by the Love that is God, reconnecting each person to the energy and force of Love—the Bread of Life. Such connection diminishes fear and reminds us to do the work the needs to be done, the work that comes from Love.

CONCLUSION

Sometimes what we seek, thinking that only our age can provide it, has been with us all along. But, in fact, we only need to pick up the pieces of history and find the images of peace that others have already provided. The lives and work of Dean Inge and Jane Addams provide us with images that, when juxtaposed, form a viable plan for social and cultural transformation that could lead to world peace.

PERSONAL REFLECTION BY ANGELA HURLEY

My passionate interest in peace has come about not as a result of a specific event, nor was it awakened at a certain point in time in my life. Instead it has developed slowly, taking the form of an ever growing awareness that I cannot condone aggression and war as ways of being in the world. My earliest memories of war come from my grandparents' home: my father's two youngest brothers fought in World War II, and there were mementos from their time in Europe scattered all through the house. In addition, the memories of WW II were fresh in people's minds and also commented upon in daily conversations. Although I was a very small child, I remember thinking that a big event had just happened. I was quite interested in the massive numbers of photos that one of my uncles had taken as he had crossed Europe with the tanks.

Certainly in this context, my earlier memory of war was positive. As I matured into young adulthood, living through the Korean War, the civil rights movement in the south and the Vietnam War, I began to question at greater length whether violence and war could be a solution to human problems. When I witnessed candlelight vigils in front of the administration building on the University of Missouri campus and saw active anti-war protests for the first time as a graduate student, I became interested in the thoughts of those who spoke out against violence. I began to set aside my father's and my own childhood advocacy of war and to see it for what I now believe it to be: an unconscionable course of action which is erroneously viewed as an attempt to solve human problems.

As my awareness grew, I made a concentrated effort to read about war, peace, and pacifist thought. The texts which have been most influential have been *War and Peace*, the writings of Dr. Martin Luther King, Jr., Pat Barker's *Regeneration* trilogy, and a children's book that is no longer in print, Louise Lawrence's *Children of the Dust*. Through a combination of philosophic thought, literature and art, individuals can perhaps come to see the uselessness and horror of war. Hopefully, this insight can encourage us to find new ways to work out differences and live with one another.

The heroic ways that some peacemakers have lived, and continue to live, also encourages those of us who are not so brave: I am thinking particularly of Rosa Parks, Martin Luther King, Jr., and the Pennsylvania Amish community that most recently set an example by forgiving the killer of a number of their children. Being able to forgive is a major component of peacemaking, and what an example these people gave to the world. What if we humans had never known the concept of war? What means would we now be using to settle our problems? Peace is a way of life, a very active and difficult one; we can shift to a more peaceful mode of living if we are committed to it. The means we now rely on is certainly not working!

14. THE ECUMENICAL PRAXIS OF PATRIARCH ATHENAGORAS I (1948-72)

PHILLIP C. NAYLOR

INTRODUCTION

I am not sure why my father made an appointment to see the Ecumenical Patriarch Athenagoras I while we were visiting Istanbul. But he did. At that time, I was eleven years old. While Dad lunched with the patriarch and other guests, my mother, my cousin, and I toured the patriarchate located in the Phanar section of Istanbul. Then the patriarch and Dad joined us. Athenagoras towered over us; he was well over six feet tall (6'-4"). His long white, wispy beard added to his physical and spiritual grandeur. His immense appearance presented an image of a prophet from the Hebrew Bible, but he also evoked simplicity and humility. Furthermore, he made me feel that I was the most important person in that room. His speech, his gestures, his hospitality, his remarkable eyes made an indelible impression. In graduate school, I wrote to him and he responded warmly and graciously. By that time, I had realized that I had had the extraordinary privilege of meeting one of the most important, and most ecumenically-minded, religious and historic leaders in modern Christianity.

My contribution to this collection of papers aims not only to survey Patriarch Athenagoras' ecumenical life and praxis—his quest to share a "common chalice"—but also to ask why he engaged ecumenism and challenged history. This paper addresses the themes of peacemaking, reconciliation, and, above all, the "healing of ancient religious animosities," a theme of this conference. The ecumenical efforts of the Catholic Church are well documented, but the corresponding Eastern Orthodox engagement has been understated and needs to be understood and publicized. This conference and this modest study provide that opportunity.

THE DEVELOPMENT OF AN ECUMENICAL PRAXIS

Aristokles Spyrou was born on March 25, 1886 in a village named Vassilikon in Epirus, a territory that was under Turkish administration.[1] Nevertheless, Greeks and Turks co-existed and cooperated. Athenagoras recalled: "The dervishes [Sufis] were very good to me. They were very tolerant toward the Christians....We had one dervish in my village by the name of Jamil. He often came to visit us at home and dined with us. My mother and sister, in particular, were very fond of him and kept no secrets from him. Jamil knew their innermost thoughts better than our village priest."[2] His mother, Helen (1863-99), "taught me the meaning of religion and worship.... Every night when we went to bed she used to sing to us ecclesiastical chants and tell us about Kosmas of Aitolia, who a century earlier had come to live at Vassilikon."[3] Kosmas had especially promoted education. Aristokles' father, Matthew (1852-1908) was the village doctor. He did not distinguish between ethnic and religious backgrounds. The future patriarch's elementary education was in Vassilikon, neighboring Konitsa, and Ioannina.

Aristokles entered the Theological School of Chalki (Halki) in 1903, located on that offshore island, from Constantinople. After receiving his degree in theology in 1910, he was ordained a deacon in March of that same year and then appointed archdeacon to the Metropolis of Pelagonia at Monastir in July.[4] Aristokles, now renamed Athenagoras, served there until 1919, when the Serbian Orthodox

---

1 Athenagoras was careful not to publicize his birthday, which was not only the Annunciation, but also Greek Independence Day. Several important works on Athenagoras' life and praxis are referred to below. See especially, Ioannes, E. Anastasiou, ed., *Athenagoras I, Oikoumenikos Patriarches: O Epeirotes* (Ioannina: Etaireias Epeirotikon Meleton, 1975).

2 Demetrios Tsakonas, *A Man Sent by God: The Life of Patriarch Athenagoras of Constantinople*, trans. George Angeloglou (Brookline, Mass.: Holy Cross Orthodox Press, 1977), 10.

3 Ibid., 11. Kosmas was canonized during Athenagoras' patriarchate in April 1961.

4 During the Balkan Wars, Athenagoras deferred Serbian soldiers from combat by having them registered as teachers (Georgiou Mode, "O Diakonos Athenagoras sto Monasteri: Anamneseis," in Anastasiou, ed., *Athenagoras I*, 101).

Church integrated the metropolis. The years at Monastir were also influential in his developing an ecumenical, transcultural conscience:

> I had some wonderful experiences of the love of which simple people are capable, of dialogue, and of my first contacts with Christians of the Western Church. I developed a strong personal contact with the local villagers, and each day, about a dozen of them would pay me a visit. When I asked them why they came to see me, they replied in their simple language, 'so that we can look at each other.' From this *looking at each other* I developed a practical philosophy: to love communication with men as I love men, as individuals, because in man I see God, and behind the miracle of human existence is God Himself.

How does one communicate with others? It is in their languages: "In order to manage to communicate with the Catholics, I became a pupil at the school of the Marian Brothers, using as an excuse that I wanted to perfect my French." After leaving Monastir, he spent time from late autumn 1918 to March 1919 on Mount Athos where he lived in isolation and meditated deeply. He "felt that a new world was being born, and that God meant us to serve this new world." [5] Athenagoras regarded himself as a monk even after becoming an ecumenical patriarch.[6] He lived an ascetic life, one of extreme simplicity. At this time he also accepted an invitation to serve as secretary to Metropolitan Meletios of Athens, who shared his ideas regarding a changing world. In this context, he learned how a metropolitan administers a church, something which proved especially useful for him. Nevertheless, the Metropolitan's reputed pro-Venezelist position led to his dismissal in 1920.[7] Meletios then organized what would become the Archdiocese

---

5 Tsakonas, 13-14. Athenagoras spoke or understood, besides Greek, Turkish, French, Spanish, English, Albanian, Russian, and Romanian (Konstantinou Demetrios Fragkou, "Paidike Elikia—Morfosis—Katartisis (Epeiros—Chalke, 1886-1910)," in Anastasiou, ed., *Athenagoras I*, 90).

6 Clément Olivier, *Dialogues avec le patriarche Athénagoras* (Paris: Fayard, 1969), 65. He took his vows as a monk while a student at Chalki.

7 Eleutherios Venizelos (1864-1936) and King Constantine I (1868-1923; r. 1913-17; 1920-22) disagreed politically over Greek involvement in World War I and also over Greek policy in Asia Minor. Venizelos eventually forced Constantine's abdication in 1917 and Greece entered the war on the side of the Allies. He negotiated skillfully at the Paris Peace Conference and Greece was awarded territory along the Asia Minor coastline by the Treaty of Sèvres (1920). After Venizelos lost parliamentary elections,

of North and South America and was soon elected patriarch. He had urged Athenagoras to continue to serve as his secretary, but Athenagoras politely refused and worked under Meletios' successor, Theoklitos.

Promoted to metropolitan of Corfu and Paxi in 1922, Athenagoras befriended Catholics, Protestants, and Jews. He intervened personally and ended an Italian bombardment of the island in August 1923 by reportedly rowing out to the attacking fleet, boarding the flagship, and castigating the admiral.[8] His inaugural address in Corfu already evidenced his ecumenical spirit: "Christ wanted one indivisible Church; instead, the Church became divided into factions. One must not hide the truth. The Church, which should have been the House of God, the Mother of all Christians, the Great Messenger of Peace, often forsook these principles and embarked on petty struggles, on missions of hatred and persecution, and abandoned the people to their own fate." [9] When he left Corfu in 1930 to become the Archbishop of North and South America, Catholics, Protestants, Jews, and Muslims attended the Divine Liturgy with Orthodox.[10]

Division caused principally by politics in Greece wracked the Greek Orthodox Church in America.[11] He immediately informed priests and communities that he would not tolerate the Church's politicization. Political and refractory priests were removed. The Church had to move on.

Constantine resumed power and pursued policies resulting in the "Catastrophe of 1922," ending the 3,000-year Greek presence in Asia Minor (dating from ancient Aeotolia and Ionia) and the aspiration of the "Great Idea" (*Megale Idea*)—a Greater Greece.

8   Athanasios I. Delekostopoulos, *Exo apo ta Teiche: O Oikoumenikos Patriarches Athenagoras I* (Athens: Alpha-Delta, 1988), 40.

9   Tsakonas, 17.

10   Ibid., 23.

11   Orthodox churches split between monarchists and Venezelists, the result being divided Orthodox communities. Athenagoras sympathized deeply with the refugees from Asia Minor, and supported institutional Venezelist political liberalism, but he also viewed the *Megale Idea* as a form of romantic nationalism which had destructive rather than constructive consequences. Athenagoras understood the dangers of nationalism. He was and continued to be an internationalist, which he perceived as a pragmatic alternative.

He loved being in America and became a citizen. The country's multiethnic, multicultural environment was invigorating and inspiring to him. Conscious of history, he compared the failure of the polyglot Ottoman Empire and to the apparently successful American experiment.[12] People could get along. He befriended presidents, yet he was not interested in social status, but in individuals. Wherever Athenagoras served, he was an initiator and an innovator. In 1931, the Archbishop inaugurated the *Orthodox Observer* monthly newspaper and the *Philoptochos Adelphotis,* the Greek Orthodox Women's philanthropic society. Recognizing the need for American-educated priests, he established Holy Cross Seminary in 1937. Athenagoras also established St. Basil's Academy and Orphanage in Garrison, New York in 1944.[13] Foreshadowing his patriarchate, he organized a pan-Orthodox convocation at the University of Chicago in 1935.

On November 1, 1948, the Holy Synod elected Athenagoras as the 268th Ecumenical Patriarch. As Professor V. Th. Stavridis of the Theological School at Chalki reflected:

> It became obvious that Athenagoras with his wide and liberal background acquired in America, was not going to follow the narrow and prejudiced concepts of the ecclesiastical tradition of the Phanar (Turkish section of Istanbul where the Patriarchate is located). He brought with him to Constantinople the enlightened spirit of the Western world, and he was determined to implement his policies with all the energy and enthusiasm that characterized him; but he also expected all those who worked with him to adopt the same standards and to strive for the same objectives.[14]

In his address from the Patriarchal throne, Athenagoras said: "We believe that only through religion and faith in God will men live in peace with each other, because religion is eternal beauty, because religion is the majesty of peace. This in fact means that it is not enough to be an idealist; man needs an iron Christian will to achieve these

---

12   Olivier, 83. Athenagoras called the establishment of a vital Greek community in America miraculous after the disaster of Asia Minor (Ibid.).

13   Athenagoras also initiated a similar social action on Corfu. He helped refugees, founded an orphanage, and reopened the Ecclesiastical School. He also inaugurated *Saint Spyridon,* a journal, and educated the clergy when he convened a general assembly in 1923 (Tsakonas, 21-22).

14   Ibid. 33, citing Stavridis, "Ho Oikoumenikos Patriarches Athnagoras ho A," *Stachys* (1972), 312.

ideals."[15] Athenagoras understood, respected, and appreciated history
and memory. He preached action rather than passivity. He was a man
engaged, but also one who wanted to transcend convention and the
atavisms of the past.

AN ECUMENICAL PRAXIS

When we think of Athenagoras' ecumenical praxis, we usually associate it with Catholicism. This paper will therefore consider that
relationship. He was, however, not only concerned with the relation
between Orthodoxy and Catholicism, but also lived up to his title as
the patriarch of the world by illustrating his respect for Judaism and
Islam.[16] He shocked the Orthodox and Christian world by praying in
a mosque. From childhood, he was personally very familiar with Islam
and respected its Abrahamic traditions. Once when he was asked a
confrontational question regarding Hagia Sophia's status as a museum rather than one of Christendom's greatest churches, he responded:
"In the time of Byzantium, Hagia Sophia was open to all. Today, as a
museum, it is again open to all."[17] He also distinguished Islam from
Turkish nationalism. He insisted on an active Orthodox presence in
the World Council of Churches, where direct contacts could be made
with Protestant churches.[18] When devastating rioting occurred on
September 6-7, 1955 in Istanbul against the large Greek community
over problems in Cyprus, it was the Anglican Church and the German
government who, under pressure from Protestant constituencies, were
especially vocal in their protests. As Demetrios Tsakonas pointed out,
"The Protestants had become Byzantines."[19]

---

15   Tsakonas, 34.

16   Valeria Martano, *Athenagoras, il patriarca (1886-1972): Un cristiano fra
crisi della coabitazione e utopia ecumenica* (Milano: Il Mulino, 1996), 183-
85.

17   "The Patriarch," *Time*, February 8, 1954, 74.

18   Martano, 179-83. In particular, see Colin Davey, "Anglican-Orthodox
Relations during the Patriarchate of His All-Holiness Athenagoras I
(1948-1972)," in Anastasiou, *Athenagoras I*, 411-22.

19   Tsakonas, 52. The riots were over Cyprus' complex decolonization. Athenagoras was not pleased over Archbishop Makarios' political involvement.
The Orthodox Church helped inaugurate the World Council of Churches
in 1948. Athenagoras encouraged an Orthodox participation the Council
(Martano, 179-83).

To Athenagoras, ecumenism also had a secular dimension. He urged Greece and Turkey to "be friends." In the 1950s and the 1960s, that would not be the case. The Patriarchate was extremely vulnerable, a fact which necessitated diplomatic sensitivity, something which he exercised skillfully and respectfully. Yet, Athenagoras was not naïve regarding the Greek-Turkish relationship. Both governments had to transcend history for practical reasons. The welfare of all in the Eastern Mediterranean was a deep concern of his. The *Megale Idea* was over with the Catastrophe of 1922 and idea of *enosis* or unity with Cyprus smacked of "pseudo-romantic" nationalism and was fraught with danger. He sought a democratic alternative: "Get together. Be friends. Advance together toward one goal—freedom of thought, freedom of belief, freedom of action."[20] Today, Greece and Turkey have cooperative, if not close relations. They recently dispatched their foreign ministers as part of a joint effort to demonstrate to the Israelis and Palestinians that cooperation and conciliation were possible, even where there is a history of enmity.

When Athenagoras was elected patriarch, President Harry S. Truman offered his own airplane to transport him to Istanbul. As the airplane approached Rome, Athenagoras requested that it circle the Vatican several times to allow him an opportunity to pray. He wanted closer relations with Western Christianity but this would have to be done carefully and by calculated steps. In 1952, Athenagoras dispatched Archimadrite Emilios Tsakopoulos, the librarian of the Patiarchate, to study at the Vatican Library. Intermediaries were used such as the Romanian theologian Archimandrite Skrima. When Pope John XXIII ascended St. Peter's throne in 1958, relations were revolutionized.[21] In January 1959, the pope announced his intention to con-

---

20 *Time*, February 8, 1954, 74.

21 Very familiar with Orthodoxy and Eastern Europe, he had hopes for a closer relationship and believed that since Athenagoras' elevation to the patriarchate that this had become possible. He found Athenagoras to be an exceptional prelate (Martano, 259). Athenagoras also promoted the establishment of a Greek church (eventually St. Andrew) in Rome. See Miltiadou A. Moutsiou, "E Idrusis Ellenorthodoxou Naou en Rome Demiourgema tes A.Th. Panagiotetos tou Patriarchou Athenagorou I," in Anastasiou, *Athenagoras I*, 189-202. For a pictorial history of the Greek Orthodox-Roman Catholic reconciliation see Aristeides G. Panotes, *Paulos VI-Athenagoras I: Eirenopoioi* (Athens: IdrymaEuropes Dragan, 1971).

vene the Second Vatican Council. One of its objectives was Christian unity. But what did this mean?

On March 17, 1959, the late Archbishop Iakovos of North and South America met privately with Pope John XXIII. The archbishop presented a message from Athenagoras in which the patriarch viewed the pope as the "second Apostle John" given his announcement of the Second Vatican Council. Pope John in his response said: "Communication with each other is the seed of unity. The slogan of the French Revolution—Liberty, Equality, Fraternity—must prevail, otherwise there will be neither peace between nations, nor unity between the Churches."[22] But what was the pope's intention? This was the first formal meeting between the "Sister Churches" since 1547. Pope John clarified that he sought dialogue. Of course, Athenagoras was very impressed and receptive. The time seemed propitious for an ecumenical initiative, given the providential presence of an exceptionally open-minded pope. But before Athenagoras could pursue this cherished dream, he had to attain another objective, one which he had been striving for since early in his patriarchate. His perspicacious foresight was again evinced.

Before the question of reconciliation with the Catholic Church could be addressed, there had to be Orthodox unification. Athenagoras measured his moves. He had to, given the autocephalous nature of Orthodoxy. The patriarch of Constantinople is regarded as the "elder brother" among brother patriarchs. His superior authority is traditional rather than inscribed in canon law. Nevertheless, Athenagoras decided to remind Orthodoxy of the ecumenical patriarchate's position in his encyclical commemorating the 1,150th anniversary of the Council of Chalc(k)edon, which confirmed the supremacy of the Ecumenical Patriarchate over other patriarchates and autocephalous churches. He sent delegations of metropolitans on official missions on his behalf to the patriarchs of Alexandria, Antioch, and Jerusalem. He encouraged the exchange of visits between the patriarchates and the Orthodox autocephalous churches with Constantinople. After assiduous care and preparation, he left the Phanar and met with the patriarchs of Alexandria, Antioch, and Jerusalem in 1959. Securing their support, he organized a Pan-Orthodox meeting on the island of Rhodes in 1961, something he had been hoping to achieve since 1952. This was the first time such a meeting had occurred since 879.

22   Tsakonas, 54.

The Russian Orthodox Church, which the Communist government had attempted to manipulate, recognized Athenagoras' primacy as the "elder brother." The Church of Greece, remained quite adamantly opposed to his internationalism. Nevertheless, the Orthodox churches met in September 1961. The reopening of formal relations with the papacy and the development of a pan-Orthodox consensus regarding the Ecumenical Patriarchate were two very significance events in themselves. But this was just the beginning. In 1963, given the 1000-year anniversary of the founding of the monastery of Mount Athos, Athenagoras convoked the second Pan-Orthodox meeting. The third meeting occurred after the historic meeting with Pope Paul VI in January 1964, the fourth, at Chambésy near Geneva in 1968.

Learning of the pope's decision to visit the Holy Land, Athenagoras acted. He proposed a meeting in Jerusalem of all the heads of Christianity, a Pan-Christian summit. The pope politely rejected this idea, but he was very willing to meet Athenagoras in Jerusalem. On the Epiphany January 6, 1964, the leaders of the estranged "Two Sisters" met in Jerusalem and they exchanged a fraternal "kiss of peace." That moment epitomized this text's title: "Justice and Mercy Shall Kiss." Their meeting was the first between pope and patriarch since 1439. At that time, the churches had failed to unite in a climate of political exigency given the strength of the Ottoman Turks and weakness of the Orthodox Byzantines. Although some Orthodox churches and prelates questioned Athenagoras' meeting with the pope, which he undertook without their full consultation, he understood the importance of this gesture. Both men developed a fast friendship. Each wanted to pursue ecumenism with determination and did so dramatically. On December 7, 1965, the pope and patriarch simultaneously lifted the anathemas cast in 1054, thereby revoking mutual excommunications. According to their joint statement, this was a "symbolic action," an "expression of a sincere mutual desire for reconciliation, and an invitation to follow up, in a spirit of trust, esteem and mutual charity, the dialogue which will lead them with the help of God to live afresh."[23] This decision did not mean the end of the schism or the sharing of the "common chalice," but it did illustrate mutual recognition of an absur-

23 E.J. Stormon, ed., *Toward the Healing of Schism: The Sees of Rome and Constantinople. Public Statements and Correspondence between the Holy See and the Ecumenical Patriarchate, 1958-1984* (New York: Paulist Press, 1987), 128.

PHILLIP C. NAYLOR

dity of history that had to be repudiated. Athenagoras hosted Pope Paul at the Phanar on July 25-6, 1967. The patriarch then visited the Vatican on October 26-28 of that year. It was the first time in history that a patriarch had visited Rome. Unity was still out of the question, but dialogue had been decisively established, and a process of reconciliation initated.

Athenagoras' patriarchate would have been significant alone because of his Pan-Orthodox unifying initiatives. But, in addition, there was his development of a close relationship with the Anglican Church, and with Catholic Rite Orthodox Churches, Nestorians, Copts, and other Monophysites.[24] The beginning of the reconciliation with Rome raised his patriarchate to the level of imitable greatness. According to Stélios Castanos de Médicis, Athenagoras was "the greatest ecumenical patriarch, perhaps since Photios [ninth century], as the apostle of peace, of social justice and of the unity of the churches of Christ."[25] After suffering a fall while visiting Chalki, the aged, yet active, patriarch intimated to his associates from his hospital bed: "I am preparing for a long journey."[26] He fell asleep on July 7, 1972.

THE MOTIVATION FOR ATHENAGORAS' ECUMENICAL PRAXIS

What motivated Athenagoras? He was a man of his times. His parents had helped cultivate openness of mind in him. He had experienced ethnic hatred in the Balkans and for that matter, in Constantinople in 1955. The late 1950s and early 1960s saw the growth of a global secular movement as well as an ecumenical one. Frantz Fanon in the *Wretched of the Earth* (1962) spoke of the creation of a "new humanity." Malek Bennabi, the influential Algerian Islamist, wrote of

24 Although Athenagoras' dramatic reconciliation with the Catholic Church has received much attention, he also developed dialogue with other churches, which had broken with the Orthodox Church centuries ago—collectively called the "Anti-Fourth Council of Chalc(k)edon (451) Churches," in general, Monophysite faiths. For a discussion of these dialogues, see Ioannou E. Anastasiou, "E Anaptuxis ton Scheseon Orthodoxon kai Antichalkedoneion kata ten Periodon tes Patriarcheias tou Oikonoumenikou Patrioarchou Athenagorou," in Anastasiou, ed., *Athenagoras I*, 285-305.

25 Stélios Castanos de Médicis, *Athénagoras Ier: L'Apport de l'orthodoxie à l'oecuménisme* (Lausanne: Editions l'Age d'Homme, 1968), 15.

26 George Dimopoulos, *From Death to Life, and from Earth to Heaven* (Brookline, Mass.: Holy Cross Orthodox Press, 1973), 40.

the emergence of a new "ecumenical man" in his work *L' Afro-Asiatisme* (1956) dealing with the Bandung Conference.[27] But, were these engaged popes and patriarch really products of their age?

Athenagoras always perceived the presence of a providential hand in his dialogical relations, especially in his work with the Catholic Church. Archbishop Angelo Roncalli spent many years as a papal representative in Eastern Orthodox countries before he was elevated to cardinal and then to Pope John XXIII. He understood Orthodoxy well. Cardinal Giovanni Battista Montini, who became Paul VI, viewed his papacy as an apostolate for ecumenism. In other words, Athenagoras found exceptional partners, who shared his wish to heal ancient religious animosities—an extraordinary confluence of kindred spirits. They viewed ecumenism strategically and pragmatically as a force for peace in a dangerous, tumultuous world.

It would be wrong to term Athenagoras the initiator of Orthodox ecumenical praxis.[28] The Patriarchal Encyclical of 1920 evinced an Orthodox interest in ecumenism, perhaps not incongruent with the new internationalism of the League of Nations.[29] Nevertheless, Athenagoras was the key to its unfolding. He stated: "I like dialogue very much." It was, for him, a means of discovery since "for the most part people's expression is unknown." Dialogue was equated with "God's

---

27 Malek Bennabi, *l'Afro-Asiatisme: Conclusions sur la Conférence de Bandoeng* (Cairo: Imprimerie Misr, 1956), 345. Like Bennabi, in his studies of history (namely *Discours sur les conditions de la Renaissance algérienne* [Algiers: En-Nahda, 1949] and *Vocation de l'Islam* [Paris: Seuil, 1954]), Athenagoras believed that "civilization is not possible without a spiritual base" (Olivier, 229).

28 Relations after Vatican I had been difficult and polemical. There were differences regarding papal infallibility, the "Filioque" formula in the Creed, the Immaculate Conception of Mary, and the Eastern Churches' loyalty to Rome. There were also the "almosts"— the various attempts at restoring dialogue. For example, while he was convalescing in Italy in 1883, Metropolitan Joachim of Dercos met with Pope Leo XIII. Joachim was elected patriarch but died prematurely (Stormon, 3).

29 See Castanos de Médicis, 35-39. The post-World War I period witnessed an increased desire of the patriarchate to enter into dialogues with other Christian churches. A deputation of five bishops from the Episcopal Church of the USA visited Europe and the Middle East—an ecumenical initiative appreciated by Archbishop Meletios who ordered Athenagoras to learn English!

blessing to receive the world."[30] Metropolitan Chrysostomos recalled that Athenagoras' faith was "simple" even "child-like." He was a risk taker who found "refuge" in the "Good Father" and the "Mother-Virgin."[31] He believed in the existence of a Church of Christ, or rather churches of Christ. He had surely reflected on St. Paul's statement, "Is Christ divided?" (1 Corinthians 1:13). His ecumenical praxis reminds us also of John Climacus's eighth rung of his *The Ladder of Divine Ascent* for monks, it described the ascent toward Christ and Salvation, toward Theosis, or being one with God. It is one of the greatest soteriological and metaphorical works produced in the history of Christian theology. Climacus (Klimakos) referred to its ninth step as the "remembrance of wrongs." He advised: "To forget wrongs is to prove oneself truly repentant."[32] Athenagoras, who regarded himself as a monk, seemed to take this advice to heart and ascended that ladder.

CONCLUSION

Patriarch Athenagoras I believed that the greatest injustice was to be enslaved by history and tradition, since it can lead to obscurantism. One of the leading clerics of the Church of Greece, Archbishop Anastasios, Professor Emeritus of the History of Religions at the National University of Athens, wrote: "We Christians have a pressing obligation to engage in dialogue with people of other religions. In order for such dialogue to be sincere, we must first have respect for the personality and the freedom of those with whom we speak, as well as sincere love and understanding. We must acknowledge the inspiration that exists in other religious experiences." He added: "Every time we engage in dialogue we also interpret and elucidate the testimony of our Christian faith....Above all, our certainty that God is *love*....If we are to be persuasive, however, what we say must grow out of our lives

---

30   Metropolitou Belgiou Amilianou, *Eis ten Mnemen tou* (Athens: Eptalofos, 1974), 113.

31   Metropolitan Chrysostomos Konstantinidou, "Athenagoras o Patriarches: Mia Morfe—Mia Analysis," in Anastasiou, ed., *Athenagoras I*, 473.

32   Father John Mack, *Ascending the Height: A Layman's Guide to* The Ladder of Divine Ascent (Ben Lomond, California: Conciliar Press, 1999, 50-51.)

and our experience."[33] Perhaps, this reflection sums up the ecumenical praxis of Athenagoras. Indeed, he was not only interested in a ritualistic "sharing of the Chalice," among churches, but also in sharing understanding and love toward others, regardless of their ethnic or cultural background. The patriarch told Clément Olivier: "I am an Easterner, I belong to the Turkish people, to the Greek people—but I am also a citizen of the world, I feel French with a Frenchman, German with a German, or Russian, or American. To each, I like speaking some words in his language, even if I do not know it well…not to confuse… [but] to share."[34] His ecumenical praxis was that of an inimitable and generous personality, a powerful pneuma (spirit) who sought action, engagement, and humanity in humility and faith.

PERSONAL REFLECTION BY PHILIP NAYLOR:

Sometimes we become resigned to life, as is often signaled by a shrug of the shoulders. Patriarch Athenagoras I opposed such an attitude. He was an exceptional man of action willing to challenge ossified attitudes and stultified atavisms. Athenagoras had the audacity to change history. His insurgent humility challenged convention. He shifted discourse and direction through his ecumenical initiatives and thereby refuted centuries of absurd anathemas and intractable traditions. With his energy, he engaged others, creating a sort of catalyzing synergy all around him; his presence was profound. I was eleven-years old when I met him. It was an extraordinary experience.

My paper briefly recounts my impressions of him, but it is not a hagiography. It chronicles Athenagoras' ecumenical pursuits. These could not, however, have been accomplished without the spiritual reciprocity and conscientious collaboration of Popes John XXIII and Paul VI. Athenagoras and his papal brothers viewed ecumenism as a liberating project, an existential praxis. Their earnest endeavors to promote spiritual co-operation and conciliation are especially inspiring in the context of today's tumultuous world as it is marked by religious radicalism and triumphalism. Indeed, their collective ecumenical enterprise remains a humanitarian as well as a spiritual imperative.

---

33   Archbishop Anastasios (Yannoulatos), Facing the World: Orthodox Christian Essays on Global Concerns, trans. Pavolos Gottfied (Crestwood, New York: St. Vladimir's Seminary Press, 2003), 152-53.
34   Olivier 227.

15. JEWS OF CONSCIENCE AND
THE REBIRTH OF THE PROPHETIC

MARC H. ELLIS

It may be true that the world is in a perpetual crisis, a "state of emergency" as the Jewish philosophers and literary critic Walter Benjamin wrote during the Nazi era. It may also be true that our traditions and identities are always at an endpoint of sorts—evolving, dying, and seemingly being reborn. Unqualified claims of continuity in tradition, identity and faith are therefore always suspect: A Jew of the fifteenth century is quite different than one from the first century, and for that matter, one from the twenty-first.

Yet, even in this discontinuity some element of association guarantees continuity, hence—the struggle in each generation to define what it means to be Jewish—or Christian, Muslim or Hindu. Why else would we struggle so mightily, with so much emotion and suffering, if affirmation of a particular identity was unimportant? How else can I articulate the meaning of the struggle to be faithful as a Jew if something of great importance is not at stake?

So, if the perpetual crisis of continuity and identity is punctuated by particular crises, perhaps these crises are actually what bind communities together. If so, the thought and action that we engage in within our lifetime is what links us to both previous and subsequent generations. Even though we cannot know how the present moment will play out in the long run, just as our predecessors could not predict our present circumstances, still, what we are left with is *this* moment. It is in the *now* that we make our distinctive contribution.

There is no question that contemporary Jewish identity is framed around the events of the Holocaust and Israel, and that present day Jewish fidelity is lived out within and around these events. There is general agreement on this fact, so much so that contemporary Jewish life is not comprehensible without reference to these two points. Some have even speculated that the Holocaust and Israel are the touchstones of a new religion, one that is paradoxically both continuous and discontinuous with historic Judaism.

Surely there is no return to historic Judaism. Still, an unexpected, and as yet unacknowledged, force has become part of the Jewish future. Within the legacy of the Holocaust and Israel, the Palestinian people loom large, their presence as a part of Jewish history is assured. Although they are seen as foreign and threatening, both culturally and politically, by mainstream Jewish thought, the Palestinians play a still more subversive role. For Jews, they are the "other" within. They challenge the very notion of Jewish identity within the structures and institutions that interpret the Holocaust and Israel.

What does their displacement and suffering mean within the narrative of the United States Holocaust Memorial Museum? The Holocaust Museum emphasizes the suffering of the Jewish people. Yet, in the shadow of the holocaust, the creation of the State of Israel was accomplished together with the displacement of the Palestinian people. This goes unmentioned in the museum's Holocaust narrative. Surely, the Holocaust and the ethnic cleansing of Palestinians during the period of the creation of the state of Israel in 1948 are two separate events. Yet, the memory of the Holocaust and what has been done in its name cannot be considered today without also remembering the tragedy that befell the Palestinians. So, too, when the memory of the Holocaust is invoked as a symbol of Jewish innocence then *and* now, the plight of the Palestinians remains before us, even if the very mention of the Palestinians with regard to the Holocaust and Israel is seen as inappropriate, even blasphemous. The force of this discourse is so powerful that we hardly even ask whose story we are asserting. But, is Jewish discourse, or even the mainstream discourse of the West, the only available or permissible one?

Surely, Palestinian discourse sees the question differently. Moreover much of the world questions Jewish empowerment in Israel and the use of the Holocaust as a locus of unaccountability for the present actions of the state of Israel.

Mainstream Jewish discourse labels other such narratives anti-Semitic, but is this appropriate? Always and everywhere? Perhaps these differing understandings of the role of narrative need to be taken into account as a critique of a newly-powerful community that seeks, like all other powerful communities, to hide aggression under the cloak of ignorance.

Some Jews see the historic and ongoing plight of the Palestinians as defining Jewish identity in light of the Holocaust and Israel. They join an ever-broadening narrative that speaks truth to power. Who are they? And what do they have to say about the crisis confronting us as a people?

To answer this, it is necessary to distinguish three broad trends in Jewish life:

First, there is the emergence and consolidation of a Constantinian Judaism, a Jewishness in league with the state and power. Constantinian Judaism, much like Constantinian Christianity and Constantinian Islam, uses religion and history to buttress positions and policies that further the advantage of a given group of insiders and dispense injustice to others under the guise of innocence and redemption. Here religion and identity are in the service of the state and power; in the twenty-first century, mainstream Jewish institutions serve the American and Israeli states. In this context, the Holocaust and Israel are seen as cornerstones of Jewish identity and projections of both Jewish ascendancy and common human decency. Any critical understanding of either event, or of how the events are used inside or outside Jewish life, is considered akin to treason or blasphemy. Included within Constantinian Judaism are the mainstream Orthodox, Conservative and Reform denominational structures, the seminaries that serve these denominations, the Anti-Defamation League and Holocaust memorial structures and outreach and many university Holocaust and Jewish Studies programs.

Second, there is the broadening progressive movement within Jewish life. In the main, this movement is known as Jewish renewal. It seeks to reinvigorate Judaism and Jewish life through modern interpretations of religion and ritual, and it stands for justice and peace within Jewish life and beyond. It also seeks to broaden the lessons that flow from the Holocaust and Israel, reaching out to others and dissenting against the unjust use of power in Jewish and non-Jewish hands. Even with this attempt to move beyond the Constantinian Jewish establishment, Jewish renewal frames its arguments within Jewish mainstream theology and thus limits the scope of dissent. In short, Jewish renewal has argued that the Holocaust mandates the creation of the state of Israel, but that the mistakes of the post-1967 Israeli occupation of the West Bank and Gaza need to be corrected with the establishment of a Palestinian state. Whereas Constantinian Judaism does not admit the validity of Palestinian aspirations, Progressive Jews do, albeit in a very limited way - one that may tend to blunt their effectiveness in questioning of this sort. In short, it is helpful to see Progressive Jews and Jewish renewal as the left-wing of Constantinian Judaism, assenting to Jewish ascendancy yet, at the same time, critiquing certain aspects of it. Though Palestinians are present in the thought of Jewish progressives, they are secondary, i.e., a certain paternalism prevails. Included with Progressive Jews and the Jewish renewal are the Israeli group, *Peace Now*, the American progressive journal *Tikkun*, Rabbis for Human Rights, and aspects of Jewish denominational and university life.

Third, there is the small but growing minority of Jews of Conscience. They have broken with Constantinian Judaism and Jewish renewal regarding these as aspects of Jewish life that do not address the crisis of the twenty-first century. For Jews of Conscience, the very limitations of the critique of Israeli and American power increasingly place Jews within the context of power structures that cannot be reformed. Or, if they are, they will continue meting out injustice. Jews of Conscience believe that a new prophetic paradigm deriving from the earlier one is needed, and that conscience is the guiding force in reclaiming aspects of the Jewish past and providing a new openness to the world. In the critique of unjust power, especially when it is wielded by Jews in the name of Jewish history, the Holocaust and Israel are placed in a new perspective and the Palestinians, with their own perspective, aspirations and destiny, are linked to the Jewish particularity of the future. Jews of Conscience see an interpreted future in which Jews and Palestinians live across *and* within borders together, in equality and dignity. But, first a reckoning with Jewish history is in order, as is a confession to the Palestinian people: The Holocaust must serve as a bridge to all who suffer injustice rather than as a means of evading accountability. Israel is not our redemption and its acts, are often, and increasingly, equally as troublesome as those of any other nation-state.

As a group, however, Jews of Conscience are fragmented, for the most part neither established nor in possession of a clear identity. They are on the fringe of Jewish life, and yet they may hold the key to the future. The Holocaust and Israel have been central to Jewish life for the last decades—its ascendancy facilitated and assured after the 1967 war—replacing, almost entirely an already disintegrating rabbinic system of thought and practice. Though this system survives and is even experiencing a renewal of sorts today, its entire sensibility is now permeated by the questions of the Holocaust and Israel, especially when it pretends to transcend these. Here I refer to the revival of various forms of Jewish Orthodoxy, including, on the one hand, those who practice a form of settler Judaism, and, on the other hand, those in the academy who found programs of Jewish studies around ancient texts and thereby aim to bypass the questions of the Holocaust and Israel.

However, Progressive Jews still retain their connections to parts of Orthodoxy and to textual renewal, and, at the same time, they attempt to deal with the questions of the Holocaust and of Israel. Their tie to the latter—what they consider to be a hallmark of authentic Judaism—seems to limit their ability to address the contemporary crisis. There is therefore a competition to define or redefine the Jewish establishment: Dissenting groups seek to find a place within an overall pattern of Jewish ascendancy. In sum, they live in the shadow of Constantinian Judaism, benefiting from its reach and affluence, all the while disputing its claim to represent univocally Jewish history and life.

Jews of Conscience understand that it is largely futile to tinker with the rabbinic system or attempt to transcend the crisis of Israel/Palestine and the subsequent effect this has had on the public carrying forth of the memory of the Holocaust. Doing so simply means that Constantinian Judaism will continue its consolidation of power and representation, regardless of the cries of dissent; in fact, it calls into question the seriousness of those cries. But, if the framework of allowable dissent dooms it from the outset, is it truly serious? Still, in the long arc of Jewish history, our individual witness is important. Perhaps even more so as it becomes enfolded within the voices of humankind throughout the ages.

16. CONFLICT, MEDIATION AND PEACEMAKING IN THE PASTORAL PRAXIS OF THE DIOCESE OF SAN CRISTÓBAL DE LAS CASAS, CHIAPAS, MEXICO

MICHEL ANDRAOS

INTRODUCTION

A new pastoral vision and process emerged in the Diocese of San Cristóbal de Las Casas, Chiapas, Mexico a few years after Bishop Samuel Ruiz came to the diocese in 1960.[1] This process developed in the midst of a social conflict marked by poverty and cultural, economic and political systemic violence in which the indigenous people of Chiapas have lived for so long. The diocese understood and supported the indigenous people in their struggle. Many would argue this support was key to the development of a new indigenous political consciousness and its accompanying resistance movements in Chiapas and beyond. Nevertheless, the situation of oppression and poverty continued unchanged and the prolonged condition of structural injustice culminated in an armed uprising led by the indigenous communities in 1994. Bishop Ruiz became the main mediator between the Mexican government and these communities in rebellion, primarily because of his long-standing commitment to a pastoral process that denounced such injustices and established strong relationships of trust with the people of the diocese.

The main thesis of this paper is that when a local church and its bishop take seriously their role of mediation and vocation of peacemaking, they can have a significant impact on the amelioration and transformation of a conflict. The history of the conflict in Chiapas is much too complex to present in detail in a relatively brief paper such as this. My intention here is rather to sketch the widely held views of

---

1 Samuel Ruiz retired in May 2000 at the age of 75, after serving for 40 years as bishop of the diocese. Felipe Arizmendi, and auxiliary bishop Enrique Díaz are the current bishops of the diocese.

diocesan sources and some sympathetic scholars about its root causes and history; secondly, I will discuss the theology of reconciliation and peacemaking of Bishop Ruiz and the Diocese of San Cristóbal, as well as their vocation of peacemaking and mediating actions; thirdly, I will outline and comment on the main features of the diocesan pastoral praxis and its impact on the transformation of the conflict in Chiapas.

BACKGROUND

The indigenous problem is at the crossroads of the problems of our whole society, and we cannot resolve it without finding a solution for the problem of our society. Trying to change the indigenous situation, without changing our social structures, is unworkable. [2]

Samuel Ruiz, 1972

On the eve of January 1, 1994, a group of a few thousand peasants, mostly indigenous, calling themselves the Zapatista National Liberation Army (EZLN) rose up in arms in the southern Mexican State of Chiapas, and declared war on the Mexican Army. They attacked army positions and occupied several of the region's cities and towns, including the colonial city of San Cristóbal, the see of the Diocese of San Cristóbal de Las Casas. The attack lasted for only a few days before the EZLN troops were forced to retreat back to their towns and communities in the jungle and the highlands. There were about two hundred casualties in all, including soldiers of both armies as well as civilians.

The main demands of the EZLN focused on: land, work, education, health care, housing, freedom, democracy and justice for the indigenous and campesino communities. Their First Declaration from the Lacandon Jungle, "Today We Say Enough is Enough!" defined them clearly:

To the people of Mexico: Mexican brothers and sisters

We are a product of 500 years of struggle: first against slavery, then during the War of Independence against Spain led by insurgents, then to avoid being absorbed by North American imperialism, then

---

2 Samuel Ruiz y Javier Vargas, "Pasión y Resurrección del Indio," in *Estudios Indígenas*, II, 1 (September 1972), 46. All quotations from Spanish sources are translated by the author unless indicated otherwise.

to promulgate our constitution and expel the French empire from our soil, and later the dictatorship of Porfirio Diaz denied us the just application of the Reform laws and the people rebelled and leaders like Villa and Zapata emerged, poor men just like us. ... They don't care that we have nothing, absolutely nothing, not even a roof over our heads, no land, no work, no health care, no food nor education. Nor are we able to freely and democratically elect our political representatives, nor is there independence from foreigners, nor is there peace nor justice for ourselves and our children.[3]

The Zapatista uprising took place mainly in the two regions of *La Selva Lacandona* (the Lacandon Jungle), and *Los Altos de Chiapas* (the Chiapas Highlands). Both regions are located within the boundaries of the Diocese of San Cristóbal de Las Casas, and their inhabitants are mostly indigenous peoples.[4]

The Mexican Army responded violently to this uprising by bombarding several villages from air and land, militarizing the region, and occupying many indigenous communities. After eleven days of fighting, and under growing national and international pressure, the Mexican government declared a unilateral cease-fire on January 12.[5]

According to the communiqués of the EZLN, this uprising came as a cry of desperation after repeated protests against the miserable so-

---

3 *Zapatistas, Documents of the New Mexican Revolution* (New York: Autonomedia, 1994), 49.

4 Chiapas has three Roman Catholic dioceses (San Cristóbal de las Casas, Tapachula and Tuxtla Gutiérrez) and several other non-Catholic churches whose members form about 40 percent of the 3.2 million population. Mexico is more than 90 percent Catholic and Chiapas has the highest percentage of non-Catholics among all Mexican states. The majority of the population in the diocese of San Cristóbal (more than one million) is divided into five main ethnic groups: Tzeltales, Tzotziles, Choles, Tojolabales and Zoques, and two other smaller groups, Mames and Lacandones. More than 30 percent of the Indigenous population does not speak Spanish. See Onésimo Hidalgo, "El Estado de Chiapas en Cifras," in Monroy, comp., *Pensar Chiapas, Repensar Mexico*, 15-27.

5 As a result of the fighting, the 1993-1994 annual report of the National Commission of Human Rights in Mexico lists 159 dead, including 16 soldiers, 38 security agents, 67 civilians, 38 unidentified bodies, and 107 wounded. According to the same source, about 48 of the dead were Zapatistas. See John Ross, *Rebellion From the Roots: Indian Uprising in Chiapas* (Monroe, Maine: Common Courage Press, 1995), 150. For a detailed report on the 11 days of fighting, see this same source, 7-153.

cial conditions which the indigenous people of Chiapas have endured for so long. The leaders of the EZLN stated that the native people of Chiapas had exhausted all possible legal means to improve their living conditions and still not gotten any results. *"Ya Basta!"* (Enough!) became their slogan. Faced with the possibilities of death either from disease and hunger, or death with dignity, they said, they chose the latter. So, they declared war against the system.[6]

This uprising had a profound impact on Mexican civil society. "Mexico cannot be the same after January 1, 1994," is a statement that was heard repeatedly there in the summer of that year and which continues to be heard today. The Chiapas uprising, according to a theological reflection paper by the Jesuit Center for Theological Reflection in Mexico City,[7] awakened many Mexican citizens to the reality of the poverty of indigenous peoples and other sectors of Mexican society.[8]

The problem of poverty in Chiapas is not new. It goes back to the time of the Spanish invasion. Since the Spanish *conquistadores* arrived in 1521, Mexico's indigenous peoples have suffered from marginalization, impoverishment, discrimination, disdain for their culture, and the imposition of new economic and political systems and a culture and religion that did not respect their way of life. The native peoples of Chiapas resisted these various forms of oppression on many occasions and in many ways. There were confrontations and uprisings in the early years after the conquest (1524-34): the Battle of Sumidero, 1693 in Tuxtla; 1700 in Chicomuscelo and Soconosco; 1712 in Can-

---

6 *Zapatistas, Documents of the New Mexican Revolution,* 49 ff.; on the use of the term "war of extermination," see the questions that the EZLN presented to Mexican civil society for national consultation on March 21, 1999 in "Chiapas al Día" Electronic Bulletin, Center of Economic and Political Investigations of Community Action, A.C. (CIEPAC), 142 (January 22, 1999), Chiapas, Mexico, available on <www.ciepac.org>; see also the EZLN "Fifth Declaration of the Lacandon Jungle," available on <www.ezln.org>.

7 "Chiapas .... Buena Nueva a pesar de Todo" (Mexico City: Centro de Reflexion Teologica, 1994), 1.

8 Mexican theologian Carlos Bravo shares the same opinion. He commented on the EZLN uprising on several occasions. See for example *Chiapas: El Evangelio de los Pobres. Iglesia, Justicia y Verdad* (Mexico City: Temas de Hoy, 1994), 9-11, 79-91.

cuc; 1869 in San Juan Chamula; 1974 in San Andrés Larráinzar;[9] and the more recent EZLN uprising. The present Zapatista uprising is the most widespread and well organized of all.[10]

Anthropologist Andrés Aubry, among others, argues that, although there were no large scale organized rebellions in the past, there has been a continuous history of resistance. He maintains that the EZLN uprising on January 1, 1994 is congruent with the long history of indigenous resistance, and describes this long movement as a "slow accumulation of force in silence."[11] The history of many indigenous communities in Chiapas—and elsewhere—demonstrates that there was no time when they were not resisting the colonizers, even when their resistance went unnoticed. According to Aubry, many native peoples have, in fact, developed a *culture of resistance* which has become embedded in their way of life, community social organization, and popular religion.[12]

---

9   Since January 1, 1994, San Andrés Larráinzar has again been a site of several confrontations between the Mexican Public Security Police and the native communities of the region. On April 7, 1999, the pro-PRI "elected" council supported by about 300 members of the Public Security Police force took back the municipal building in San Andrés which had been occupied by the members of the "autonomous municipal council," chosen by the community according to traditional customs. The following day, April 8, about 3,000 pro-Zapatista indigenous people marched peacefully, regained control of their municipal building and re-installed their "autonomous council." *La Jornada*, April 9, 1999, 3, 4 and 5.

10   On the various rebellions throughout the history of Chiapas see Elizabeth Pólito Barrios, "Las Autonomías," in *El Caminante, Boletín Interno de la Diócesis de San Cristóbal de Las Casas*, 2ª Epoca, (May 1996), 37-44; Andrés Aubry, "La Historia de Chiapas Identifica a Los Zapatistas," in CENCOS *Iglesias* (Sept. 1994), 25-35; Jan de Vos, "The Battle of Sumidero, A History of the Chiapanecan Rebellion Through Spanish and Indian Testimonies (1524-34)," in Kevin Gosner and Arij Ouweneel, eds., *Indigenous Revolts in Chiapas and the Andean Highlands* (Amsterdam: CEDLA, 1996), 9-25; Kevin Gosner, "Historical Perspectives on Maya Resistance," in Gosner et al., eds., *Indigenous Revolts*, 26-42; Jan Rus, "Whose Caste War? Indians, Ladinos and the Chiapas 'Caste War' of 1869," in Gosner et al., eds., *Indigenous Revolts*, 43-77.

11   Aubry, "La Historia de Chiapas," 29.

12   For studies on the cultural resistance of the indigenous communities of Chiapas, see Antonio García de León, *Resistencia y Utopía: Memorial de Agravios y Crónicas de Revueltas y Profecías Acaecidas en la Provincia de*

During the 1970s, the indigenous communities of Chiapas experienced a new social awakening. Many believe that this was encouraged in part by the consciousness-raising popular education programs promoted by the pastoral workers and the catechists of the Diocese of San Cristóbal. According to many diocesan sources, and some external observers of this process, one of the most significant turning points in the history of collaboration between the diocesan teams and the indigenous communities was the First Indigenous Congress that took place in 1974.[13] At the Congress, representatives of the government of Chiapas and of the marginalized indigenous communities met face-to-face. The State Governor inaugurated the Congress, and senior officials were present at all its sessions. They heard the plea of the indigenous communities, their analyses of their problems and their demands. The Congress provided an opportunity for the communities to speak loudly and clearly through the voices of their representatives and the government heard them. But there is little evidence that the government really listened and responded to their outcry. This Congress was a missed historic opportunity and the events of 1994 demonstrated that the Mexican government failed to respond to it appropriately. It might have been the beginning of a genuine reconciliation and peacemaking process in Chiapas and beyond.

MEDIATION, PEACEMAKING AND
THE ROLE OF THE LOCAL CHURCH

On January 21, 1994, twelve days after the cease-fire between the EZLN and the Mexican government, a statement from the Diocese of San Cristóbal declared that Bishop Samuel Ruiz had accepted the role of mediator in the peace process between these two parties.[14]

Chiapas Durante los Ultimos Quinientos Años de su Historia (México City: Ediciones Era, 1985); Jean De Vos, La Paz de Dios y del Rey: La Conquista de la Selva Lacandona (1525-1821) (Mexico City: Secretaría de Educación y Cultura de Chiapas, 1980).

13 For a detailed description of the Indigenous Congress and a listing of bibliographical sources, see Michel Andraos, "Indigenous Leadership in the Church: The Experience of the Diocese of San Cristóbal de Las Casas, Chiapas, Mexico," in Toronto Journal of Theology, Spring 2005, vol. 21(1), 58-59.

14 CONAI, Archivo Histórico Serie: "Senderos de Paz," cuaderno no. 1 (Mexico City: CONAI, 1999), 14-15.

Don Samuel would carry out this service as bishop, not as judge, and without renouncing his prophetic responsibility. The diocesan statement proposed a framework for the dialogue and an explanation of the meaning of mediation and peacemaking that he had hoped the process would foster.[15]

In a message delivered on a day of reconciliation and peace held in the Cathedral of San Cristóbal on January 23, 1994, Don Samuel declared that he and the diocese had accepted the task of mediation. He explained his understanding of it by saying

> Our local church, and particularly I as its pastor, wants to assume the calling from God who calls us to be ministers of reconciliation. Supported by all of you, I have agreed to take on the task of mediation which the Mexican government and the Zapatista Army of National Liberation asked of me. Above all, and in ecclesial communion, I feel called by God to do this work. … But I want to make it very clear that I participate in these negotiations not as a judge but as a bishop who does not renounce his prophetic vocation which has its basis in the ultimate commitment to the Father of our Lord Jesus Christ and his cause, which is the fullness of life for all his children, particularly for the people who have lived deprived of it.[16]

The desired peace, asserted Don Samuel, cannot be imposed; nor can it entail a return to the pre-war status quo which was a bitter nightmare for the majority of the people in Chiapas. This is not the kind of peace that God desires. In a significant diocesan document on mediation and the role of the local church and its bishop, Ruiz argues that the root causes of a conflict are: structural injustices, lack of democracy, and violation of human rights. Conflicts, he pointed out, "create irreversible processes which generate deep change and necessitate new situations. … Peace can only be built by dealing with the causes [of a conflict]."[17] Working for peace first requires an analysis of the conflict as it is related to existing, unjust structural conditions. When con-

---

15   CONAI, *Archivo Histórico*, cuaderno no. 1, 16-19.

16   CONAI, *Archivo Histórico*, 16.

17   Samuel Ruiz, "Mediating High Intensity Conflicts: One Bishop's Perspective on Mediating High Intensity Social Conflicts," in Michel Andraos, *Praxis of Peace: The Pastoral Work and Theology of Bishop Samuel Ruiz and the Diocese of San Cristóbal de Las Casas, Chiapas, Mexico*, (Unpublished dissertation, University of St. Michael's College, Toronto, 2000), Appendix II, 220. For a version of the original document in Spanish, see Samuel

flicts arise, the document argues, it is a sign that there are "structural deficiencies as well as deficiencies on the part of social and political actors. ... Creating peace is impossible without creating new political and social forces who work for the common good."[18] The document emphasizes the significant and uniquely prophetic role local churches can play in mediation:

> In several armed conflicts, the services of churches have been required to support mediation efforts. The trustworthiness of the churches in these conflicts is due not only to the fact that they fill the vacuum left by political and social actors, or to the absence of strong parties or to the inability of the forces to commence dialogue. All these elements help explain the presence of the churches, but the constant throughout the world is the churches' own specific identity in the mediation role they play. There exists an awareness concerning the distinct character that churches have [which is] prophetic, not political. Their trustworthiness has a lot to do with their ability to provide disinterested service. The church is not an actor which seeks to capitalize upon its capacity for mediation, nor to strengthen its own projects. The church understands that its only project is peace, and therefore can contribute to peace through its role of mediation objectively and neutrally, and with greater commitment.[19]

In Don Samuel's view, churches are called to be prophetic. Part of their prophetic ministry and mission of service (diakonia) to the world is their contribution to reconciliation, social transformation, and peace-making. Churches can contribute to the creation of the conditions and space for civil, political and social forces to come together and become co-participants in building peace.[20] According to Ruiz, this pastoral ministry of the church is deeply rooted in the ecclesiology of Vatican II and of the Latin American Bishops' teachings of the last three decades. The activities of the church such as liturgy, evangelization, service and catechesis ought to be directed to accomplishing this goal.[21]

Ruiz, "Mediación de Conflictos de Alta Intensidad," in CENCOS-Iglesias (December 1995), 3-5.

18   Ruiz, Ibid., 220.

19   Ruiz, Ibid., 220-221.

20   Ruiz, Ibid., 221.

21   Ruiz, Ibid., 221.

Bishop Ruiz argues that "the work of peace and mediation is profoundly ecclesiastical and profoundly episcopal." It is rooted in following the model of Jesus, the Mediator *par excellence*. Peace building and reconciliation are realized through mediation which is an ecclesial service to the community. Mediation strives to unite and reconcile the community through actions aimed at strengthening just social structures and promoting justice and peace. By providing this service, the church and its bishops help to create social actors and situations that promote the emergence of new alternatives to the situations which generated armed conflict. He argues that churches must take upon themselves the tasks of mediation and embrace this service to society. If they do not, they are neglecting of one of their most vital tasks, namely defending life.[22]

A pastoral letter from the Diocese of San Cristóbal, *Del Dolor a la Esperanza*, affirms the awareness of this local church of its mission of peacebuilding.[23] The letter notes that peace is an essential component of the reign of God, as it is founded on justice, equality and love. For this reason,

> faithful to the word of God and to the values of the reign of God, as bishop and Church we prophetically assume the difficult task of mediation in the Dialogue for the purpose of achieving peace with justice and dignity. ... This task is full of misunderstandings, accusations, and calumnies, but is also seen as necessary by some. ... The building of the reign of God requires a transformation of the present social, political, economic and cultural conditions. And more than anything else, it also requires a transformation of the hearts of each person, family, community and of all our country.[24]

A significant component of lasting peace is reconciliation. Bishop Ruiz argues that it has two dimensions, the personal or spiritual and the social. There is no reconciliation without restitution in concrete social, political, economic and cultural terms. Peacemaking and reconciliation, which include establishing social justice, building democracy, and protecting human rights, are fundamental to proclaiming the reign of God in history. In his words:

---

22   Ruiz, Ibid., 221-223.

23   Samuel Ruiz and Raúl Vera, *Del Dolor a la Esperanza*, pastoral letter from the Diocese of San Cristóbal de Las Casas (December, 1998).

24   Excerpts from *Del Dolor a la Esperanza*, no. 4, in *El Caminante*, bulletin of the Diocese of San Cristóbal de Las Casas, March 13, 1999.

Reconciliation assumes a concrete change in our relationship with
God and the people; it is not just a mere change of feelings; it consists of the transformation of an objective situation. Peace with God
is intimately related to inner peace and social peace; it cannot be
separated from these two aspects. Where social, political, economic,
and cultural inequalities exist, there is a rejection of the God of history.[25]

I have thus far presented a summary of the theology of peace of the
Diocese of San Cristóbal and Bishop Ruiz. The peacemaking ministry
of the church is a praxis that takes place in a concrete historic context
and becomes an essential component of proclaiming the good news of
the reign of God—the good news of peace to the poor. This will be the
focus of the remaining part of this paper.

PEACEMAKING AS A PASTORAL PRAXIS

The Mexican Dominican theologian and human rights activist, Miguel
Concha, argues that the pastoral process of the Diocese of San Cristóbal has evolved in response to the prolonged, structural and historic
violence endured by the indigenous people of Chiapas. Peace cannot
be restored there by military means; a military solution can only aggravate the vicious spiral of violence. As Concha notes, "we all want
peace, but not merely at any price. We want true peace which is born
of justice for all and the recognition and respect of all the human
rights for all. A peace that requires the end of violence, and the end of
the causes of violence." [26] According to him, eliminating the causes of
violence requires urgent social change, change aimed at removing the
causes of poverty, not only in Chiapas, but in all of Mexico.[27] However,
the diocesan pastoral process and the indigenous peoples' perspectives
on peace are not the only visions for peacemaking; there are others as
well.

The conflict there is complex. It involves many actors and occurs
at many levels of society. On the one hand, the Mexican government
(local and federal), supported by the economic elite, large landowners,
the Mexican armed forces and police want to re-establish and impose
the "peace" of yesterday. They want a return to the *status quo*, based on

25   CONAI, *Archivo Histórico*, cuaderno no. 1, 17-18.
26   Miguel Concha, "Paz Verdadera y Vida Digna para Todos," in CENCOS
      Iglesias (Jan. 1994), 4.
27   Ibid. 6.

the old social relations of power with the campesino and indigenous communities and their organizations. And they want this without having to make any significant structural changes to the economic, political and social order. The main axes of the government's national "peacebuilding" process are the promotion of market economy, globalization and free trade in Chiapas and the Central American region, as well as projects such as Plan Puebla Panama.[28] The continued extensive presence of the Federal Mexican Army in Chiapas supports the implementation of this national policy. On the other hand, civil organizations and movements are struggling to establish processes of economic, political and social transformation in which all participate. These processes aim at building a new society based on true democracy, justice and peace and so take into consideration the interest of those at the bottom of the social and economic order.[29] The work of mediation, reconciliation and peace which the Diocese of San Cristóbal has been promoting represents the interests of the indigenous people and supports their civil organizations and social movements. The commitment to such indigenous communities has long been a focal point of the diocesan pastoral work and has guided its vision of mediation and peacemaking. Aubry notes that these new civil society movements and organizations in Chiapas - "the new Chiapas" as he calls them—call into question the entire Mexican social system insofar as they propose new and alternative models for local economic and social organization.[30]

The long pastoral praxis of the diocese (since the early 1970s) aimed at transforming the systemic structures that supported violence and at building those which would support justice and peace. Its multiple dimensions included the diocesan option for the poor, respect for indigenous cultures and religions, and a commitment to the people in

---

28   See Miguel Pickard, "The Plan Puebla Panama Revived: Looking Back to See What is Ahead," in La Cronique de Amériques, 12 (April 2004), 1-7.

29   See Pablo Latapí, "La Paz de Don Samuel," in Chiapas: El Evangelio de los Pobres, 159-161; Andrés Aubry, "Para un Retrato del Mediador," ibidem, 163-167; Samuel Ruiz, "Mensaje para la Reconciliación y la Paz," ibid., 169-174; Jorge Santiago, "El Momento Actual de Chiapas: La Construcción de la Sociedad Civil," in CONAI, Archivo Historico, Cuaderno no. 2, 193-204.

30   Aubry, "Para un Retrato del Mediador," 165.

their struggles, all of which are defining theological and pastoral principles of this praxis. One key aspect of this process is that it developed a praxis which involved concrete historic, strategic and transformative pastoral work and ongoing theological reflection. All of these were carried out by thousands of trained, mostly indigenous catechists and several hundred indigenous deacons and all of which were supported by the diocesan structure. This concrete, historic, multi-dimensional pastoral process has continued over several decades, and was unwavering in its denouncement of the structures of violence, in its commitment to educating the people and supporting the social movements through which they sought to develop an alternative, new society. It expands the horizon of theology and the praxis of peacemaking and offers an inspiring example to the universal church.

This long pastoral process prepared the way for Bishop Ruiz and the diocesan teams to do the work of mediation in the conflict between the EZLN and the Mexican government after January 1, 1994. Insofar as they accepted responsibility for the service of mediation from the very early days of the conflict, they helped reduce the level of violence, fostered concrete hope, and were able to propose new alternatives for building peace. Certain facts about the Chiapas situation were remarkable: A cease-fire was reached after only 11 days of fighting, and national and international civil societies were engaged as actors in the process of reconciliation and peace building. This mediation made several peace agreements possible between the government and the EZLN, the most important of them being the San Andrés agreement on Indigenous Rights and Culture which was signed in February of 1996. However, the Mexican government did not fulfill these agreements. Instead, it launched a low intensity war against the people of Chiapas, one which is still ongoing.[31] The indigenous communities have declared "war" against the Mexican army and system, but their main demand has been dialogue. But, even in the context of this extreme conflict, the deep ethical commitment and moral credibility of Bishop Ruiz and several other diocesan mediation organizations have helped reduce the violence, opened possibilities for dialogue and introduced a new strategy for building peace.

---

31 See *Militarization and Violence in Chiapas*; *Ni Paz Ni Justicia* (San Cristóbal de Las Casas: Centro de Derechos Humanos Fray Bartolomé de Las Casas, 1996); and *Chiapas: La Guerra en Curso* (Mexico City: Centro de Derechos Humanos "Miguel Agustín Pro Juárez," 1998).

Don Samuel denies having a pre-existing elaborate theoretical definition of peace which served as an ideal or model for the diocesan praxis.[32] In fact, his early theological reflections do not include a distinct discourse on peace. The discourse which he developed is, however, well-rooted in the long history of the diocesan pastoral process, its social vision, spirituality, popular education programs, organization and leadership development. One could say that, even though the language of peace was not explicit in his theological and pastoral discourse of the 1970s and 1980s, peacemaking was nevertheless always at the center of the diocesan pastoral process. It was merely worked out more explicitly as the situation unfolded.

CONCLUSION

The present bishop, Felipe Arizmendi, and auxiliary bishop, Enrique Díaz, continue to support formally the diocesan praxis that began with Bishop Ruiz. The diocesan pastoral praxis was formalized in the Third Diocesan Synod, which was concluded in the year 2000, after five years of deliberations. The agreements of the synod are recognized in the newly published pastoral plan of the diocese, which attempts to put its decisions into practice.[33] The diocesan pastoral process does not represent the totality of social forces working for justice and peace, but it certainly makes a significant contribution to this movement. The struggle for peace with justice and human dignity and the resistance of the indigenous people of Chiapas continue. In spite of enormous local and global challenges, their efforts continue to be marked by renewed creativity and resilience. Their dream of a new Chiapas and a new world still motivates their peaceful struggle—and they themselves continue to be an important source of hope for our church and for the world.

ABOUT THE AUTHOR

Michel Andraos is an Associate Professor of Cross-Cultural Ministries at Catholic Theological Union in Chicago.

---

32   Samuel Ruiz, interview with the author, in *Seeking Freedom*, 51.

33   See Diócesis de San Cristóbal de Las Casas, *Plan Diocesano de Pastoral*, (Diocese of San Cristóbal de Las Casas, 2004).

242   MICHEL ANDRAOS

PERSONAL REFLECTION BY MICHEL ANDRAOS

Having been born and raised in Lebanon, my interest in doing theology of peace is not a just an academic exercise or a curiosity. It is
rather rooted in my experience of the great injustice of international
politics and in deep desire to see Christian churches and communities
become more aware of their vocation of social peacemaking, especially
in places where they have historically contributed more to creating social injustice and conflict than to building peace. Certainly, observing
the pastoral process in the Diocese of San Cristóbal de Las Casas,
Chiapas, Mexico for the last twelve years has profoundly shaped my
understanding of what I call a "pastoral praxis of peace." However, I
take the main challenge of peacemaking to be developing a praxis that
is sustainable, since social transformation is always a very long-term
endeavor. All pastoral processes that take peacemaking seriously in
situations of structural injustice and conflict must be prepared to survive for a long time while resisting social evil and oppressive power
structures. This reality is often underestimated. As the present case
study and several other situations around the world will reveal, this is
a significant theological and pastoral challenge.

PART 3
PEACEMAKING THROUGH EDUCATIONAL INSTITUTIONS AND ETHICAL BUSINESS PRACTICES

17. TEACHING PEACE IN A DANGEROUS WORLD

NATHAN TIERNEY

We live in dangerous times. Terrorism, religious and ethnic violence, new kinds of nuclear threats, environmental
deterioration, population pressures on natural resources,
new projections of force by both current and emerging powers, increased international hostilities, the expanding reach of organized
crime—all of these point to a world of multiple threats and challenges.
Further, they are all being profoundly shaped by the defining shift of
our times: globalization. The current trend of economic, cultural and
political forces to by-pass national borders and create new congeries
of power of global scope is likely to continue at an increasing pace
throughout the 21st century. Old certainties and patterns of response
have become problematic, and many of our institutions of governance
at both the national and international level are becoming more and
more dysfunctional.

In such a world, peace education is needed more than ever. But if it is
to address the current dangers effectively and respond to the underlying global pressures realistically, peace educators will need to re-think
some of their assumptions, methods and pedagogies. In this paper I
would like to propose five specific changes to peace education practice which I believe will empower our vocation for this global century.
Some of these changes are already underway while others have barely
begun. Some will be received with widespread agreement, even if their
practical implementation will require prolonged and dedicated effort.
Others will, I expect, be vigorously disputed since they challenge some
of the basic valuational framework of much of the peace education
that has been practiced since the Second World War.

I. COSMOPOLITANISM

First, peace educators should deliberately educate for a cosmopolitan
perspective. The vast majority of the world's people still see global
events solely through the lens of their own group or nation. This is
rapidly becoming untenable. Monocular vision is not only a main

cause of violent conflict, it is also such that it is unable to perceive possible solutions to global problems.

The idea of cosmopolitanism has a long history. Deriving its meaning from its Greek roots, *kosmos* (world) and *polites* (a citizen), it expresses the attitude of mind and habits of action of a world citizen: a person of no fixed residence or national identity, one who is nowhere a stranger, and everywhere at home. Though this may seem to be an innocuous and apparently timely idea, it has in fact been the subject of lively debate, often even hostility. It has been opposed by both national realists and communitarians. On the one hand, realists argue that, in our dealings with other countries, we should always put our national interest first since other nations certainly do. On the other hand, communitarians such as Michael Walzer and Amatai Etzioni argue that a universal perspective is neither possible nor desirable. From what values and principles would such a perspective be derived? In what way could it claim legitimacy over against the self-conception of particular cultures? Does it not require a conception of rights-possessing individuals which ignores the communal embedding of the self?

These objections may have some weight, but I do not think they are ultimately decisive. I agree that cosmopolitan principles cannot have the *sui generis* authority that some of their more Kantian proponents claim for them, yet I believe that it is within our capacity to develop universal values and principles appropriate to global ethics and global politics *from the ground up*. In fact, the current world situation demands that we do so. The cosmopolitanism appropriate to peace education is an *evolutionary cosmopolitanism* rather than one which is imposed from above. Two of its central features are a systems approach to identifying global problems and an intercultural approach to resolving them.

The systems approach is necessary because many of our problems today have global aspects that are simply beyond the capacity of nation-state politics to resolve. Systems thinking involves the capacity to see things as parts of wholes, to give attention to processes, the ability to trace interactions and interrelations across local categories and contexts, the clarification of high leverage factors in complex situations, and the provision of a unifying narrative. It works from the ground up when empirical and inductive methods are used to arrive at basic principles which are themselves always open to further testing and refinement.

But the systems approach is only part of the puzzle. Indeed, if it were the only strategy of cosmopolitanism, it would lead to all sorts of disasters, ranging from the destruction of local communities to the rise and domination of world tyrants. Human beings are cultural beings, not merely parts of systems. They attain their understanding of their world within more or less local relationships, with more or less local sets of significations and patterns of conduct. This is not some unfortunate circumstance that is to be overcome by some transcendent world view, but the lifeblood of a meaningful existence. That is why the second element of a healthy cosmopolitanism must be an *evolutionary interculturalism* which understands globalization as a process for which each culture must evolve its own subroutines of intercultural exchange suited to its own sense of identity.

A truly global citizen must have a foot in both global and local processes, understanding the systemic issues but recognizing that all solutions will require the cooperation of local processes. Cultures are not static. They are in a state of constant change, even as they retain their most ancient cultural tropes and strategies of identification. Similarly, the self-descriptions of their citizens are both fluid and multiple. These cultural facts provide the opening for intercultural progress. There are forces of evolution as well as devolution in any society, and the cosmopolitan peace educator will identify the former and participate with them in working for a better world.

A case in point is inter-religious conflict. The lack of a sufficiently intercultural approach has been evident in the failure of a great many of the peacemaking efforts of international bodies. Internationalism (as opposed to cosmopolitanism) has frequently taken the view that because these conflicts are given religious significations, religion itself is the problem; therefore negotiations should be restricted to so-called practical matters, and orchestrated as much as possible by neutral third parties with credentials from approved international bodies. In hindsight, the cultural naiveté of this view is breathtaking. Religious meanings form a considerable part of the core of self-understanding of most cultures, and they involve a level of intellectual and spiritual depth that require years of study before they can even be partially understood—let alone bypassed. To be sure, because of its intense personal and cultural potency, religion is capable of generating violent antagonisms among people who feel its power but who have not yet arrived at the level of self-reflection which would enable them to embody higher religious ideals. Interfaith antagonism is not essential to religion, and the antagonisms that do arise between proponents of different faiths require religiously-educated responses if they are to be part of any general peace process. One important implication of the evolutionary intercultural approach, then, would be to encourage and support the already active interreligious peacebuilding efforts and to generate new and more extensive interreligious programs.

Cosmopolitanism in this sense seems to be both possible and necessary in the age of globalization, and it is to educators that the responsibility for this primarily falls. An important part of this process is the development and articulation of a global ethic which can guide both systems thinking and intercultural exchange. Several projects which aim to work in this direction are already underway. There is much more common ground between cultures than either national realists or communitarians acknowledge. Shared global values can assuredly be developed which all functional cultures could eventually endorse, while still permitting considerable variety of interpretation and implementation in diverse cultural contexts.

A global ethic can recognize shared values while at the same time respecting the diverse ways in which those values might be culturally embedded and expressed. It would take a multi-layered approach, with more general values governing, but not determining, the legitimacy of culturally more specific layers. A possible outline of a global ethic which could form part of peace pedagogy might be as follows:

1. *Core values:*
   respect for the dignity of all human beings
   responsibility for one's and actions and relationships
   concern for the welfare and happiness of others.
2. *General standards of human interaction:*
   human rights, reciprocity, community, principles of justice, freedom, security.
3. *Culture-specific norms, codes and practices:*
   marriage and courtship customs, gift giving, rules of hospitality, religious ceremonies and practices, etc.
4. *Practice-specific norms, codes and practices:*
   accounting, engineering, medicine, education, dancing, fishing, etc.
5. *Group-specific norms, codes and practices:*
   corporations, universities, villages, voluntary organizations, etc.

6. *Personal values, projects and relationships:*
  personal interests and ideals, careers and ambitions, families, friendships, etc.

The upper levels identified here express more generality and objectivity, the lower ones, more particularity and subjectivity. The former are thus more absolute, the latter, more relative. Moving up the ladder conduces to integration, moving down, differentiation. If a way of achieving a lower level value (e.g. a personal interest in money) is in conflict with a higher level one which is in conformity with core values (e.g. honest accounting methods), then we know that it is wrong. There can still be conflict between levels, of course, since there will be a variety of ways in which a higher level value can be modeled; not all models are consistent with each other. But such conflict is due not to any supposedly absolute cultural relativity in the nature of value, but to the variety of concrete ways that different personalities and cultures express those values. Similarly, two culturally distinct value formations on the same level can be mutually exclusive in their practical implications. However, as long as they are both consistent with a higher level value which is in conformity to core values, this mutual exclusivity need not generate conflict. Diversity of this kind is an important social good. Difference, in itself, does not have to produce conflict. Conflict will properly arise if one or more of the ways of embodying values are inconsistent with core values.

2. REALISM

Second, peace education needs, in the words of John Paul Lederach, "a dose of realism". He states: "Ours are professions afflicted with a proclivity toward the promise of great change. It is true. Our rhetoric comes easy. If constructive social change rolled forward as easily as our words and promises pour out, world justice and peace would have surely been attained by now." [1] In their hearts, most peace educators are idealists of one sort or another, and idealism is a wonderful thing. It provides a large perspective and purpose to our lives which takes us out of our self-concern and gives us hope and inspiration for the future. But it may also involve attitudes which can get in the way of success. There is a temptation to treat our ideals as blueprints rather than sources of inspiration, to allow them to ossify into ideologies which can exclude cooperation with those who do not happen to share our

particular vision of perfection. There is also a temptation to factional-
ize ourselves under absolute banners that create divisions rather than
heal them. This kind of idealism can cause us to become impatient
concerning the small and difficult steps that are the only path forward
to even partial realization of our goals. Finally, such idealism can even
lead to cynicism, self-righteousness and despair in light of the realization that the world obstinately refuses to re-make itself overnight in
the image of our ideal.

A case in point is the way that peace educators treat the idea of
nonviolence, which is certainly one of our most profound and moving
ideals. There is a tendency to broaden the concept so that it becomes
virtually identical with the real peace for which we are striving, i.e.,
to include not just physical violence, but all forms of "psychological"
and "structural" violence, the latter being extra-psychological in nature.
There is, indeed, such a thing as structural violence, but one should
use the concept sparingly. Racism and sexism are psychologically violent. Laws which are designed to exclude certain members of a population from receiving benefits that others enjoy are structurally violent.
But speech that some might be offended by, or laws with which one
disagrees, might be uncivil or unjust and yet not violent. Much of what
is called "psychological violence" is perhaps better treated under the ru-
bric of training for civility rather than for nonviolence. Similarly, much
of what is called "structural violence" is often better understood not by
reference to the ideal of nonviolence, but as a violation of justice.

When we paint with too broad a brush, important differences between these phenomena are overlooked, and we are seduced into an
absolutist rhetoric that is both impractical and subtly divisive. We pro-
nounce a "decade to end violence" and are surprised that few take us
seriously. The truth is that the impulse to violent response is a very real
part of our biological make-up, without which we would undoubtedly not have survived as species. But our growing interconnectedness
makes the task of restraining and transforming that impulse (rather
than, as is impossible, eliminating it from our cultures) more urgent
than ever. Further, an absolutized commitment to an overly-broad notion of nonviolence tends to obscure and distort the valuable function
performed by conflict in human life. Conflict can sometimes be appropriate and healthy because it allows us to clarify our disagreements
over ideas and policies. The suppression of this kind of conflict in the
name of nonviolence can itself be a very subtle form of violence. The

goal of peace education is not to eliminate conflict; sometimes, indeed, it should seek to encourage it. Rather, the goal is (again, in Lederach's phrase), to *transform* it into something constructive.

3. IDEOLOGICAL INCLUSIVISM

Third, peace educators should not allow themselves to be burdened by the political and theological frameworks within which they operate. They should also encourage cooperation between peace educators who come from a variety of religious traditions, and political orientations and who take different starting points. There are, for example, a host of governmental peace education projects. The various religious traditions also have a long history of peace education efforts. There are interfaith projects, there are pacifist and non-pacifist peace traditions of peacemaking and also liberal, internationalist, socialist, feminist, anti-war and conservative peace educators. Each of these contributes a great deal, but they have thus far failed to provide a synthesis or a strategy appropriate to a global society. Often, they are unfortunately reduced to squabbling among themselves. The fault lies not in their intentions, nor in their skills as peace educators, which are often exemplary, but rather in their insistence on implementing their own framework of valuation in a particular way. The result is the implicit or explicit assignment of blame and the curtailment of cooperation with other peace educators who do not share their assumptions or doctrines. The language of peace education inevitably occurs in larger social contexts, so we must be very careful that the framework we draw on does not exclude or dis-invite those who would otherwise share in our practical and constructive efforts. Peacebuilding is a recognizable necessity for all of us, whether religious or non-religious, Democrat or Republican, Western or Eastern.

The majority of today's peace educators undoubtedly see themselves as situated on the left of the political spectrum. There are good historical reasons why this is so, but our current global context makes such a posture ever less useful. Centrists and conservatives interested in working for peace are quickly made to feel unwelcome at many peace gatherings by gratuitous hostile remarks about the Bush administration, capitalism, and Western culture in general. No doubt these are sincerely meant, and are often little more than a form of unconscious group bonding intended to demonstrate one's attitudinal credentials; still, they are exclusionary and counterproductive. They establish unnecessary boundaries, inhibit cooperation across political lines and severely limit the resources of the peace movement. The truth is that being a peacemaker does not require one to adopt either leftist or a rightist views. It is perfectly compatible with liberalism in the classic constitutional sense (i.e., as involving a commitment to the rule of law, government based on free and fair elections, consent of the governed, toleration, freedoms of religion, speech and assembly and the recognition and protection of human rights). It is *also* compatible with conservative positions on certain issues such as skepticism about the integrity and efficacy of some international bodies such as the UN and ICC, an emphasis on the importance of tradition, endorsement of an activist military role in support of democratic governments and a federalist conception of global governance. Peace educators need to become better at separating their political convictions from their primary peace making endeavors.

In this connection, I would particularly urge more cooperation between pacifist and non-pacifist peacebuilders. Historically, much of post-WWII peace education, which itself is a deeply sourced and honorable movement, has been conducted along pacifist lines. It has represented the highest ideals of Christian life with courage, integrity and love. But there are two other peace traditions within Christianity, namely, Catholic Just War theory and the Christian realism of Martin Luther and Reinhold Niebuhr. In their own way, these traditions recognize nonviolence as our highest ideal, but believe that responsible peace-seeking in a fallen world requires that we be prepared, under specific conditions and in certain circumstances, to face violence with violence.

In St. Augustine's words:

> In dealing with this 'condition of war' we must of course pray for peace and hope for peace but we must also be prepared to deal with the wars and discord that will inevitably affect our lives. Certainly, we should be messengers of peace, but we must also be able and willing to respond to attacks against those we love, those under our care, against those ideals to which we have dedicated our lives. When wars are waged for such good and noble purposes, they must be said to be righteous wars.[2]

There are many people who yearn for peace and work for it, but nevertheless believe that democratic nations today need to have significant armed forces available to them. In the words of Trotsky, "You may not be interested in war, but war is interested in you."

It is not my purpose here to argue the relative merits of these positions, but only to point out two things. First, a great deal can be accomplished by way of peace education without insisting that either of these is the only right answer; it is better to unite than to fight. Second, all three positions have a role to play in any long-term dialogue among peacebuilders. Pacifism keeps Just War theory and Christian realism honest, demanding that it give a rigorous account of its motivations in terms that demonstrate commitment to the ideals they espouse. Conversely, Just War theory and Christian realism keep pacifism grounded in the real world, insisting that they resist the temptation to ignore a complex reality or avoid necessary tasks for fear of dirtying their hands.

4. PRACTICAL MULTICULTURALISM

Fourth, peace education should be much more multicultural in its methods. Too often it is carried out within the context of a single culture. There is a great need, particularly within the university setting, for coursework to be embedded in cultures other than the one in which students have grown up. The process of students striving to understand each other is not just a side-issue in peace education, but central to its mission; indeed, it models the process of dialogue that is requisite for peace in a global era. The call for a more multicultural pedagogy is nothing new. It has now become so universal that it is a virtual shibboleth of current educational theory. Still, it is hard not to take a very jaundiced view of the courses in multiculturalism that already abound on university campuses. They are frequently inspired by the noble idea of making students more reflective about their own culturally-based presuppositions, but are often abstruse and jargon-filled, ideologically one-sided, and themselves monoculturally preoccupied with issues which are unique to Western intellectual history.

Two examples of successful multicultural peace education programs with which I am familiar are the *Neve Shalom/Wahat Al-Salam* project in Israel, and the Study Abroad program developed by Eastern Mennonite University. Neve Shalom ("Oasis of Peace") is a village community of fifty families in rural Israel, started in the 1970s. Half of the families in this community are Jewish and half are Palestinian. They work and learn together in their School for Peace. Classes are

conducted bilingually and there is a bicultural emphasis. In each classroom, a Jewish teacher and an Arab teacher instruct in their own language and all students are taught both Arabic and Hebrew. Dialogue
is framed around issues of common concern such as land, security,
rights and equality. Arab and Israeli values are given an equal voice.
The fact that they live together in one community creates an opportunity to overcome the limitations created by ideological frameworks
and to begin to construct a truly common peace perspective.[3]

The Eastern Mennonite Future Generations Program, founded in
1992, sends students overseas to learn and work with local students
in such places as Vietnam, Nepal, China and Afghanistan. Dan Wessner, Director of Academic Programs, developed a peace curriculum
specifically aimed at development education. His approach is grounded in his six years of classroom experience in north and south Vietnam.[4] Recognizing that his American and Vietnamese students both
suffered from superficial knowledge of the other's culture, and that
their learning was being greatly influenced by the fact that their respective cultures were vastly different in power and outlook, he developed a curriculum which was intended to break through the hidden
barriers to genuine communication and cooperation. Two pillars of
this pedagogy are Intercultural Communicative Competence (ICC)
and Critically Embodied Studies (CES). ICC aims at creating and
strengthening three skills: establishment of relations, communication
with minimal distortion of meaning, and an achieved level of concord
among participants in dialogue. The goal of ICC is the development of
a world view that blends insider and outsider perspectives into a still
larger one. CES encourages students to move beyond a merely theoretical understanding of the other's narrative to a point where the suffering and struggle of the other is taken on and lived as one's own. This
opens a dialogic space in which each tradition's spiritual resources can
be employed to transform that struggle in peaceful ways, without fear
of cultural colonization. It does, however, require genuine cultural im-
mersion, equal parts reflection and action, and a conception of development as liberation. Like the Neve Shalom/Wahat Al-Salam project,
it conceives of its peace curriculum as directed toward very concrete
ends which are informed by deep spiritual and educational values.

5. ENGAGED EDUCATION

Fifth, peace education must involve engagement and be linked to the multiple peace efforts which exist today. In practical terms, this means that it should be self-consciously training peacebuilders. Its goal should be to train students to take up active roles in peacebuilding both in governmental and nongovernmental agencies. Practice-oriented internships which work within both of these should be built into the educational process. Specifically, the two areas in which peacebuilding experience is most needed are in development education and reconciliation efforts. The first addresses the stresses which occur in a society and which can erupt into bloody conflict, and the second seeks to remedy the effects of such conflict. Training for practical peacebuilding in these arenas is probably the most effective thing that peace educators can do.

The systemic problems that are currently creating the dangerous conditions which now prevail in our world are best addressed by governmental agencies: there are some things that only national governments and intergovernmental organizations (IGOs) like the UN and World Bank can do. Yet, there is much cause for legitimate complaint with these institutions; they can be arrogant, overly centralized, bureaucratically encumbered, and self-serving. If they are to work more effectively, they should be staffed by people who are more deeply educated in peacemaking and, at the same time knowledgeable of the agencies' operations. It is at the intercultural level, however, that our needs are greatest. Work at this level is best done by private individuals and nongovernmental organizations (NGOs). The number of NGOs in the world is very large—the United States alone has thousands of them—and a subgroup of them has been working in the area of global peace and justice for years, e.g., Human Rights Watch, Doctors Without Borders, Amnesty International, Transparency International, Anti-Slavery International, the Association for the Prevention of Torture, the Coalition to Stop the Use of Child Soldiers, etc. These organizations have done a great deal of good work, though sometimes in a fitful manner, frequently at cross purposes with each other, and often when burdened by narrow and sometimes heavily ideological perspectives.

Peace education programs can increase their effectiveness by establishing multiple relationships with NGOs, from internships and exchange programs to cooperative action projects. In turn, educational institutions can offer a unifying framework within which non-governmental peacebuilding agencies can situate, coordinate and redefine their efforts. These efforts need not be restricted to peace studies programs, but can also be embedded in a variety of disciplines: business schools, schools of education, humanities and creative arts programs. We have had critical thinking across the curriculum, writing across the curriculum and ethics across the curriculum. Perhaps it is time for peacebuilding across the curriculum. An expanded and more inclusive peace curriculum—one which is open, engaged, and free of self-righteousness—is our best hope in these dangerous times. The desire for peace is an almost universal one. If, by building upon what they have learned, peace educators are able to adjust their practice to current global conditions and work cooperatively in keeping with the best practices of both governmental and nongovernmental organizations, this century might be the most remarkable one yet for the human race and for our planet.

NOTES

1. Lederach, John Paul, 2005. *The Moral Imagination: The Art and Soul of Building Peace*. New York: Oxford University Press, p.22.
2. St. Augustine, 1991. *Contra Faustus*. 22.74. Translated by John Langan in "The Elements of St. Augustine's Just War Theory" in William S. Babcock (ed.), *The Ethics of St. Augustine*. Atlanta: Scholars Press, p.171.
3. For more information, contact American Friends of Neve Shalom/ Wahat al-Salam. *www.oasisofpeace.org.*
4. See Wessner, Dan. "Venues and Ethics of Intercultural Communicative Competence". Documents from 2003 International Conference on Religion and Globalization, Payap University, Chiang Mai, Thailand: http://isrc.payap.ac.thai

18. INTERNATIONAL TRADING PARTNERS CAN LEAD THE WAY TO PEACE

LEE B. THOMAS, JR.

AND

PAUL J. WEBER

In 1776, Adam Smith published *Inquiry into the Nature and Causes of the Wealth of Nations*. In this seminal work, he demonstrated why trade among private individuals and privately owned business was the key to public wealth creation. His insights led to the destruction, but not the disappearance of mercantilism, a system of state controlled and subsidized manufacturing and trade. Few people today remember that Smith was not a trained economist but a moral philosopher. He was not much interested in the accumulation of personal wealth, but in understanding why some nations climbed out of poverty and others did not.

Smith was, however, concerned for the under-class. He blamed the great disparity in income, which he regarded as a moral wrong, on imperfections in the system. In his view, these imperfections were most frequently caused by various forms of government interference such as tariffs and quotas.[1]

There were however many consequences of capitalism, as his new system began to be called, that Smith did not foresee. He did not anticipate the human and environmental costs of the Industrial Revolution. But, curiously, he did observe that the worst enemies of capitalism would be capitalists trying to subvert competition and create monopolies. He therefore advocated government regulation of industry. What Smith could not possibly have dreamt of was globalization with all of its various modes of social and economic interconnectedness and instantaneous mass communication that facilitate and speed the development of large, sophisticated, truly international businesses. Hence, he also did not consider the idea that international businesses might pursue peace and justice.

Subsequent history and business practices have led many people who are interested in peace and justice to consider multinational businesses to be among their enemies, or, at best, a necessary evil. This paper argues that this is an antiquated viewpoint. International and multinational businesses can and should be instruments of both peace and justice. We propose to outline in brief form some of the steps that have been taken to further this end and also to sketch out what we take to be some of the challenges that lie ahead.

International business is extremely complex. In order to produce their goods and services, both the largest and smallest companies rely on other independent companies around the world. In earlier times, almost all companies bid one source against another and awarded contracts on the basis of price. W. Edward Deming (1900-1993) recognized that price was only one of many considerations in this, or rather that the nominal cost of a unit did not include such things as quality, innovation, or reliability, all of which can have a major impact on a company. He therefore advocated single sourcing and developing partnerships throughout the supply chain. Deming was primarily concerned with product quality and on time-delivery, but the same possibility of partnering exists with respect to environmental and human rights issues.

Deming introduced the concept of Quality Circles, a production system that enables people at the lowest level to make decisions in their areas of responsibility, corresponding to the principle of subsidiarity. Its buzzword is "Worker Empowerment." An example will serve to illustrate this: A company for which Lee serves as Chair of the Board, Universal Woods Inc., sometimes sends a production worker to visit customers when there is a quality issue. Not only does that worker have the best knowledge of products and customer needs, but he or she can also help develop a partnership with the customer. The common thread that runs through all of Deming's work is cooperation rather than confrontation.

Interestingly enough, Deming had trouble getting clients in the United States, but, when Japanese companies that were struggling with quality control after World War II tried Deming's principles, they so improved their profitability that soon General Motors and Ford were seeking to learn what they had done.

Currently, a number of individuals are trying to apply these same principles to the idea of creating international trading partnerships that help facilitate peace. The significance of this effort and of Deming's principles is not to be underestimated: If we are to be successful in this endeavor, we must work with business people, with multinational corporations, not against them.

Peace is only possible where there is justice. The amount of injustice in the world is so great as to make our task huge and its solution by no means certain. In Lee's world travels, searching for sources of raw materials and markets, he has seen sweatshops, some of which are several decades old. Even now similar conditions continue to exist. In one factory in India, which was still doing lead pot heat-treating, workers were breathing lead fumes and did not have shoes to wear. You can imagine what happened when some of the molten lead was spilled. In a Chinese factory which ground pliers, the grinding dust was so thick one could hardly breath. Silicosis was known to be a serious health hazard in that area, causing all kinds of lung ailments, including cancer. In that same factory, a woman was holding a cold chisel while a man hit it with a sledgehammer—with no protection for her hand. We cite these examples here as we have experienced them personally. At the same time, we know that the problems of injustice are not merely personal, but systemic.

As a general principle, nations have tried to deal with such injustices through government-to-government diplomacy and by means of coercion. However, private businesses have a critical role to play here as well. During the days of apartheid in South Africa there were all kinds of systemic injustices. The United States government called for a boycott of the country's products. One business leader who was trying to move the private sector toward constructive change was Leon Sullivan, an African-American preacher and social activist. General Motors had been severely criticized for its policies in South Africa. Board members invited Leon Sullivan to join the Board of Directors and work with them on improving their performance. The result of this was the Sullivan Principles, which required that, in order to do business with GM, a company had to practice no discrimination in the work place. Of course, the real world of business is messy and imperfect, so this standard was difficult to measure or enforce. Nonetheless, the Sullivan Principles gave companies a concrete set of standards that enabled them to do business while working toward the good. Most international drug companies continued to do business in South Africa on humanitarian grounds, but they have now adopted these principles.

Have such companies been helpful in ending the injustices of apartheid? World consensus seems to be that they were at least more helpful than harmful.

A further example from Lee's experience may clarify my point here
further.

While General Motors and the drug companies were struggling for
proper leverage, a Black businessman from South Africa approached
a German subsidiary of Vermont American Corporation, a company
which Lee headed, wanting to buy a turnkey operation to manufacture
files for use in metalworking in South Africa. The boycott was in effect and it seemed unlikely that our parent company in the U.S. could
have made the sale. However under the principle of subsidiarity, the
German company was allowed to make the decision. They went ahead
and sold the equipment. At that time we suspected that the South African company employed only Black people. So be it. In the real world,
making ethical decisions on behalf of justice is never as clear-cut as we
would like.

Let us return now to the larger theme of international businesses as potential partners for peace. "Subsidiarity" is a word used by
UNCTAD[2] to describe the desirable degree of decentralization that
allows local subsidiaries of multi-national companies to make decisions without complying with the requirements of headquarters. Thus
they can be responsive to the demands of local customs and local
government. This can, however, be very much a two-edged sword depending on corruption levels, the nature of local customs and the commitments of local leaders to social improvement. But it is increasingly
difficult for even local suppliers to hide bad practices. Today, even small
companies tend to be international. Universal Woods, headquartered
in Louisville, Kentucky, for example employs about 50 people. Yet it
has a worldwide distribution network including India and China. It is
sourcing wood products in China. In other words, globalization is the
new dimension that makes work for peace and justice a far more realistic goal in international business than it has been in past decades.

Globalization, and the global communications infrastructure that
makes it possible, have introduced an important variable into the cal-
culus of business decisions, namely, worldwide publicity. And, public
scrutiny of sweatshop labor, discrimination, unsafe working conditions, and the lack of transparency can substantially affect profit mar-
gins. In their work, *Global Business Regulation*, John Braithwaite and

Peter Drahos have shown how global institutions such as the World Trade Organization, the Organization for Economic Cooperation and Development, the International Monetary Fund, Moody's, and the World Bank as well as various non-governmental organizations and significant individuals who play watchdog roles can bring about effective regulation of international business.

How does this work? Global companies are responsible for their products or services regardless of whether they produce them internally or through a program of outsourcing. They therefore seek to ensure that price, quality control, and a good reputation, all intersect. At the same time, they try to avoid being victimized by unscrupulous suppliers and buyers who offer inferior goods produced under unjust conditions at lower prices. Ethical companies are willing to take steps to ensure that does not happen.

Some companies use the following model to achieve this goal. In order to facilitate quality control, The International Standards Organization, ISO, located in Geneva, Switzerland, developed a set of production standards in 1994 called ISO 9000. ISO 9000 does not fix absolute standards. Instead, companies that wish to be certified set their own, measurable goals. ISO 9000 relies on a management system that can realistically measure progress toward them. Most very large companies in the developed world require their sources to be ISO 9000 certified, whether they are located next door or in developing countries. Some small firms have argued that ISO 9000 is too bureaucratic and expensive, but many global companies seem to find it cost effective.

ISO developed ISO 14000 in 1996 and revised it in 2004. This is an environmental standard which is based on the same principles as ISO 9000 and intended to improve company performance in this area. Instead of placing external demands on companies, it measures progress toward various goals. European companies have been much faster to sign on to it than have American firms, although General Motors did so relatively early.

The most immediately effective force for change in business practices is government regulation. In general, European governments tend to be more demanding with regard to environmental and human rights issues than does the United States government. The Swedish government is a case in point. Still, progress is being made overall, even if it could be happening faster.

However, there are other forces besides government that encourage companies to be more concerned with these issues, forces that have fewer directly negative consequences for business. As mentioned, international publicity is one of them. Consumer pressure is another. While some consumers are more concerned than others about these questions, most want to do business with ethical companies. Investor pressure is another force for change. Today, over 10% of all money management firms and their procedures require some sort of ethical evaluation. And, this is an area that is ripe for expansion. For example, KLD is a private company that does extensive research for potential investors on companies.[3] Human rights issues are high on its list of concerns. There are no perfect companies just as there are no perfect individuals, of course. Still, such research is a step in the right direction as it allows investors to make properly informed choices. KLD is not the only company providing this kind of service. S.i.R.i. located in Geneva, Switzerland does the same kind of work, except that it tends to focus on companies that are headquartered in Europe and Japan.

The Council on Economic Priorities started out as a non-profit organization which worked on human rights issues and rated companies. It was in competition with KLD. In the mid-1990s, it devised a standard patterned after ISO for adjudicating human rights issues(SA 8000). It soon dominated the organization and Social Accountability International was set up as a separate entity; simultaneously, the Council on Economic Priorities ended its operations.[4]

SA 8000 is far more demanding than the ISO standards in that it lays out specific goals to be achieved in a reasonable length of time. These include:

No child labor (under age 15)

No forced labor

A safe and healthy work environment

Freedom of association

No discrimination based on gender, caste, race or ethnic group

No corporal punishment or abuse

No more than 48 hours of work per week, with voluntary overtime of no more than 12 hours at premium pay; always one day off per week.

A living wage with some extra pay for discretionary spending.

Finally, there must also be a management system to provide for continuous improvement.

Does this seem overly idealistic? Instantaneous compliance with all of these standards is clearly too much to expect. One calculation estimated a living wage at about $2.25 an hour when, in fact, the average hourly wage in the country under discussion was only $.50. An abrupt adjustment of this magnitude could have numerous unintended consequences for the economy as a whole. Other problems abound as well. In China, freedom of association is prohibited as is unionization. The best one can expect to achieve there is a workers' council which hears grievances and communicates these to management without revealing their source. In the Arab world, progress toward guarantees of equal rights for women, toward the day when there is no gender discrimination, is far too slow. Nonetheless, SA 8000 is designed to establish goals for companies and to measure progress toward them.

Once a company has agreed to participate in SA 8000 or ISO, regular monitoring is required if that company is to maintain its status. Auditing for ISO and SA compliance requires a different set of skills than does auditing financial statements. Since a big part of the job is evaluating the management systems of local entities, thorough familiarity with local language is important. Certification auditing firms that have a multitude of local offices around the world have therefore emerged. Transparency is what is fundamentally at issue here. The public has a right to know that companies are doing what they say they are doing. Had Enron fully disclosed to investors what they were doing with regard to their "special purpose entities", they might still be in business.

Unfortunately, some large American companies viewed SA 8000 as a threat to their short-term profitability and lobbied the United States government to produce legislation which would dilute its effect. With its help, they established an "Apparel Partnership," an organization which was described as part of an effort to eliminate sweatshops. The problem was that it said nothing about a living wage, did not provide for regular audits and avoided the issue of transparency. The late Phil Stern, then head of Citizens Against PACs, wrote a book entitled, "Still the Best Congress that Money can Buy," in which he argued that some companies generally do the right thing with respect to their international partners, but others are prone to be less conscientious.

A level playing field is not something that can be taken for granted in international business. Shortly after this, several trade associations in the United States followed up on this with similarly watered down programs. The result has been a significant setback for SA 8000 in the United States, even though faster progress has been made in Europe. Toys 'R Us, Avon, Chiquita and Dole are the most well-known companies to have signed on to and stayed with SA 8000. The purchasing arm of the United Nations is also certified. And, all participants mandate that their sources also become SA8000 certified. Even though the number of certified factories is not increasing as fast as we would like it to, it is expanding worldwide.

A second major challenge has arisen in recent years. According to a recent issue of *Business Week*,

> Codes of conduct have been an important part of efforts to improve labor standards in global supply chains.[5] Over the last ten years, these codes and systems for their implementation have proliferated. Brands and retailers are faced with multiple industry standards and suppliers are confused by the numerous codes and initiatives. Local organizations are frustrated by the many initiatives making demands on their time. Better coordination and cooperation is essential to address this confusion. It is also important to develop a shared understanding of the ways in which voluntary codes or labor practices and their implementation result in better working conditions.

The confusing proliferation of such codes has allowed some major players such as Wal-Mart and Target to opt out of any cooperative system whatever by claiming they have their own standards, conduct their own audits and monitor their own results. None of this leads to real transparency, of course, and the rest of the world is left to take such companies at their word.

Out of this frustration, however, one phenomenon has arisen which is of interest: The Joint Initiative on Corporate Accountability and Workers Rights. It represents the first successful effort to unite leading code-of-conduct organizations into a collaborative program. The initiative brings together six American and European organizations: a. Clean Clothes Campaign (CCC), b. Ethical Trading Initiative (ETI), c. Fair Labor Association (FLA), d. Fair Wear Foundation (FWF), d. Social Accountability International (SAI) and e. Worker Right Consortium (WRC).

The Joint Initiative on Corporate Responsibility and Workers Rights cannot require instantaneous compliance with all of the SA 8000 standards. Reasonable progress toward the goals should, however, improve morale and worker participation as well as profitability. The result is a win-win situation for all but the most unscrupulous. If corporate behavior is going to contribute to world peace, it must be such that people everywhere can look forward to a better tomorrow. In the battle for peace and justice across the world, businesses are frequently —and correctly—seen as part of the problem. However, this can and must change. Instead they must become a part of the solution—and they can indeed. Moreover, the peace and justice community can use newly developed technologies to ensure that communication in our globalized world has a profound impact on this process.

We propose that those interested in peace and justice engage still more actively to encourage partnerships between international businesses, their sources, their workers and consumers, all of whom subscribe to ethical principles governing commerce in goods and services. The level of interconnectedness that is developing worldwide makes it possible to set a realistic goal for the future of mankind: Adequate wealth for all—something that Adam Smith could only dream about.

NOTES

1. See Adam Smith *The Theory of Moral Sentiments*.
2. UNTAD is the arm of the United Nations that oversees the conduct of transnational corporations. However, their power is limited to that of persuasion. Eduard Dommen of that organization was helpful in developing the SA 8000 standards.
3. KLD, 500 Atlantic Avenue, Boston MA.
4. Social Accountability International, 220 East 23rd Street Suite 605, New York, NY 10010
5. See *Business Week*, May 23, 2005.

ABOUT THE AUTHORS

Paul J. Weber, PHD was Distinguished Professor of Political Science at the University in Louisville, KY. He was Director of the McConnell Center for Political Leadership, 1990-2000, and Executive Director of the Grawemeyer Awards, 2000-2004. He published numerous articles and books, including *Unfounded Fears: Myths and realities of a Constitutional Convention* (1989), *Equal Separation: Understanding the Religion Clauses of the First Amendment* (1990), *The Power of Ideas* (2000), and *Faith-Based Initiatives and the Bush Administration: the good, the Bad and the Ugly* (2003).

Lee B. Thomas Jr. served as President and CEO of Vermont American Corp. from 1962 to 1984 and Chair from 1984-1989. He is currently Chair of Universal Woods, Inc., Chair of the J and L Foundation and Executive in Residence at Bellarmine University all of Louisville, Ky. He was Chair of the Board of the Council on Economic Priorities at the time it negotiated the SA 8000 universal workplace standards for global business in Geneva, Switzerland (1997). He is the author of *Global Partnerships: Opening the Way Toward Economic Justice and World Peace.* Friends Journal, 2004.

19. IMAGINING PEACE:
ALIENATION AND THE CONSUMER

L. GEORGE THOMPSON

"What difference does it make to the dead, the orphans and the homeless, whether the mad destruction is wrought under the name of totalitarianism or the holy name of liberty or democracy?"
Mahatma Gandhi, *Nonviolence in Peace and War*

"The wages you failed to pay the workmen who mowed your fields are crying out against you. The cries of the harvesters have reached the ears of the Lord Almighty." James 5:4,6

I. VIOLENCE, ITS ROOT CAUSES AND
THE SWEATSHOP PROBLEM

Violence does not only happen in war. We commit acts of violence daily when we speak falsely or harshly, when we pollute, when we impoverish. Traditionally, violence is understood as one person's harming another. But, in today's world, where our environmental pollution reaches farther than the eye can see, where one's words can travel around the world instantaneously, where our economic desires and choices create a chain of events invisible to us, violence has taken on forms that we could never have imagined in the past. It is therefore that we are able to identify them, that we can understand how we contribute to the net amount of violence in our world, and that we begin to imagine how we can stop it and draw on the power of the human imagination to bring about peace. If there is one problem around which the world's religions may become united, it may be the need to uncover the violent attitudes and actions that we continually commit without being aware of the fact that we are doing so. I would like to participate in the quest to do this by focusing here on one of these forms of violence, one in which most of the world's peoples seem to participate unconsciously.

Our most accurate studies tell us that over half of the garment workers in the United States are trapped in illegal working conditions.[1] In a five-county study in the Los Angeles area, 78 percent of all garment production facilities were in violation of five out of ten safety guidelines.[2] To understand this, first consider the estimates in the U.S., and then imagine what it must be like to work in a situation where there are no labor unions, where inspection guidelines are not enforced, and where government does not intervene to ensure safe and humane working conditions. We have all bought and worn clothes supplied by the sweatshop industry, so, if these studies are even remotely accurate, we must all be answerable for the human havoc wreaked by such industries.

Once, after I had presented on this issue, an audience member asked, "Is there any possible way *not* to contribute to this?" This question is important for two reasons. First, because this is almost invariably the first question asked, and second, because when one looks at such situations closely, the answer is entirely obvious: If one wants to stop being an accessory to such suffering, one can simply do so. Still, I would add that I do not in any way believe that this is an easy task, or one which has no consequences. But I would also claim that, unlike other, more difficult changes in lifestyle, if people decide to stop buying clothing from sweatshop-related stores, there are plenty of alternative ways to provide clothing for themselves and plenty of time to decide on how to go about doing this.[3] Still, until one actually comes to the realization that one *can* stop, the whole idea seems utterly fantastical, so it is no surprise that this is always the first question that comes up in discussion. One cannot conceive of not buying clothing if one has become accustomed to shopping, let alone find creative alternatives. In terms

1   Robert J.S. Ross, *Slaves to Fashion* (Ann Arbor, MI: The University of Michigan Press, 2004), 35.

2   U.S. Department of Labor. "U.S. Department of Labor Announces Latest Los Angeles Garment Survey Results." Press Release, Office of Public Affairs, May 27. Available at <hhtp://www.dol.gov/dol/opa/public/media/press/opa/opa98225.htm>. Accessed July 2, 1998. Quoted by Ross, *Slaves to Fashion*, 31.

3   Today, creative alternatives to this are more readily available. Besides the dozens of thrift shops in each major city, fair trade stores are opening everywhere. A good source is The Conscious Consumer at _http://newdream.org/consumer_. In local Milwaukee, see Wisconsin Network of Peace and Justice _http://test.wnpj.org/_.

of peacemaking, this means that one cannot conceive of breaking this chain of violence.

This illustrates an amazing fact about our industrialized culture: We consumers in major first-world countries do not think that we *cannot* contribute to sweatshop violence and at the same time sustain our quality of life. We seem to be thoroughly convinced of this, and choose to ignore the ways in which our lifestyles contribute to the problem. Indeed, we seem to blind ourselves to the corrupt functioning of the economic and political system when in fact its continued functioning depends on our willing cooperation with it.

Analysis and discussion of the sweatshop problem has traditionally focused on the factory worker overseas and the economic policies of multinational corporations. The consumer's contribution to it is often, if not always, overlooked. One is hard pressed to find discussions of consumer responsibility in applied ethics textbooks. I would note here in passing that Marxism is not something I subscribe to; indeed, I take the entire Marxist enterprise to be flawed in many respects. His language of alienation is, however, not entirely inappropriate to a more complete analysis of the sweatshop problem which factors in consumer attitudes. In fact, it is extremely useful in framing such an analysis. When Marx writes, "Political economy conceals the estrangement inherent in the nature of labor by not considering the direct relationship between the worker (labor) and production," this resonates with the situation of the consumer in America at present.[4] Together with him I would therefore assert that the modern global economy conceals the estrangement inherent in the nature of the consumer society by not considering the direct relationship between the consumer and the sweatshop worker. When Western consumers are confronted with complete and accurate information, information which can influence purchasing decisions, they often react by either becoming hostile to the information itself (or denying its truth altogether), or by feeling that somehow their autonomy has been impinged upon and their purchasing power limited. Their condition of alienation in the marketplace has piqued the imagination; still, they do not make the connection between our attitudes and actions and the violence they entail.

To understand this phenomenon of consumer alienation in Western cultures, one must first reflect on Marx's own thinking about alien-

---

4 Karl Marx, *Economic and Philosophical Manuscripts of 1844*, trans. Martin Milligan (New York: International Publishers Co., 1964), 109-110.

ation and its causes. He developed his thinking on it in the context
of 19th century England, and so it is reflective of the conditions that
prevailed there in factories.

II. THE PHENOMENON OF ALIENATION

Alienation describes a certain *kind* of relationship between two sub-
jects, one marked by a loss of connection or by estrangement. Under
such conditions, a residue remains, one that reminds that person that
she is alienated and that alienation is a perversion of natural human
relations. More exactly, it involves a distortion of *perspective*; a physical
relationship exists between the subject and object, but intellectually it
is not acknowledged. In what follows, I discuss the various aspects of
alienation, its outward manifestation, and finally its causes as Marx
understood them.

According to Marx, three aspects of alienation tend to blend together: the development of a sense of distance from the object, detachment from that object, and unnaturalness. First, the worker is severed
from the object of his labors (the completed product) and develops a
distant view. He or she sees it appear in the distance, pass by quickly,
and disappear once more. Second, the worker experiences a *detached*
relationship to the creation of products. Whether or not he or she is
sick one day, or even if he or she is fired, work continues on entirely
impersonal terms. Third, an air of *unnaturalness* permeates the work
setting. When a carpenter builds a chair, he is creating an extension
of himself. It is the result of his own artistic and productive work. By
contrast, the factory worker "puts his life into the object; but now his
life no longer belongs to him but to the object."[5]

Also important is the fact that alienation has three consequences: estrangement, powerlessness, and the desire for further uninvolvement.
First, the worker becomes hostile and *estranged* from what has become
a very unnatural work environment; "[i]t's alien character emerges
clearly in the fact that as soon as no physical or other compulsion exists, labor is shunned like the plague."[6] Secondly, he or she experiences
a sense of *powerlessness* and becomes estranged from him- or herself as
a human being. Thirdly, the worker desires to be uninvolved with the
process of labor. J.C. Kumarappa writes that, ideally, labor is like fine
desirous food to the soul that "nourishes and enlivens the higher man

5 Ibid., 108.
6 Ibid., 111.

and urges him to produce the best he is capable of." [7] But the labor of the factory, of the assembly line, particularly of the sweatshop, is hardly desirable food, it is more like a "plague." The effects of alienation are readily apparent in most work situations. The worker feels silenced, hates the work, and becomes so estranged from the entire process that he or she does not even feel as if she is alive while at work.

Finally, Marx identifies three systemic causes of alienation: the system is *overwhelming, demanding,* and *inhibiting.* First, it is *overwhelming* in that the worker finds herself presented with crushing challenges; the only choices available are to work under exploitive and abusive conditions or not to work at all. The sounds from the factory floor are deafening, and the voices of the inspectors in the glass room above are hardly audible. Second, the economic system *demands* alienation on a certain level; "[t]he political economy conceals estrangement inherent in the nature of labor." And, to reveal the estrangement that it entails and to find it unacceptable is to turn off the factory, to bring production to a stop.[8] Finally, the corporate/big business community *inhibits* meaningful relationships with workers. The massive size of the factory, the impersonal assembly line procedures, the fact that the workers never see the finished product or meet those to whom it is sold and the fact that they never meet the person who is their actual boss all contribute to a general condition of alienation. These causes combine to produce a kind of hopelessness, a situation in which it seems impossible to put an end to the alienation that has come to define the situation.

III. ALIENATION OF THE MODERN CONSUMER

Marx's use of the term 'alienation' has been widely adopted and it is employed in a variety of contexts. But does it applied to the modern consumer? Clearly, he or she does not work on an assembly line in a deafening factory without any unions, but instead shops in malls that cater to his or her every need. Is there even a remote similarity between these two circumstances? There may be. In what follows, I will seek to demonstrate that the consumer is also subject to conditions of

---

7　J.C. Kumarappa, *Economy of Permanence* (Rajghat, Kashi: Sarva-Seva Sangh Publication, 1958), 4th ed. Quoted in E.F. Schumacher, *Small is Beautiful* (Harper and Row, 1973), 56.

8　Marx, Ibid., 109-110.

exploitation. To begin, I offer a brief discussion of what I take to be the causes of alienation in the modern consumer society.

The causes of consumer alienation are very similar to those which pervade the system as a whole. Just as the worker finds a system of labor and production that causes her alienation, so, too, is the consumer confronted with a vast economic system that depends on, and thus *demands*, the habitual purchase of goods. The Western market economy thus revolves around the consumer.[9] If the consumer were not alienated and were actually able to make an autonomous ethical choices about all of his or her purchases, if access to critical information about the history and genesis of the items on the market were guaranteed, then the economic machine would come to a halt. Garment stores would grow quiet, that is, assuming that consumers would choose not to participate an economic cycle which is fundamentally immoral. In other words, the ongoing success of the market depends on the consumer not caring about the genesis of the product or the conditions under which it was produced.

Closely related to the market's dependence on the consumer and the demands it places on him or her, is the fact that consumers are encouraged to depend on it for their way of life. The importance of our initial question ("Is it possible for one *not* to participate in the cycle that supports sweatshops?") thus becomes clear as well. How can I *not* buy clothes from these stores? The sweatshop industry is built on the fashion industry, and, as long as consumers demand the latest fashions, as long as they *need* them, at least some will not *want* to know about sweatshops.

There is also the fact that the global economic community *overwhelms* the consumer. The worker depends on the factory for a livelihood. But she is overwhelmed by even the adverse forces at work in the local economy as they are arrayed against her, by a factory that treats her with little respect, and by the fact that she is caught up in a cycle of exploitation perpetuated by the global economy. The consumer feels entirely insignificant and even irrelevant. Dependent on the corporate market, the consumer is one among billions and so his expenditures seem to be of little value; the sheer proportions of the modern multinational corporation are overwhelming.

---

9 See Naomi Klein, *No Logo* (Toronto: Vintage Canada, 2000), for good examples of how far corporations go to control consumers' buying habits.

Even if one does want to learn the facts about sweatshops, they cannot simply be found in the phone book. Nor do they welcome visits
from local citizens. Instead, the entire sweatshop industry is embedded in a global community which *inhibits* and degrades human relationships. Just as the worker sees only a small part of the entire system,
(she carries out a single function on the assembly line); so, too, does
the consumer witness only one part of the economic machine (at the
point of purchase). The consumer thus becomes equally as alienated
as the worker. How does one even begin to have a relationship with
the worker across the ocean or in urban ghettos? How does one even
begin to understand the conditions that person faces on a daily basis?
And, merely learning about sweatshops, is by no means the same thing
as knowing the real facts about the horror across the ocean or hidden
in our own society: It is actually very easy to hide things in the global
market—and very hard to find them.

Thus, it is evident that the consumer is subject to all of the conditions which foster alienation. In fact, the ongoing success of the
economic/philosophical system *depends* on the alienation of the consumer, conversely, the consumer's perpetuating his lifestyle *depends*
on his continuing to be alienated. And, the consumer finds himself
overwhelmed by the conditions of marketplace, and by living in a global
context which only inhibits the development of human relationships
and thus facilitates and deepens human alienation.

As noted, my claim is that all of these conditions also contribute
to the alienation of the consumer. He or she develops a sense of distance and detachment because of the global market, something which
is unnatural in itself. This relationship is marked by *distance* because
there is either a huge physical distance between the worker and the
consumer (via oceans or megalopolises), or an enormous social void
between the two (the middle and upper classes are separated from
lower classes). The relation between them is marked by *detachment*.
Given his distance from the global market and the vast, complicated
economic system, the consumer does not see himself in a relationship
with the sweatshop worker; the consumer does not feel like he affects
the worker in any way. Furthermore, this dissociation is *unnatural* because one side of the market depends on the consumer (for income),
and the other depends on the sweatshop worker (for labor and output).

This is reflective of our previous earlier analysis of alienation: Distance, detachment, and unnaturalness are its primary features. The consumer feels estranged from the worker and wishes to keep her, and the truth about her life and work, at a distance. Thus, even for the consumer, the market is overwhelming; he or she is powerless to change anything. The billions of dollars and massive collections of malls, factories, etc. that make up the economic system tend to obliterate individual identity and obscure the facts of one's participation in the system. In point of fact, the consumer becomes *uninvolved* in the plight of the sweatshop worker as a result of all of these pressures. Nevertheless, I would argue that total estrangement is not really possible.

The similarities between Marx's analysis of the worker and our analysis of the consumer are notable. In fact, we seem to demand - and expect—both to be alienated from each other. The worker must be alienated if a factory is to produce its maximum output. Modern economic attempts to gauge alienation in factories and in fact, to encourage it in order to maximize output are evidence of this. [10] In a similar fashion, the consumer *also* must continue to be alienated from the worker if he or she is to consciously engage in consumption. If direct contact with the workers and methods of production were possible, if the consumers had complete and accurate information at their disposal, a much greater premium would be placed on the corporations ensuring that all aspects production were in fact managed in an ethical fashion. Instead, we find consumers who know absolutely nothing about *what* they are buying or from *whom* they are buying it.

Marilyn Frye describes the oppression of women in a famous bird cage analogy. When you are very close to the cage, you can only see one wire at a time. You wonder why the bird does not simply fly away. But when you step back and see all the wires at once, the actual facts of the situation become obvious. [11] If the consumer is aware of only a single point at which a purchase is made, the consumer sees only one of the wires on the cage. But given the distance, detachment, unnaturalness, estrangement, powerlessness, and non-involvement which market

10   Bronfenbrenner, for example, does not even see alienation as a problem that must be solved. He is perfectly willing to let alienation exist to maximize production. Martin Bronfenbrenner, "A Harder Look at Alienation", from *Ethics* ,Vol. 83, No. 4 (Jul., 1973), 267-282.

11   Marilyn Frye, *The Politics of Reality: Essays in Feminist Theory* (Freedom, CA: The Crossing Press), 6-7.

conditions cause, and also given the overwhelming, demanding, and inhibiting effects of global community, it is clear why the consumer has an unnatural relationship with the worker, the producer of his clothes.

Lastly, I would ask whether it is possible for one *not* to participate in the destructive cycles associated with sweatshop labor. My answer to this question is in the affirmative: If you want to stop, stop. There are plenty of fair trade shops in major cities, more websites are appearing everyday. Every town has a thrift shop, and every city has many of them. But this is still not the point. If one really wants to stop participating in such a destructive and dehumanizing economic cycle, it only takes a couple of hours on the internet or phone to discover creative alternatives. Are you willing to exert yourself in this way? Or does the thought of doing this seem confusing or even annoying? Maybe others can and should solve this problem.

There is only one way to end the process of consumer alienation, namely to break down these walls. One must go the distance, become a member of the world community, and realize that both worker and consumer have a natural place in the market. The walls came down for me when a friend introduced me to his Cambodian fiancée whose family had worked in sweatshops across the ocean—a life changing moment.

If we continue to participate in such cycles of alienation, we are covering up one of the greatest forms of violence of our time. We must reclaim our imaginations, recognize these forms of violence for what they are, and be accountable for our own participation in them. In order for dialogue to even begin between Catholic, Protestant, Muslim, and Hindu, the first-world citizen must be able to breakdown the walls of alienation in the marketplace and acknowledge his own contribution to human suffering of this sort. Only then can we begin to move toward peace.

PART 4
CONCLUSION

20. THE LIES OF WAR:
DISSECTING THE "JUST WAR" EUPHEMISMS AND
BUILDING AN ETHICS OF PEACE

DANIEL C. MAGUIRE

My comments today are dedicated to a ten year old Afghan boy, Mo-
hammed Noor. He was having his Sunday dinner when an American
bomb struck. He lost both eyes and both hands. Who, with this child
in mind, would dare sing "God bless America" and thereby make God
a co-conspirator with the American war machine. The sightless eyes of
this child should haunt us to the end of our days. It should sear on our
souls the absolute need not merely to pray for peace, but to do something
to make it happen.

The Prussian officer Karl von Clausewitz famously saw war
as an entirely rational undertaking, a "continuation of policy
... by other means." The sanitizing implication of this was, as
Barbara Ehrenreich has noted, that war involves "the kind of clear-
headed deliberation one might apply to a game of chess ... no more dis-
turbing and irrational than, say a difficult trade negotiation—except
perhaps to those who lay dying on the battlefield."[1] The disguisers of
war have framed it in such non-toxic terms, and have so successfully
defanged it and anointed it with respectability that we find ourselves
using the word in all sorts of innocent and lovely contexts: "the war on
poverty," "the war on cancer," "the war on illiteracy," etc. Indeed, war can
even be armchair spectator entertainment. It is socially acceptable for
people to become "Civil War Buffs," or "Revolutionary War Buffs," yet,
if people were to announce themselves as "prostitution buffs" or "rape
buffs" their perverted absorption with such human disasters would
raise eyebrows.

---

1   Barbara Ehrenreich, *Blood Rites: Origins and History of the Passions of War*
    (New York: Henry Holt and Company, 1997) 7.

278   DANIEL C. MAGUIRE

War is so thoroughly suffused into all levels of our cultural imagination that it crops up in even the gentlest of contexts. In his prize-
winning book, *We are Not Alone*, Walter Sullivan writes beautifully
of the intelligence of dolphins. He alludes to the possibility that we
may some day be able to communicate extensively with them and train
them for complex tasks. But, this tantalizing prospect led him immediately to thoughts of war and warmaking. Dolphins could be used "by
one government to scout out the submarines of another ... to smuggle
bombs into enemy harbors ... serve on underwater demolition teams
... [be taught to] sneak up on hostile submarines and shout something
into the listening gear." He notes, however, that there are worries that
the dolphins might demur, that "they might prove to be pacifists."[2]
Their non-human consciousness might be less amenable to violence
than we are.

Our haughty species should be slow to speak in demeaning terms
of "descending to the level of animals." The human being, says Erich
Fromm, "is the only mammal who is a large scale killer and sadist." He
cites evidence supporting the claim that, if we had the level of aggres-
siveness that chimpanzees do in their natural habitat, our world would
be a kinder place by far.[3]

"WAR" ... WHAT IS IT REALLY?

The reality that "war" euphemizes is that of *state*-sponsored violence,
though non-state actors may now mimic state violence. Such a description opens the door to an honest moral evaluation of it. What is it
really that we are talking about? Violence: It kills people and destroys
the earth. The question before us is therefore whether that kind of
destruction can ever be called "just."

Unfortunately, the venerable and all too infrequently challenged
"just war theory" has contributed to our facile acceptance and even
sanctification of war. Combining the word "war" with the word "just"
helped to baptize war. It made it seem rational and good as long as certain amenities were observed. The reality of it is, however, most often
hidden from public view. The much abused word "war" is no longer
descriptive of the mayhem and slaughter we are wreaking when we "go
to war." If "just war theory" were called "justifiable slaughter theory," or

2 Walter Sullivan, *We Are Not Alone*, (New York: Signet Book, 1966), 245.
3 Erich Fromm, *The Anatomy of Human Destructiveness* (New York: Holt,
   Rinehart and Winston, 1973), 105.

"justifiable violence theory," we might have made a more honest assessment of it. The slaughter and the human and ecological destruction we are contemplating when we are planning wars may in some way be justifiable, but at least we should be honest with ourselves and get clear on what exactly it is we are justifying. Language sans legerdemain.

Military strategists, and the ethicists who are embedded with them, drape an even thicker tissue of lies around military violence. They refer to it as "the use of force"—a term that sugar-coats it handsomely. "Force," after all, is official and respectable. A forceful personality, a forceful argument—these can be quite admirable. But the fact of an atomic bomb hitting the population centers of Hiroshima or Nagasaki, or the brutal leveling of Falluja in Iraq or of the dehumanizing conditions in settlements in Palestine—these require a more honest description. "Force," like war, is a malicious euphemism. It averts our eyes from horrors of the sort described by Archbishop Desmond Tutu: "Some two million children have died in dozens of wars during the past decade .... This is more than three times the number of battle field deaths of American soldiers in all their wars since 1776 .... Today, civilians account for more than 90 percent of war casualties."

THE POLICING PARADIGM

The real question here is this: When, if ever, is *state-sponsored violence, involving as it does slaughter and environmental destruction,* justifiable? There may be situations in which it is. I will argue that it might be justified as collective international police action to respond to actual (not imagined) threats and attacks. However—and this is key—it can only be justified by the same argument that justifies violent action by police, namely, in a communitarian context within an enforceable framework of law. Justifications for war, however, often prove to be shady rationalizations for failed efforts at building peace. It might be more truthful to say that war is the pit we fall into when we avoid the tedious and unglamourous work of peace-making and justice-building. Some slaughter might have prevented greater slaughter in 1994 in Rwanda, where there was no real international interest in supporting the peace and reform efforts in the years preceding the carnage. But such a failure should not be hidden by facile "just war" arguments for the "use of force." The allegedly "justified war" usually masks an unconscionable failure to do the advance work of peacemaking; it also covers up for a total lack of effective statecraft.[4]

The policing paradigm for justifying state(s) sponsored war is brilliantly enshrined in the Charter of the United Nations. It was meant to put an end to the vigilante approach to war which Adolph Hitler represented, as well as to the "preemptive war" policy of George W. Bush. In the view of the United Nations, state-sponsored violence can only be just in a communitarian setting under the restraints of enforceable international law. The United Nations was founded precisely to make this possible. Nations, such as the United States, long accustomed to vigilantism in the international arena, have frustrated the United Nations and its Charter. This is a sad irony, particularly since The United States was a principal shaper of its policing paradigm for justifying war.

Richard Falk writes:

> World War II ended with the historic understanding that recourse to war between states could no longer be treated as a matter of national discretion, but must be regulated to the extent possible through rules administered by international institutions. The basic legal framework was embodied in the U.N. Charter, a multilateral treaty largely crafted by American diplomats and legal advisers. Its essential feature was to entrust the Security Council with administering a prohibition of recourse to international force (Article 2, Section 4) by states except in circumstances of self-defense, which itself was restricted to responses to a prior 'armed attack' (Article 51), and only then until the Security Council had the chance to review the claim.[5]

But, this noble, civilizing moment in human moral history has been seriously denigrated and all of us must shoulder the blame for this. It is no wonder that Pope John Paul II called George Bush's vigilante invasion of Iraq "a defeat for humanity."

The primary challenge faced by contemporary ethicists is to rethink and reframe the problem of the morality of war. It is a fact that Catho-

---

4   See Stanley Hauerwas, Linda Hogan, Enda McDonagh, "The Case for the Abolition of War in the Twenty-First Century," forthcoming in *The Annual* of The Society of Christian Ethics. This paper argues brilliantly that "war possesses our imaginations, our everyday habits, and our scholarly assumptions."

5   Richard Falk, "Why International Law Matters," *The Nation*, March 10, 2003, 276, #9, 20.

lic moral theology has never risen to the challenge put to it by Pope John XXIII in his 1963 encyclical *Pacem in Terris*. There he said that, in our age, "it is irrational to believe that war is still an apt means of vindicating violated rights."[6] The Second Vatican Council called for "an evaluation of war with an entirely new attitude."[7] In their pastoral letter, "The Challenge of Peace," the U.S. Catholic Bishops appealed for "a fresh reappraisal which includes a developed theology of peace."[8] It is a scandal that these appeals to Catholic moral theology have gone almost unheeded, while an inordinate and embarrassing amount of attention has been paid to what I call "the pelvic issues" of masturbation, homosexuality, and abortion.

In his powerful new book, *The New American Militarism*, Andrew J. Bacevich, a Catholic and a retired officer, now professor at Boston University notes how the Protestant religious right pushed for the American invasion of Iraq and even for the concept of preventive or preemptive war. Writing as "a Catholic author" he says that "the counterweight ought to have been the Roman Catholic Church ... [which] was eminently well-positioned to put its stamp on public policy." It failed to do so. He puts major blame for this on the hierarchy. I put it on American Catholic theology and uninvolved Catholic citizens.[9]

BRED FOR VIOLENCE

Language and thought never arise in a sociological vacuum. And, except in moments of true creativity, all theory is essentially autobiographical. Our stories themselves inform our choice of words and frame our discourse. A strong penchant for violence toward one another and toward the rest of nature seems tragically kneaded into our historically-formed collective consciousness. Maybe the apocalyptic voices, chilling as they are, deserve a hearing. Georg Henrik von Wright says with stoical calmness:

---

6 John XXIII, *Pacem in Terris*, April 11, 1963: AAS 55, 291.

7 Walter M Abbott, S.J., General Editor, *The Documents of Vatican II* (New York: Herder and Herder, 1966), "The Church Today," 80, p. 293.

8 The Challenge of Peace: God's Promise and Our Response, National Conference of Catholic Bishops, May 3, 1983, # 24.

9 Andrew J. Bacevich, *The New American Militarism: How Americans are Seduced by War* (New York and London: Oxford University Press, 2005), 250-51.

> One perspective, which I don't find unrealistic, is of humanity as approaching its extinction as a zoological species. The idea has often disturbed people. ... For my part I cannot find it especially disturbing. Humanity as a species will at some time with certainty cease to exist; whether it happens after hundreds of thousands of years or after a few centuries is trifling in the cosmic perspective. When one considers how many species humans have made an end of, then such a natural nemesis can perhaps seem justified.[10]

Vaclav Havel warns that if we endanger the Earth she will dispense with us in the interests of a higher value, namely, life itself. Lynn Margulis joins this grim chorus by saying that the Earth did very well without us in the past and it will do very well without us in the future. And, not all religious scholars rush in with gospels of consolation either. If we are the "missing link" between apes and true humanity, as Gerd Theissen puts it, our species is morally prenatal and yet armed to the teeth, with the end of our existence stored and ready in our nuclear silos and other species dropping around us like canaries in a doomed mine.[11]

Some scholars think our passion for war is innate and irrepressible. Thus, in his 1960 study on the statistics of violent conflicts, L.F. Richardson searched for the causative factors of war and concluded that wars are largely random catastrophes whose specific time and location we cannot predict, but whose recurrence we must expect just as we expect earthquakes and hurricanes.[12] This led one writer in *American Scientist* to see the nations of the world as banging "against one another with no more plan or principle than molecules in an overheated gas."[13] Lastly, these dismal views are supported by a study showing that hu-

---

10   Quoted in Goran Moller, Ethics and the Life of Faith: A Christian Moral Perspective, (Leuven, Belgium: Peeters, 1998), 35.

11   Gerd Theissen, *Biblical Faith: An Evolutionary Approach* (Minneapolis: Fortress Press, 1985), 122.

12   L. F. Richardson, *Statistics of Deadly Quarrels*, (Pacific Grove, California: The Boxwood Press, 1960.) Quoted in Vaclav Smil, "The Next 50 Years: Fatal Discontinuities," in *Population and Development Review* 31 (2): June 2005, 225.

13   B. Hayes, "Statistics of Deadly Quarrels," *American Scientist* 90. 200, 15.

mans have been at peace for only 8 percent of the past 3,400 years of their recorded history.[14]

Both the contemporary situation and the facts of history lend credence to this bleak picture. As of January 2002, there were 38 significant conflicts ongoing, and 24 others precariously suspended, e.g., that between England and the Irish Republican Army. And, again, religion is listed as at least a partial cause in sixteen of the 38 ongoing conflicts.[15] Indeed, it is often the problem, not the solution. Since 1945, 135 wars, most of them in the poor world (often erroneously referred to as the "developing" world), have taken the lives of more than 22 million people, "the equivalent of a World War III."[16]

IS THERE ANY HOPE?

Is there any hope for this blundering species that dares to call itself *sapiens*? Are we destined to drown in the blood of our own belligerence? We have created the means to bring about the end of the world and stored them in our nuclear silos, planes, and submarines while, at the same time, unrelentingly double-basting our planet with heat- trapping carbon dioxide. Having already extinguished many other species, we are technically poised to extinguish our own.

And yet there is hope. As Vaclav Smil writes, the historical "success of our species makes it clear that humans, unlike all other organisms, have evolved not to adapt to specific conditions and tasks but to cope with change. This ability makes us uniquely fit to cope with assorted crises and to transform many events from potentially crippling milestones to resolved challenges."[17]

Hope may be found in reflection on both the present and the past. Today, there are stirrings of what has been called a "moral globalization" process. Ironically—and perhaps happily—the havoc being wreaked on the children and people of Iraq by the U.S. war machine, has birthed a fervent and growing outcry for peace. In the largest call for peace in human history, on February 15, 2003, demonstrations in

14   R. Paul Shaw and Yuwa Wang, *Genetic Seeds of Warfare: Evolution, Nationalism, and Patriotism* (Boston: Unwin Hyman, 1989), 3.

15   "The World At War—January 2002," *The Defense Monitor*, XXXI, No. 1, January 2002.

16   Michael Renner, *Critical Juncture: The Future of Peacekeeping*, Worldwatch Paper, 114, May 1993.

17   Vaclav Smil, art. Cit., 208.

DANIEL C. MAGUIRE

80 nations around the planet pleaded with the American giant not to embark on this lie-laden venture into killing. In recent years, 16 tribunals of conscience have met in Barcelona, Tokyo, Brussels, Seoul, New York, London, Mumbai, Istanbul, and in other cities. In the words of Arundhati Roy, their purpose has been to show "faith in the consciences of millions of people across the world who do not wish to stand by and watch while the people of Iraq are being slaughtered, subjugated and humiliated."[18]

Also encouraging are the heroic Israeli soldiers, dubbed "refuseniks," who are asserting that conscientious objection is also the right of soldiers. The idea of the soldier as automaton, with no more conscience than a fired bullet, is the keystone of military culture. These Israeli soldiers are challenging it in a revolutionary way, saying they will no longer participate in the occupation and humiliation of the Palestinian people. In the spirit of the ancient Hebrew prophets, they are asserting that soldiers are persons, not pawns. Jail will likely be their portion, but veneration is what they are justly due. Some U.S. soldiers are beginning to make similar assertions, saying that blind obedience is as immoral as slavery. (See www.swiftsmartveterans.com)

I draw hope also from the Manresa Project because it really believes that 'justice and mercy will kiss' and that peace may be born from this embrace. There is this—and more—which can provide a sort of transfusion of hope into our veins.

NO MORE "SUPERPOWERS"

Our human failure is, ironically, also teaching us to seek peace. The United States, the alleged "superpower" lost its first war in Vietnam and now, for the first time in its history, it is losing two wars simultaneously in Iraq and Afghanistan. There is nothing in these two debacles that merits the name of victory or even provides us with a means of understanding of what "victory" could possibly mean. Such wars are not winnable in principle. The fact that the alleged "superpower" is suffering a streak of losses to guerilla-based insurgencies is very suggestive of a realignment of power worldwide.

First of all, it reveals that war has mutated. Guerillas, with the unmatchable trinity of advantages—invisibility, versatility, and pa-

18   Quoted in Richard Falk, "The World Speaks on Iraq," *The Nation*, 281 # 4, August 1/8, 2005, 10.

tience—have "put to rout" the "arrogant of heart and mind." The supposedly weak have "brought down monarchs from their thrones," (Luke 1:51-52) to borrow a phrase from Jesus' revolutionary mother, Mary.

Secondly, this is a wake-up call for Americans concerning their declining democracy. As Yale professor of international relations, Bruce Russett, notes, democracies "more often win their wars—80 percent of the time." The reason is "they are more prudent about what wars they get into, choosing wars that they are more likely to win and that will incur lower costs."[19] Unfortunately, this does not describe our 2 billion dollar per month fiasco in Iraq, or the quagmire of Vietnam.[20] It appears that the U.S. now goes to war in the same way autocracies do, often on a pretext. In our current situation, the ingredients for proper democratic decision-making concerning war are missing: a free and seriously critical press, broad participation in any war effort by the citizens, and proper declaration of war according to the Constitution. Congress has not declared war according to Article 1, Section 8 of our Constitution since World War II. Instead, it violates the Constitution by passing ad hoc resolutions that hand over their war-declaring powers to a single individual, the president. This is exactly what the founding fathers sought to avoid.[21] As professor David Kennedy writes, today "thanks to something [called] the 'revolution in military affairs,' ... we now have an active-duty military establishment that is, proportionate to population, about 4 percent of the size of the force that won World War II ... and today's military budget is about 4 percent of gross domestic product, as opposed to nearly 40 percent during World War II."[22] If we add to this an indifferent public minimally inconvenienced by the war because it is being fought by the children of the poor, the presence of a group of ruthless ideologues and war profiteers in high office, we then have autocracy unleashing itself

19   Glen Stassen, Editor, *Just Peacemaking: Ten Practices for Abolishing War* (Cleveland: The Pilgrim Press, 1998), 106.

20   Cf Linda Bilmes, "The Trillion-Dollar War, *The New York Times*, August 20, 2005. Projecting out to the year 2010 Bilmes shows that the cost of the war will reach the 1.372 trilllion mark.

21   Robert Previdi, "America's Path to War," *The Long Term View*, Massachusetts School of Law at Andover, Vol 6, #2, 92-105.

22   David M. Kennedy, "The Best Army We Can Buy," *The New York Times*, July 25, 2005, A 23.

on the world—and three lost wars in a row! Democracy is like swimming: you keep working at it or you sink.

THE POWER OF NONVIOLENCE

There is, however, some good news. Happily, in our day, the myths of the non-utility of nonviolent power and of nonviolent resistance are being debunked. Mohandas Gandhi, Martin Luther King, and Nelson Mandela demonstrated to the world the power of nonviolent resistance. And, dictators such as Ferdinand Marcos have been driven out almost bloodlessly, as have at least seven Latin American despots. As Walter Wink writes, "in 1989-90 alone fourteen nations underwent nonviolent revolutions .... "[23] Gene Sharp lists 198 different types of nonviolent actions that are on historical record but neglected by historians and journalists. They apparently prefer to report on the flash of war.[24] "Britain's Indian colony of three hundred million people was liberated nonviolently at a cost of about eight thousand lives ... France's Algerian colony of about ten million was liberated by violence, but it cost almost one million lives."[25]

Compare these successful cases of nonviolent resistance with the quagmires America created in Vietnam, and has now created in Afghanistan and Iraq. The Israeli occupation of Palestine is also a case in point: Who are the realists, the prophets of Israel, Jesus, the Buddha, and Gandhi? Or, the warriors of the Pentagon and the Likud?

Also helpful here is the fact that the American empire is being exposed for what it is even as it declines. Our post-World War II boom began to be reversed in the 1970s and this trend has continued apace. The essence of empire is "the domination and exploitation of weaker states by stronger ones."[26] All of these tendencies are present in spades in the current American situation. We have 800 military installations in 130 countries and our Special Forces operate in nearly 170 nations. We spend more on our military than eighteen other leading nations

23   Walter Wink, *Jesus and Nonviolence: A Third Way* (Minneapolis: Facets Books: Fortress Press, 2003), 1-2.
24   Gene Sharp, *The Politics of Nonviolent Action* (Boston: Sargent, 1973); See also Ronald J. Sider and Richard E. Taylor, *Nuclear Holocaust and Christian Hope* (Downers Grove, Ill.: InterVarsity, 1982).
25   Walter Wink, *Jesus and Nonviolence*, 52.
26   Chalmers Johnson, *The Sorrows of Empire* (New York: Holt, 2004), 28.

combined. If nations won't allow us on their territory, we invade them. Or, we threaten to boycott them out of our market. We use 20 percent of Okinawa's arable land for our military bases and if Okinawans protest, they are threatened with denial of access to American purchasing power. What we cannot buy we conquer. It is amazing that anyone could miss the fact that when oil-hungry Americans invade oil-rich Iraq, they have oil on their minds. Many of the billions of dollars poured into Iraq have disappeared like water on a desert floor, as have weapons intended for Iraqi "allies." More successful empire-builders would consider our effort botched.

We have overthrown twenty-five governments since 1945, but would take a dim view of any nation that tried to overthrow ours.[27] We flood the world with our culture and technology as empires do. American Christians should be sensitive to the charge of empire building. Jesus died fighting the Roman empire.

All empires mask their true purposes with some sort of noble pretense: to promote the revolution of the proletariat, to take on, in Kipling's phase, "the white man's burden," to promote une mission civilatrice, to spread democracy and freedom, and now to "fight terrorism," while defining terrorists as any who resist, by means foul or fair, the intrusions of empire. Terrorism amounts to the killing of innocent people for the purpose of persuading their government to do what terrorists want. A classical example of "state terrorism"—the worst kind—was the American bombing of civilians at Hiroshima and Nagasaki. Those two events and many more, defined the U.S. as a terrorist nation. As Peter Ustinov, actor and playwright aptly said: "terrorism is the war of the poor and war is the terrorism of the rich."

Empire is always animated by hubris. American hubris is, however, being undermined by embarrassing data. Of the twenty-two richest nations of the world, we are first in wealth but last in developmental assistance. In other words, among those twenty-two rich nations we are the stingiest. The United States devotes a smaller percentage of national income to development assistance than nearly any other

27 See William Blum, Rogue State: A Guide to the World's Only Superpower (Monroe, ME.: Common Courage Press, 2000), and Chalmers Johnson, Blowback: The Costs and Consequences of American Empire (New York: Holt, 2000). Johnson's book, written two years before September 11, 2001, predicted "blowback" (a CIA term) from Osama bin Laden due to U.S. Middle-East presence and policies.

developed nation—less that one-tenth of one percent (.1 percent), as compared to Denmark's .97 percent, Sweden's .89 percent, France's .55 percent, and Germany's .31 percent. Even in *absolute* terms, excluding U.S. aid to Israel and Egypt, (largely military aid which is used in Israel to oppress Palestinians and in Egypt to suppress democracy), the United States—with its 300 million people—spends less on development assistance than does Denmark, a nation of five million."[28] Meanwhile, we licentiously squander billions making war on oil-rich Iraq.

Successful empire depends on the illusion of moral and cultural supremacy. That illusion is being vaporized by our bellicosity and penury. The emergence of hard truth is always good news.

THE RENEWABLE MORAL ENERGIES OF RELIGION

As John Henry Cardinal Newman reminded us, people will die for a dogma whereas they will not stir for a conclusion. Nothing so activates the will as does the tincture of the sacred. This can be negative as well as positive. The poet Alexander Pope reminds us that the worst of madmen is a saint gone mad, and, in the past as well, religion has often been invoked and co-opted in support of war.

But, we need to think positively about religion as well. In the past, it also caused humankind to turn in the direction of peace. In other words, there are success stories in our history, situations in which religion played a leading and positive role.

Three hundred years before Jesus was born, a powerful prince Ashoka in India was dominating much of India by military force. After his last big battle, he walked among the dead in the battlefield where a hundred thousand men had fallen. Instead of feeling triumphant, he felt repulsed. He then converted to Buddhism and, for the next thirty-seven years, pioneered a new mode of government, one of true compassion. He left a legacy of concern for people, animals, and the environment. He planted orchards and shade trees along roads, encouraged the development of the arts, built resthouses for travelers and watering sheds for animals and devoted major resources to the poor, the aged and the sick. As Duane Elgin says in his hope-filled book, *Promise Ahead: A Vision of Hope and Action for Humanity's Future*, "Ashoka's

28   Laurie Ann Mazur & Susan E. Sechler, Paper No. 1, "Global Interdependence and the Need for Social Stewardship," 1997, Rockefeller Brothers' Fund.

political administration was marked by the end of war and an emphasis on peace."[29] His governmental officers were trained as peacemakers
"building mutual good will among races, sects, and parties."[30]

What was the result of all this? His kingdom lasted more than two
thousand years until the military empire of Britain invaded India.
Britain's empire based on "superpower thinking," did not endure, nor
did those of Alexander the Great, Caesar, Genghis Khan, Napoleon
or Hitler. Historian H.G. Wells is known to have said that, among all
the monarchs of history, the star of Ashoka shines almost alone. But it
need not. We can almost hear the prophets of Israel crying out to us:
"Have you ears and cannot hear? Have you eyes and cannot see?"

THE BIBLICAL DEMURRAL

The ancient world cynically declared what seemed to be the natural
law of social evolution: *si vis pacem, para bellum* (if you want peace,
prepare for war). On this view, given the tough world we live in, war
is the only way to peace. The Biblical writers, would, however, register
major dissent here: They would say: *si vis pacem, para pacem!* If you
want peace, prepare for it and build it. "Seek peace and pursue it" (Ps.
34:14). You have to plan for it, and work at it. Peace does not happen
just because individual human beings are nice. We can't obtain it merely by praying for it. It is a social, economic, and political arrangement
that must be assiduously and ingeniously forged. As the rabbis put it,
"All commandments are to be fulfilled when the right opportunity ar-
rives. But not peace! Peace you must seek out and pursue."[31] We will
not stumble upon it by luck. Rather, like a city, it will come to be only
if it is constructed brick by brick.

In this connection, Abraham Heschel cites a dramatic fact: The Israelites "were the first [people] in history to regard a nation's reliance
upon force as evil."[32] Nothing in their environment was conducive to
this insight. Any sociology of knowledge is hard pressed to explain
how these simple tribes, surrounded by superior and hostile forces,

29   Duane Elgin, *Promise Ahead: A Vision of Hope and Action for Humanity's Future* (New York: Harper Collins, 2000) 117.
30   Ibid.
31   Pinchas Lapide, *The Sermon on the Mount: Utopia or Program for Action?*
(Maryknoll, N.Y.: Orbis, 1986) 35.
32   Abraham Heschel, *The Prophets* (Philadelphia: Jewish Publication Society of America, 1962), 166.

could dream a dream of peace in a way that was unmatched in history, yet increasingly seen as largely common-sensical. The Israelites did not just criticize the security-through-arms illusion; they offered an alternative. Peace can only be the fruit of justice. In essence, Isaiah says that justice is the only road to peace (Isa. 32:17)—a statement that, in and of itself, deserves a Nobel Peace Prize.

The Hebrew Bible does not resort to hints and indirect statements when it speaks of peace. It rather offers an epochal breakthrough in moral brilliance, one that is loud and to the point. Also, its writers are not speaking about an internal, spiritual peace of soul as subsequent centuries of Jewish and Christians have tried to do to escape its challenge. Their biblical position pioneered in ancient Israel and embraced in early Christianity is that trust in arms for safety will not work and represents a moral failure and a collapse of imagination. Unlike Tacitus who thought that the gods were with the mighty, the prophets insist that the power to kill is not sacred. God is not on the side of the mighty; indeed, God abhors them and will abandon them, not bless them, when they neglect justice and seek peace by war.

The message that is thereby brought home by this is that violence does not work; it bites back at you. As the Jewish-Christian Apostle Paul put it: "If you go on fighting one another, tooth and nail, all you can expect is mutual destruction." (Gal. 5:14) In short, the Bible rejects the use of military power.

"Neither by force of arms nor by brute strength" would the people be saved (Zech. 4:6). "Not by might shall a man prevail" (1 Sam. 2:9; RSV). Military power will be discredited: "The nations shall see and be ashamed of all their might" (Mic. 7:16). "Some boast of chariots and some of horses, but our boast is the name of the Lord." Those who boast of state-of-the-art weapons will therefore "totter and fall, but we rise up" (Ps. 20:6-7). "Their course is evil and their might is not right" (Jer. 23:10; RSV). The song of the military (usually translated as ruth-less) will be silenced, and fortified cities will become heaps of ruin (Isa. 25:5, 2). Reflecting Israel's history, the primary weapons of oppressive royalty, horses and chariots, are to be despised (see Exod. 14:9, 23; Deut. 20:1; 2 Sam. 15:1; 1 King 18:5; 22:4; 2 Kings 3:7; 18:23; 23:11). As Walter Brueggemann puts it: "Horses and chariots are a threat to the social experiment which is Israel. ... Yahweh is the

sworn enemy of such modes of power." [33] God orders Joshua to dis-
arm. "Hamstring their horses and burn their chariots" (Josh. 11:6).

"There is no peace for the wicked" (Isa. 57:21). Conversely, if we do
not have peace, it is our fault. We have taken the wrong approach. "Because you have trusted in your chariots, in the number of your warriors, the tumult of war shall arise against your people and all your for-
tresses shall be razed" (Hos. 10:13-14). For leaders to ask their people
to trust in arms for their deliverance is "wickedness" and "treachery"
(Hos. 10:13). Arms beget fear, not peace. You cannot build "Zion in
bloodshed" (Mic. 3:10). Therefore, "I will break bow and sword and
weapon of war and sweep them off the earth, so that all living creatures may lie down without fear" (Hos. 2:18). It is notable here that
distrust of arms is seen as a norm for "all living creatures," not just for
Israel. War delivers peace to no one. From a Biblical perspective, there
are many modes of power; the resort to violence is the most delusional
and least successful.

PACIFISM VS. PASSIVE-ISM

The Jesus movement extended the Biblical injunction against the power of killing as the path to security. "How blessed are the peacemakers; God shall call them his children." (Matt 5:9) There is, however,
one text, which seems to have muddied the Christian contribution to
peacemaking. It makes it appear that Jesus opposed resistance to evil.
In fact, what he opposed was violent resistance. He himself was an
active nonviolent resister against empire and precisely this led to his
death. It is a remarkable fact of history that his movement survived
longer than Roman rule itself did.

This widely misunderstood text is Matt. 5: 38-42: "You have learned
that they were told, 'Eye for eye, tooth for tooth.' But what I tell you is
this: Do not set yourself against the man who wrongs you. If someone
slaps you on the right cheek, turn and offer him your left. If a man
wants to sue you for your shirt, let him have your coat as well. If a man
in authority makes you go one mile, go with him two." As professor
Wink notes, this text has been interpreted so badly that it has become
"the basis for systematic training in cowardice, as Christians are taught

33   Walter Brueggemann, *Revelation and Violence* (Milwaukee: Marquette
University Press, 1986) 25-26.

to acquiesce to evil." [34] It has been used to urge cooperation with dictators, submission to wife battering, and helpless passivity in the face of evil. Associating Jesus and his teachings with such pusillanimity is an outrage.

Wink puts the meaning back into these texts. "Turn the other cheek" was not in reference to a fist fight. The reference is to a backhanded slap of a subordinate where the intention was "not to injure but to humiliate." Abject submission was the goal. Turning the other cheek was the opposite of abject submission. Rather, the message was "Try again .... I deny you the power to humiliate me." The aggressor is a failure, his goal is not achieved. His "inferior" is not cowering, but rather treats the insult to be trivial.[35] Gandhi understood this perfectly: "The first principle of nonviolent action is that of non-cooperation in everything humiliating."[36] This is courageous resistance, not passivity.

Similarly, the person being sued for his clothing was an outrage in Jesus' day. The poor were strapped with debts, and would, as a result, lose their land, their homes, and even their clothing. As Wink explains, if a man is being sued for his outer garment, he should yield it and then strip himself naked and say, here take my inner garment too. "Why then does Jesus counsel them to give over their undergarments as well? This would mean stripping off all their clothing and marching out of court stark naked! Imagine the guffaws this must have evoked. There stands the creditor, covered with shame, the poor debtor's outer garment in the one hand, his undergarment in the other."[37] Nakedness was taboo in that society and the shame fell less on the naked party than on the person viewing or causing the nakedness (Gen. 9:20-27) This was therefore not an act of submission, but, as Wink calls it, deft lampooning. In fact, it amounted to nonviolent resistance.

There is also the notion of 'going the second mile ...'. By law, Roman occupiers could force a person to carry a soldier's heavy pack, but only for a mile. The mile limitation was a prudent ruling aimed at minimiz-

34   Walter Wink, *Engaging the Powers: Disarmament and Resistance in a World of Domination* (Minneapolis: Fortress Press, 1992), p. 175.
35   Ibid.
36   Mahatma Gandhi, in *Harijan*, March 10, 1946, quote in Mark Juergensmeyer, *Fighting with Gandhi* (San Francisco: Harper & Row, 1984), 43.
37   Ibid., 178-79.

ing rebellion. There were two gains for the Roman soldier in this. He could hand over his 85 to 100 pound pack and gear and he also could reduce the vanquished to a pack animal. But when they reach the mile marker—and the soldier could be punished for forcing that person to walk more than a mile. The victim had the right to say "Oh, no, I want to carry this for another mile!" Again, as Wink points out this nonviolent resistance put the Roman infantryman into the position of pleading with a Jew to give back his pack! There is more than a little humor in this way of discomfiting oppressors.

Again, this does not amount to an act of submission, but rather to an assertion of human dignity by the apparently powerless. Jesus knew that violent resistance to the Roman Empire was fruitless. The recent history of his own land had demonstrated this.

During World War II, the Danes did not try to fight the German army, but allowed them in. Everyday, the Danish king would lead a quiet walk through the city of Copenhagen with the citizens in good order behind him. It was peaceful, but the message to the occupiers was, "You do not own us and you have not captured our spirits." This must have affected even the minds of the Nazis, as nonviolent resistance always seeks to do. The same hopeful spirit showed through when the Danes got word from a friendly German officer that the Germans were coming for their Jews. Using everything that could float, the Danes transported their Jewish compatriots across the sea to neutral Sweden, thereby saving most of them.

Jesus' message then is roughly, "Don't return violence with violence. It will get you nowhere. Instead, oppose evil in any way you can." Even Gandhi said that if there were only two choices in the face of evil, cowardice or violence, he would prefer violence. But there is the third option of ingenious, persistent, creative nonviolent resistance—in Biblical terms, "the way of the Lord."

This message is concretized in an important book produced by twenty-three Christian ethicists and entitled *Just Peacemaking: Ten Practices for Abolishing War*[38] It is very readable, written to inform the consciences of citizens so that they can meet their primary duty, namely, to be the conscience of the nation and move war-addicted governments toward peacemaking.

38   Glen Stassen, Editor, *Just Peacemaking: Ten Practices for Abolishing War* (Cleveland: The Pilgrim Press, 1998.

Citizenship in religious terms is not a privilege; it is a vocation, one to which a serious duty to learn is attached. Failure to respond to those duties amounts to corrupt living. The Christian scriptures are ingenious in their assessment of acts of omission: They tell us more about our level of moral development than do acts of commission. The story of the Good Samaritan (Luke 10:29-37) does not condemn the "robbers" (whose sin is obvious) but rather focuses on "the priest" and "the Levite" who ignored the plight of the half dead victim and "passed by." Self-indulgence and inaction seem to go hand in hand with willful political ignorance. Beguiled by the policy of "bread and circuses," such citizens regarded governmental evil as none of their daily business.[39] The consciences of such individuals are, however, politically dead. They may be pious and "religious" people just like "the priest" and "the Levite," but they are the goats not the heroes of the Good Samaritan story.

CONCLUSION: SOME THOUGHTS ON SHEDDING TEARS

The tearless are the enemies of peace because they do not respond appropriately to the evils that peacemaking must address. Tears, after all, are very Christic. Jesus looked at the city and wept, heartbroken over the fact that we do not know the things that make for peace. (Luke19:41:42) Jeremiah said that unless our eyes run with tears, we will come to a terrible ruin. (Jer. 9:18-19) I was amazed, as a young Catholic boy, when I saw on the back of the *Missale Romanum* a prayer for the gift of tears. And it said, "Oh God, strike into the *duritiam*, the hardness of my heart and bring forth a saving flood of tears." And as a little boy, I thought, "Who wants tears? When you grow up you don't have them anymore, especially if you are a man." But precisely this is the problem. If you are without tears, we are living a tragedy; we are not Christ-like. Maybe we cannot even call ourselves Christian. "How blest are you who weep ...." (Luke 6:21) Jesus wept. He looked at Jerusalem and said, "If only you knew the things that make for your peace, but you don't." And he broke down sobbing.

To update that text, let us hear Jesus say, "America, America, if only you knew the things that make for your peace, if only you could see that the answer is not in your weaponry and economic muscle. If only

39   See Daniel C. Maguire, *A Moral Creed for All Christians* (Minneapolis: Fortress Press, 2005), 17.

I could, like a mother hen, wrap my wings around you, wings of justice and peace and compassion, if you could use your great talent and wealth to work to end world hunger, world thirst, world illiteracy, no one would hate you, no one would crash planes into your buildings, you would know *Shalom.*" That is the promise of Isaiah 32:17: Plant justice and compassion, and then and only then will peace grow. Then you could burn those chariots in a holy fire and you would be secure.

There is an illness in this land of ours that makes the Bible's peacemaking message "a hard saying." I'll call it ICS: Imperial Comfort Syndrome. When you are living in an extremely advantaged imperial situation, basking in unearned and purloined privilege as we are in the United States, you become very comfortable. This particular illness, ICS, does not result in fever or in cold chills. Its symptoms are rather tepidity and a dull, crippling kind of depression. It also has numerous other consequences. In many recent elections, for example, as many as sixty percent of eligible American voters didn't even show up. In Revelations 3:15, 22, the author puts these words into the mouth of God. "I know all your ways. You are neither hot nor cold. How I wish you were either hot or cold. But because you are lukewarm, neither hot nor cold, I will spit you out of my mouth …. Hear, you who have ears to hear, what the Spirit says to the churches."

LIST OF CONTRIBUTORS

Michel Andraos, Ph.D.
Catholic Theological Union
5401 South Cornell Ave.
Chicago, Illinois 60615-5698
(773) 324-8000
mandraos@ctu.edu

Brian Bloch
ISKCONResolve
http://www.iskconresolve.com/index.php
bbloch@pamho.net

John Patrick Donnelly, SJ
History Department
Marquette University
P.O. Box 1881
Milwaukee, WI 53201-1881
(414) 288-3554
john.p.donnelly@marquette.edu

Michael Duffey, Ph.D.
Theology Department
Marquette University
P.O. Box 1881
Milwaukee, WI 53201-1881
(414) 288-3748
michael.duffey@marquette.edu

Marc H. Ellis, Ph.D.
Director, Center for Jewish Studies
Graduate Faculty, Philosophy Department
Baylor University
One Bear Place #97174
Waco, TX 76798-7174
(254) 710-3609
Marc_Ellis@baylor.edu

Edward Grippe, Ph.D.
Norwalk Community College
188 Richards Ave
Norwalk, CT 06854
(203) 857-7000
egrippe@nctc.commnet.edu

Patrick J. Hayes, Ph.D.
Department of Theology and Religious Studies
St. John's University
Staten Island, NY 10301
t1010wins@aol.com

Veena Rani Howard
University of Oregon
Eugene, Oregon 97403
(541) 346-1000
veenahoward@msn.com

Angela Hurley, Ph.D.
Transylvania University
300 North Broadway
Lexington, KY 40508
(859) 233-8300
ahurley@transy.edu

Hideyuki Koyama, Ph.D., SJ
Sophia University
7-1 KIOI-CHO, CHIYODA-KU
TOKYO, JAPAN 102-8554
81-3-3238-3179
k-hideyu@hoffman.cc.sophia.ac.jp

Jane E. Linahan, Ph.D.
Contact information not available.

Daniel C. Maguire, Ph.D.
Marquette University
Theology Department
P.O. Box 1881
Milwaukee, WI 53201-1881
(414) 288-5508
daniel.maguire@marquette.edu

Nancy M. Martin
Department of Religious Studies
Chapman University
1 University Drive
Orange, CA 92866
(717) 997-6608
nmartin@chapman.edu

Phillip C. Naylor, Ph.D.
History Department
Marquette University
P.O. Box 1881
Milwaukee, WI 53201-1881
(414) 288-3561
phillip.naylor@marquette.edu

Ayse Sidika Oktay
Assistant Professor
Faculty of Theology
Department of Philosophy & Religious Sciences
Suleyman Demirel University
Isparta, Turkey 32260
asoktay@gmail.com
askotay@ilahiyat.sdu.edu.tr

Irfan A. Omar, Ph.D.
Theology Department
Marquette University
P.O. Box 1881
Milwaukee, WI 53201-1881
(414) 288-3746
irfan.omar@marquette.edu

Deborah S. (Nash) Peterson
Theology Department
Marquette University
P.O. Box 1881
Milwaukee, WI 53201-1881
(262) 250-0140
deborah.peterson@marquette.edu
dpeterson@milwpc.com

Terrence Rynne
Marquette University
P.O. Box 1881
Milwaukee, WI 53201-1881
terrence.rynne@mu.edu

Lee B. Thomas, Jr.
Bellarmine University
2001 Newburg Rd.
Louisville KY 40205
(502) 452-8131
leet@bellarmine.edu

L. George Thompson
Contact information not available.

Nathan Tierney, Ph.D.
Philosophy Department
California Lutheran University
122 Garden Valley Court
Napa, CA 94558
(707) 259-9485
tierney@callutheran.edu

Paul J. Weber, deceased

INDEX